Grab Success by the Horns

Powerful Lessons You Can Learn From Proactive People

Barbara Siskind & Barry Siskind

Manor House

Library and Archives Canada Cataloguing in Publication

Siskind, Barbara

Grab success by the horns : the proven proactive approach : get what you want in business and life / Barbara Siskind and Barry Siskind.

Includes bibliographical references.
ISBN 978-1-897453-47-6

1. Success. 2. Self-actualization (Psychology). I. Siskind, Barry, 1946-

II. Title.

BF637.S8S587 2010   158.1   C2010-907095-X

Printed and bound in Canada

Cover design: Michael B. Davie and Donovan Davie
Cover illustration by Doug Thompson
To see more of Doug's work visit www.thompsonimagery.com

Published November 28, 2010, Manor House Publishing Inc.
Released in the US market, May 2011

We gratefully acknowledge the financial support of the Government of Canada through Book Fund Canada, Dept. of Canadian Heritage.

Copyright 2010 / All rights reserved / first edition / 240 pages

No part of this book may be reproduced or transmitted in any form or by any means, without the express written permission of the publisher.

Manor House Publishing Inc.
www.manor-house.biz
905-648-2193

Grab Success by the Horns

For Joan McKnight, 1951 - 2006

Other Books by Barry Siskind: ***Bumblebees Can't Fly; Eagles Must Soar; The Successful Exhibitor; Making Contact; Master the Art of Networking to Develop New Business Needs; Uncover Hidden Opportunities and Enhance Your career; The Power of Exhibit Marketing; Powerful Exhibit Marketing***

Acknowledgements

There are always so many people to thank once you have reached the end of a project like this.

We want to start with the People of Action, the people you will read throughout the book. Many of them gave of their time and candidly shared their stories with us. Others were the result of research. In either case we owe a debt to all of them for leading extraordinary lives.

Without their stories, this book would not have happened. The internet played an important role. The World Wide Web is probably the most important tool for writers since the typewriter. The whole world is out there for the asking. If this book has whet your appetite then perhaps you will start searching for more people who will move you closer to the success you deserve.

Some of the research was conducted by Geoffrey Siskind and Mark Silverberg — thanks.

Nancy Carroll's wisdom, judgment and her sharp editing pen were indispensable. Even when we thought she was wrong — she was right.

We owe a debt to Michael Davie who found us when we were struggling to find a good home for this book. Michael's proactive approach with us and in building his publishing business is what we hope to inspire in our readers. Thanks Michael.

Then there are those close to us whose love and acceptance fills our every waking hour: Jillian, Geoffrey, Mark, Bob, Cory, Lynda, Suzanne, Carol, Zoë (big), David, Aidyn, Zoë (little), Moses, Daniel, Colin, Charlie, Rachel and Katelin. Thanks guys.

Barbara Siskind
Barry Siskind
2010

Grab Success by the Horns

TABLE OF CONTENTS

OVERVIEW   11

PROLOGUE   13

INTRODUCTION   15

Chapter 1
EMBRACE HOPE   23

Chapter 2
THE COURAGE TO ACT   49

Chapter 3
STAY IN THE GAME   81

Chapter 4
WHEN OPPORTUNITY KNOCKS – ANSWER   111

Chapter 5
PURSUE HAPPINESS WITH GUSTO   143

Chapter 6
SUCCEEDING IN AN IMPERFECT WORLD   175

Chapter 7
TURN YOUR PROACTIVITY INSIDE OUT   205

ABOUT THE AUTHORS   237

Grab Success by the Horns

Overview

This book is for those people who want to take charge of their career in sales.

Arthur Conan Doyle, in his book *The Sign of Four,* had Sherlock Holmes explain to Watson, "How often have I said that when you eliminate the impossible, whatever remains, however improbable, must be the truth." [1]

But the truth is often masked and what should be obvious, often isn't. The net result is that people through their own inaction miss opportunities to take charge.

I am intrigued with the role of pro-activity in the development of a sales career path. I speak with thousands of workshop participants each year and listening to their rationales for inaction often leaves me shaking my head in disbelief. They may say, "I don't want to rock the boat," or "let's see if I can build a consensus first," or "what will so and so think?"

I have based my career success, which has spanned 40 years, on pro-activity. Not only does taking action give me what I want, it gives me a daily semblance of control. It's not always easy and it certainly isn't always safe, but those that don't take action view the world with bewilderment, unsure of where they fit in and willing to settle for second best. Not me and not the readers who take the steps they learn in **Grab Success by the Horns** seriously. We are people of action who are prepared to step up to the plate and have the career in sales we want.

Just talking about control makes many sales people feel helpless. How can we control anything when the world and its problems seem so much greater than any one individual? What control can we possibly have when global warming threatens our existence, acts of terrorism affect our safety, and big government and big business dictate every facet of our lives; from how we act to what we consume? The big picture can seem so depressing and beyond our control that we often feel helpless and fail to take action in the areas we can control. We put

---

[1] Arthur Conan Doyle, 1890.*The Sign of Four* (Berkeley,1986).

off starting that new business or making the next cold call. We postpone having that talk with our boss. We ignore destructive behaviors by customers. In many cases, we just give up on life go to work and do our job. We never see the potential that could be ours if only we could reach out and grab hold of our brass ring.

So, is control nothing more than an illusion? Many seem to think so, and it's in this belief that many sales people fall into a self-defeating trap. They lose hope and are no longer motivated to even try.

Knowing that we are in control is the first step towards becoming great in the sales arena. It's a scary world we live in, yet I continue to find relief by taking control through action. I think that many other people might also find this solution. Building a successful career in sales through action is the focus of **Grab Success by the Horns**. It is an opportunity for readers to learn that nothing is impossible—if you do something about it.

Sun Tzu wrote, "Even a one thousand mile journey starts with a single step." [2]

Readers will see how everyone from ordinary folks to cultural icons (who, after all, were once just ordinary folks themselves) have faced challenges and took action that put them back in the driver's seat. This book offers an opportunity to learn why some people act and others don't. It is a chance for readers to be more than inspired. It is an opportunity to take the lessons learned and integrate them into the steps that will give readers the tools they need to take charge of their sales career.

We all hold the key to our epitaph. Either we can take action to make things better or we can sit back and let life take its toll. If the latter describes you, then this book will give you a chance to take a heroic step forward. Millions of people have moved beyond the safe comfort of the tried and true into the realm of the unknown. They've taken chances. While all of their stories are unique, what they all have in common is never having said, "If only I had ..." Some succeeded and some failed, but they all tried. Making the effort is what this book is all about.

---

[2] Sun Tzu, *The Art of War (Filuguarian,* 2007).

Prologue

How will history remember your sales career? When your children and your grandchildren talk about you, what do you think they will say? What would you want them to say?

When you were a child, do you remember being taught that if you rowed your boat gently down a stream, your life would be but a dream? Was that your impression of how the world of business worked? Do you still sing this song to your children even though you have learned that a gentle stream often turns into rapids, which lead to a waterfall, and then out to the ocean where it becomes part of a big body of water?

Water is the most powerful force on earth. It covers 70 percent of the earth's surface and yet nothing in the water stays the same. When we think about selling, we often talk about going with the flow, letting the river carry us along. When things go wrong, we refer to it as rowing upstream without a paddle. Using metaphors like this can be disastrous. They're an excuse for inaction – changing the course of the river is not going to happen overnight. Watch beavers construct a dam. They go about their work one stick at a time and eventually they have a dam that changes the course of the entire river. As long as you live convinced that your sales career is totally out of your control and that you are a victim of the world, you will never be the captain of your own ship.

So, what kind of salesperson do you want to be? How do you want your family, your employees, your friends, and your peers to think about you? And most of all, how do you want to think about yourself?

The motivation for action stems from a cacophony of sources. The people of whom you are about to read have been chosen to illustrate such career motivators as helplessness, hope, fear, loyalty, opportunity, and purpose. Successful sales people are like sponges, taking in lessons that seem, at first blush, unrelated.

The people you are going to meet in this book will act as your case studies. The narrative examines the back-story to find the less obvious reasons and causes behind these proactive people's motivation. As you learn the motivations behind these proactive people who have made a difference, you can decide what actions work for you. You have the power to change; you are the author of your life's story. Life is filled with wonderful opportunities; they are yours for the taking. All you need to do is follow the lessons you will learn in this book, add a bit of courage, and you will have what you need to create a life you never thought possible.

Grab Success by the Horns

Introduction

"My parents brought me up to think we could all change the world."
- **Richard Branson** [3]

Your house is on fire. Your worst nightmare has come true. Your personal treasure trove of memories and the life you have built is engulfed in a sea of red and orange flames. The heat is unbearable. There are fire trucks pouring tons of water on your hopes and dreams. Everything you own is in that house and all you can do is watch.

But wait. What is that? You hear a familiar sound. You hold your breath in disbelief. Recognition is instantaneous. Your child is screaming. "Mommy, Daddy! Help me!"

In a heartbeat, this nightmare has turned into every parent's horror. A child, your child, is in trouble. "Oh my God," you say out loud as you run toward the flames.

A voice yells, "Don't go in there; you'll get killed!" Without thinking, you run towards the house. Your focus is only on one thing — your child is in trouble.

A firefighter puts his hand on your shoulder and repeats, "Don't do it; we'll get him out." But you push his hand aside. You are blind to the consequences. You ignore common sense and the experience of professionals who have dealt with life-and-death situations many times. None of their wisdom matters. It's your child's life at stake and, like a kamikaze pilot unconcerned with personal risk; you rush headlong into the unknown.

Was your decision to take action right or wrong? It doesn't matter. You had a critical mission — to save your child. There was no inner dialogue. There was no choice. You reacted to a primal need. You just did it. Fortunately, very few of us are ever in a life-and-death situation where the results of action versus inaction have such grave consequences. Someone who instinctively dives into a river to save a drowning stranger might say when asked, "I didn't think about it; I just did what I had to do." There are people who take stray animals home

---

[3] A great source of Branson's quotes is www.thinkArete.com

because their hearts, not their heads, say, "You can't leave that poor animal out there to die." We act spontaneously when we help an old person cross a busy street or give a homeless person money to buy food. Some people, when faced with a unique set of circumstances that fate has thrown in their path, feel a deep need to react. Yet, there are many others who, when faced with similar circumstances, don't react. These people just watch and wait for others to take action. What stops them from reacting, from helping those in need?

Threatening situations, or a multitude of everyday situations, we are all faced with, are a few of the many factors that can undermine our taking action. A perceived lack of power, fear, inbred messages, and peer pressure can all affect our ability to take the next selling initiative. Each day we face situations that require us to act. For instance, Bill, a good friend of mine, was nearing retirement. His health was good and his mind was active. Retirement was a step into the unknown. How would he fill each day? Where would he meet people to talk to? What purpose would his life serve?

Bill had always been a productive citizen. He held a middle-management job with a large international company. He had traveled extensively and often had to make crucial decisions. But no decision was ever as difficult for Bill as the one he now faced. So, Bill sat down with Mary, his wife, and they talked.

"How do you want to spend the next ten years?" Mary asked.

"That's what we're here to talk about," Bill said with a touch of sarcasm.

"Yes, but the real question is what would you like to do that you've never had a chance to try," Mary said with a mischievous look on her face.

"Well," Bill started, "I've always wanted to run my own show; a small business where I can be the boss. That's what I really want."

"So, what's stopping you?"

"Money? We have our retirement savings. I could use that, but what if we lost it all? Then where would we be?" Bill asked.

"Okay, Mary persisted. "If money weren't an issue, what else is stopping you?"

"I've been in marketing all my life, what do I know about production?"

"What else?"

"I'm sixty-five years old and I don't know if I want to spend that much time committed to a business."

"Okay. Anything else?" Mary probed.

"Nope."

"So, you want to start your own business, but money, expertise, and time are stopping you right?" Mary inquired.

"Yeah, that's right," Bill agreed.

"Okay, let's see if we can come up with a plan that works with these obstacles," Mary suggested.

And they did. Bill went out and found an interesting small business for sale. The owner, like so many who run small businesses was simply overwhelmed trying to do everything. When Bill suggested he take him on as a partner with expertise in marketing, the owner realized this might be his perfect solution. And it worked for Bill too.

This new venture was a shared partnership, which limited Bill's investment to 50 percent. Because the company had a good track record, Bill was able to finance most of his investment with his bank, leaving his retirement savings in tact.

His new partner, suddenly freed from marketing his business, was able to turn all his attention to production. As partners they both shared in the success of the company which meant they could both enjoy the flexibility of time away from the office, knowing the business was in trusted hands.

Sometimes we respond to our needs or the needs of others and sometimes we don't. But we can only justify inaction to a point. When passivity is no longer an option, we do something.

For many, the decision to run into a burning building is simply not an option. No matter what the circumstances, they would opt out while others will take immediate action. It's as if the action of helping is hard wired into their mental computers. Like the rest of us, firefighters, police officers, pilots, racecar drivers, and emergency workers feel fear and have a strong will to live. At the same time they are dedicated to helping others as well as themselves in life-and-death situations; putting their life on the line is their only option. Years of training have taught them how to react on instinct. They make split-second decisions without considering their own survival. Their own well being is not part of the equation. They just do what they need to do at the moment. They have chosen work that requires immediate action.

But all actions have this in common: they set a course of action that changes everything by setting into motion a sequence of events that is unstoppable. For instance, you could take an action that will save the planet or one that will make your next sales call more enjoyable. Each decision creates another ripple in the pond of experience. There are countless books that chronicle the activities of people who have performed great feats. Many of these individuals have become part of our folklore and their stories are recounted in books, songs, or even movies of the week. But what about the actions of people like you and me— regular folks who act and produce results that most of us never hear about? These stories are inspiring. The focus of this book is not simply these individuals' stories. Rather, through these stories you will gain useful information to help move you from inaction to action.

What do Lance Armstrong, Nelson Mandela, Martin Luther King, Terry Fox, Mother Theresa, Bono and Erin Brockavitch have in common? They all acted in extraordinary ways that changed the course of the world. They gave us a view of a world without hunger, poverty, and disease, a world of possibilities and endless selling opportunities.

Many of us are temporarily moved to action, but once the initial impetus wears off we go on with daily lives. Remember how we were all moved to help the victims of the Tsunami that hit on Christmas Day, 2004? Billions of dollars in donations raised. Many of us comfortably sat back, picked up the phone and made our pledge. We felt like we accomplished something important, but there's more to being a Person of Action (POA) than writing a check. The same holds true of customers who need your attention. You can sit back and delegate work to others, or you can get your hands dirty and get the job done.

In a speech delivered in Michigan, former US president Bill Clinton said, "I really believe the 21st century will, more likely than not, be the most exciting time ever in all of human history to be alive." [4]

Your choice is to sit back like a Monday morning quarterback critically replaying all the moves, or you have to learn how to tap into your internal resources and take action.

---

[4] William Jefferson Bill Clinton in a speech to the 100th anniversary meeting of the American Society of Agricultural and Biological Engineers.

Sometimes, in the heat of a friendly debate I speculate about what motivates some people to take action. Perhaps they have unbridled passion or were personally hit by a tragedy. Some chalk it up to a calling, while others talk about purpose. Some talk about desperation and others mention a lack of choices. It's hard to know what motivates people, but one thing is for sure, such people command respect. Are Persons of Action exceptions to the norm? Are most of us destined to be part of the "silent majority" and let others do all the work for us, or do we all have a POA within us? Friedrich Nietzsche wrote, "For every man there exists a bait which he cannot resist swallowing."

We All Need a Superhero

When I was growing up, my hero was Superman. He was super smart and everything a hero was supposed to be. He was perfect. He had great strength. He was "faster than a speeding bullet, stronger than a locomotive and able to leap tall buildings with a single bound." He was my generation's hero. If I could be anything I wanted, would I be Superman? But instead, I was Superman's alter ego, Clark Kent – a mild mannered reporter who sat back and fought injustice vicariously. All I really needed was a telephone booth and a red, white and blue leotard and cape and away I went in my imagination.

Society needs heroes — people who are mythical yet real and can accomplish superhuman feats, who can overcome obstacles and touch issues and win. Heroes are good role models of persons who take action so it's only natural to turn our attention to them. The dictionary defines a hero as (a) "a legendary figure endowed with great strength or ability, b) an illustrious warrior, c) a man admired for his achievements and noble qualities and d) one that shows courage." [5]

According to Jung, a hero "can only follow an alien impulse within him and follow where it leads, sensing that his work is greater than himself, and wields a power which is not his." [6]

---

[5] *Microsoft Encarta College Dictionary* (St Martins Press, New York).
[6] Carl Gustav Jung, 1875 – 1961 a prolific writer and analyst. In his book, *Man and His Symbols*, (Doubleday, (1964) he identified various human archetypes one being the hero. The hero according to Jung is the one type that often engaged in fighting his own shadows. This archetype can be seen in movies and books one of the most popular enactment of the archetype is Luke Skywalker in the Star Wars series.

Superman, like all heroes, had a firm grasp on moral values. Superman fought for "Truth, Justice and the American Way." [7]

Like Superman, all heroes need to stand for something. Their values must be unshakable. Imagine Superman saying, "I'm bushed. I've been saving people all week. Tonight I'm going to stay home, order a pizza, and watch TV."

True heroism is reserved for a select few who, through their actions, set themselves apart. Their undeviating commitment to strong values, even in the face of opposition, inspires us all.

The Courage to Act

The one trait that all heroes possess is courage. Courage is often thought of as a rare characteristic that's extremely difficult to acquire. It is something to which many aspire, yet few acquire. Superman had courage. But why wouldn't he? Nothing except Kryptonite could hurt him. The rest of us are not so lucky. We often confuse real courage with what we see portrayed in the media or on the screen. Courage is more than a dramatic scene. It's more than a cop who walks into a deserted building armed with nothing but a gun and a flashlight. Courage is acting boldly, even when there are knots in your stomach, whether your actions are selfless or selfish. Courage is pushing the envelope of what is safe and comfortable. It's taking a chance on something that might fail. Courage is talking to your kids about sex and drugs. Courage is standing your ground with an unreasonable customer. In essence, it's all about love: the love of justice, principles, other people and ourselves. An anonymous writer once said, "Courage is what you would do if you knew your children were watching." [8]

What Would You Do?

Here's a quiz. What would you do in each of these situations?

1. Imagine you work in law enforcement, assigned to the vice squad in the area of child pornography on the Internet. Your mission is to catch as many of the bad guys as possible. But the job is just too big. The Internet is worldwide, your budgets are shrinking and everyone is telling you the job is impossible. What would you do?
   a. Continue doing the best you can with the resources you have.

---

[7] There is no shortage of information on the Internet about D.C. Comic's Superman created by Jerry Siegel and Joe Schuster.
[8] I wish I could find the source of this terrific quote. It's right on.

b. Find another job that promises more satisfaction.
c. Contact Bill Gates and see what he can do for you.

2. Imagine you and your child are on a shopping trip. On the way back to your car, two ruffians overtake you, throw you and your child in the back of the car and head out along the highway. These abusive people tell you to sit quietly and do nothing and no one will get hurt. What would you do?
   a. Sit quietly and do what you are told.
   b. Try to strike a bargain with the kidnappers.
   c. Quietly call 911 on your cell phone.

3. Imagine you are the spouse of a high-level executive who heads an institution in a very conservative industry. You hear of an ongoing hate campaign against a religious group to which you don't belong. You live a privileged life, but you want to do something. What would you do?
   a. Ask your spouse to make an anonymous donation to the cause.
   b. Leave the solution to others more capable of handling it.
   c. Help your spouse to organize other CEOs in a special task force.

4. You are a six-year-old out for a walk with your mother. You see a homeless person asking for money. Your mother explains what it means to be homeless. What would you do?
   a. Give the homeless person your allowance.
   b. Ask your parents to help the homeless person.
   c. Arrange to ask the leader of your country for help.

How did you do? Did you find some answers absurd? Were others simply out of the question? Were some simply too risky? Some of the POA's you are about to read about chose "c."

Their journeys make compelling reading, but there is more in store for you. Motivation is more than following a few simple steps. It requires a deep understanding of what you need to do to motivate yourself.

The best way to discover what motivates you is to learn what others have done and why they did it. Here are some samples of what's in store:

You will meet some proactive people, including a policeman who approached the world's wealthiest man to ask for help with the issue of child pornography.

You will meet a child who, by the age of ten, had raised $500,000 for the homeless, an entrepreneur who started a small business, and a sculptor who left a well-paid job to do his art full-time and the wife of a banker who used her position of power to fight anti-Semitism.

You will also meet a former president of the United States who redefined the role of ex-presidents by picking up a hammer to provide affordable housing for hundreds of thousands. You will meet a Harvard University scientist who developed a device that has saved millions around the world and an actor who used his love of acting to help other struggling actors.

Hannah Taylor, our first POA, wasn't afraid to take risks, nor were the other POA's you will read about in these pages. Follow their stories, but more importantly, look for the factors that led each to action.

By examining the stories behind the actions of individuals who have changed their own lives, and the lives of others, you will learn the key to unlocking your own door to a more fulfilling life. You will find your own inner strength to do the things that you have always felt deep inside that you should do. Never again will you fall victim to that malady of regret, which is synonymous with the words, "I wish I had done something."

Very few of us remember the people behind yesterday's headlines. While the accomplishments are significant, the people are soon forgotten. Does that mean that we should not strive to change the world? Not at all. Even though the chances of hearing your name remembered throughout history are slim, reaching for the stars is a worthwhile pursuit. Or, you can set your sights on different goals.

Whether you choose to become a superstar in your field of endeavor, to change the world to make it a better place, or to create a legacy that will be remembered by a select few, the choice is yours. You can sit on your couch immersed in a 500-channel universe as the real world passes you by, or you can get up and do something to change the world, your community, or your own life.

The pages that follow will motivate and inspire you to choose the path of proactivity.

Grab Success by the Horns

Powerful Lessons You Can Learn From Proactive People

Barbara Siskind & Barry Siskind

Manor House

Grab Success by the Horns

1
Embrace Hope

"Trust your instincts. Your mistakes might as well be your own, instead of someone else's."
- **Billy Wilder**

I have learned some of my most important lessons in life from my children. All too often we short-circuit our sales career when we add layer upon layer of excuses justifying why we cannot do this or that. Children have a way of looking at the world for what it is, and they can often cut through the muddle and aim directly at the problem.

Hannah's Story

We'll start with the real story of a six-year-old girl from Winnipeg, Canada. Her name is Hannah Taylor.

One day, Hannah was returning from a mother-daughter Christmas manicure when she saw something at the side of the road that would shift her outlook on life completely. Hannah had never seen someone eating from a dumpster.

"What's he doing?" Hannah innocently asked her mom.

Hannah's mom, Colleen, explained that he was looking for food, that he was homeless and had no choice. They then proceeded to drive back to their comfortable home in an affluent area of Winnipeg.

But Hannah's questions didn't stop. For the next year, every time Hannah would sit down with her mother to eat she would ask, "What is that homeless man eating?" And at bedtime she would ask, "Where is that man sleeping?" And when she felt loved by her family she would ask, "Who loves that homeless man?"

---

[9] Billy Wilder, 1906 – 2002 was an Austrian born motion picture director and producer.

The following year, Hannah entered Grade One at an affluent, all-girls private school. It had a large iron fence that separated it from an impoverished area of Winnipeg. As Hannah and her mother drove up to the school gates, they passed a woman carrying all of her possessions in tattered shopping bags. Hannah begged her mother to do something to help the woman. Her mother told Hannah that she couldn't stop the car and that there was nothing she could do.

"But Mom, you have to do something!" Hannah cried. The car sailed through the gates towards the school, leaving the woman behind them.

That night, when Colleen was putting Hannah to bed, they talked about what they had seen that day. Hannah's heart was heavy.

"Maybe if you do something to help her," Colleen began, "your heart will feel better."

At school, Hannah took part in a photo exhibition called "The Power of Passion." When asked what passion meant to her, Hannah replied, "Passion to me is something that you really want to do, is good for the world, and makes a lot of other people happy."

After seeing that homeless woman outside the gates of her school, something clicked for Hannah: She had found her passion. The next day, Hannah went into her father's home office and sat down at his desk. She began preparing a presentation for her Grade One class on homelessness.

Hannah's mother realized that this wasn't just a passing phase. Hannah spent the next year talking about homelessness to anyone who would listen. Hannah's mother wanted to help her daughter, but didn't know where to turn. Coincidentally, Hannah's grandmother called to say that she'd just seen a television report about a homeless shelter and perhaps Colleen could help Hannah better understand what it was like by seeing homelessness firsthand.

Colleen took Hannah to the shelter. As she and Hannah walked through the doors, a feeling of sadness and hopelessness overcame them both. Colleen looked down at Hannah, who looked surprisingly calm and relaxed.

"I feel so good that the homeless have a place to go," Hannah told her mom.

Many of Hannah's questions were answered on this trip to the shelter, but her mission to do something was only just beginning. Hannah would later explain that her goal was to get people to care about homeless people in their community and around the world. "Because they really need our help, and even though they might look different from us or wear clothes that aren't as good as ours, it doesn't matter 'cause we're all the same inside."[10]

Hannah knew that she had to take her message to the people who were important, and for her, the most powerful person in the world was her father. She saw him get up every morning, put on a suit and head downtown to go to work. "Downtown, that must be where the powerful people are," she thought to herself. "That's who I need to ask to help."

With the aid of her parents, she began inviting some of Winnipeg's most influential businesspeople out to lunch to tell them about homelessness. And each, in turn, were charmed by Hannah's passion, and responded with some sort of positive action. But this wasn't enough for Hannah. This exercise of explaining homelessness to powerful executives one at a time was becoming exhausting. "What if we could just take all these big bosses out to lunch at once?" Hannah mused to her mother. "We could give them sandwiches and juice boxes and talk to all of them!" And so Hannah's idea for the "Big Bosses Lunch" was born.

At the first Big Bosses Lunch, Hannah hosted 100 CEOs from Winnipeg's business establishment. The little girl's earnestness, and more importantly, her message, moved and charmed them. At the end of Hannah's, talk one of the executives pointed to one of Hannah's drawings that she had made for the occasion.

"How much for that drawing?" he asked.

"Let your heart decide how much it should cost," Hannah replied.

The man thought for a moment and then answered, "How about $10,000?"

---

[10] This quote is directly out of the mouth of a six year old. Amazing. Check out her website www.ladybugfoundation.com.

Hannah held several more of these Big Bosses lunches, each one raising a tremendous amount of money through sales of her art and contributions.

One day, while in the kitchen watching her baby sister eat food from a baby food jar, Hannah suddenly had an idea: The baby-food jar would be perfect for collecting money! She also thought the cause should have a mascot. The perfect mascot was a ladybug. Hannah and Colleen began painting hundreds of ladybug jars and distributed them to anyone who would take one. All the money was distributed through the "The Ladybug Foundation." To date, the foundation and Hannah's family has made over 5,000 jars and the Ladybug Foundation has raised over $300,000.

But the story doesn't end here—it gets better. When the Canadian Prime Minister's office heard that Hannah was going to be traveling to Ottawa, Hannah and her mother were invited to attend a luncheon hosted by Prime Minister Paul Martin. Hannah had no idea what a Prime Minister was. Colleen explained that he was someone who held a lot of power in Canada.

"Well, if he has so much power, then I need to speak at his luncheon," Hannah said to her mother.

Colleen responded by trying to explain that things just didn't happen that way, but Hannah wouldn't let up and cajoled her mother into asking.

Colleen sheepishly dialed the number of the Prime Minister's office. Her daughter's request to speak at the luncheon was met with silence at the other end of the phone. Forty-five minutes later, the Prime Minister's office phoned back to say yes.

Hannah sat beside Prime Minister Martin at the luncheon held at a Chinese restaurant filled to capacity with 500 of the country's most powerful politicians and business leaders. Hannah would later talk about how she viewed the Prime Minister as "just a regular guy with a pretty big job."

Hannah's speech that day made such an impact on the Prime Minister that he gave her his direct phone number and told her she could call him anytime. A year later, the day before the federal election, she used the number and left a message. "Good luck tomorrow,"

Hannah said into his answering machine. "And even if you don't win, you'll be okay."

Still, one of the hardest things for Colleen was explaining to Hannah that homelessness may never go away and the best you can do is make it a little bit better.

Hannah's answer: "I want to find a cure for it."

Last Christmas, Hannah asked Santa to build a house for all of her homeless friends. When her mother read this, she told Hannah that Santa couldn't do everything. So Hannah asked Santa for sleeping bags for the shelter to keep everyone warm. Colleen called up a manufacturer of sleeping bags and explained what Hannah had asked for. The supplier sent Colleen 100 sleeping bags. At Christmas, Hannah went to the shelter to give them out. It was the best present she had ever gotten. To thank her for all her hard work, the homeless people at the shelter passed around a ladybug jar of their own as a small way to help each other.

Once, when Hannah was at a shelter handing out pie, she asked the first man in line what kind of pie he would like. The man looked shocked. "I have a choice?" he stammered back. No one had ever given him a choice before. "Of course, you have a choice," Hannah replied and smiled back at him.

This work comes naturally to Hannah and yet is so hard for many of us. "They need money, that's true," Hannah says. "But mostly what they need from us is love. And we need to treat them like they are family. Like a brother or sister. Because you'd never let a brother or sister sleep in a garbage can, or eat out of one. And that's the most important thing we can do. Give them love."

Hannah can take the hand of the Prime Minister or the hand of a homeless man, and to her they are equal. Some days, all Hannah can think about is helping the homeless. On other days, she's a regular kid and it's all about her new rubber boots. Hannah says that if you don't want to help her cause through the Ladybug Foundation, it would be good enough if you just cared about something. Anything. It would be enough to just care about the person standing beside you.

Hannah Taylor is a person of action (POA). She saw something that really disturbed her. We all face similar situations when we are troubled by something. How many of us simply drop a coin in a cup, avoid eye contact and move on? How many times have you been bullied at work, taken abuse from an unappreciative customer, or didn't pursue a just cause? All the while knowing it was wrong, and yet you did nothing. Why?

By contrast, there are those special, proactive individuals like Hannah, who do something to fix what they perceive to be wrong.

Hannah was motivated by her own uneasiness that just wouldn't go away. Hannah's mom was key in providing support and encouragement. What motivates such a young person to take action when a much easier road would have included a life built around friends and school? There are countless stories of young people whose actions have produced amazing results. When we are faced with career choices, we can learn from their unobstructed childhood enthusiasm to take some action, no matter what the odds. Here is another example.

Samantha's Story:

It was 1982 and ten-year-old Samantha Smith was confused. She understood that relations between the two most powerful countries at the time, the United States and the Soviet Union, were not good and that they engaged in something called a "Cold War."

The leaders of both countries said they'd never start a nuclear war. Why, then, Samantha wondered, did they both continue to stockpile nuclear weapons? We often give children false security by saying, "Don't you worry, everything will work out." When Samantha asked her mother to write to the new president of the Soviet Union, Yuri Andropov, her mother in her wisdom said, "Why don't you?" So, in the winter of 1982, Samantha Smith sat down to write her letter.

Dear Mr. Andropov,
My name is Samantha Smith. I am ten years old. Congratulations on your new job. I have been worrying about Russia and the United States getting into a nuclear war. Are you going to have a war or not? If you aren't, please tell me how you are going to not have a war . . . . God made the world for us to live together in peace and not fight.
Sincerely,
Samantha Smith

---

[11] Samantha Smith died in 1985 in an airplane crash. She was 13 years old. If you want to learn more about this remarkable young woman, check www.Samanthasmith.info

Samantha sent the letter and felt satisfied. Her life in Grade Five at Manchester Elementary School in Manchester, Maine returned to normal. But little did Samantha realize the tremendous impact the letter would have on her future.

In April 1983, she was called into the principal's office. Her immediate thought was, "What have I done wrong?" However, to her surprise, she wasn't in trouble at all. There was a phone call for her. On the other end of the line was a reporter from United Press International.

"Did you write a letter to President Andropov?" the reporter asked.

"Yes," Samantha replied.

The reporter went on to explain that he had seen a copy of it in the official state newspaper of the Soviet Union. Samantha was shocked. Up to that moment she wasn't sure that President Andropov had even received her letter!

When she got home from school that day, she told her mother what had happened. Then Samantha sat down and wrote another letter, this one to the Soviet ambassador in Washington, D.C. She hoped that he could tell her what was going on. A few days later Samantha received another phone call, this time from the Soviet Ambassador telling her that a personal letter to her from President Andropov was on its way. On April 25th, Samantha and her father stopped by the post office to pick up the letter.

By the time Samantha arrived home, her front yard was crowded with reporters and photographers from all over the country. In the midst of this media frenzy, Samantha coolly answered questions about the letter she had written to President Andropov and his response.

In President Andropov's lengthy letter, he compared Samantha to the fictional character Becky Thatcher in Mark Twain's famous novel, Tom Sawyer. 12He called Samantha "courageous and honest." [13] He told her that the Soviet Union was "trying to do everything it could to

---

[12] Mark Twain, The Adventures of Tom Sawyer, University of California Press, 2002.

[13] Mark Twain, *Tom Sawyer, The Adventures of Tom Sawyer*, (University of California Press, 2002).

avoid a war between the countries." When the reporters asked what she thought of Andropov's response, she said it read like "a letter from a friend."

Andropov invited Samantha and her family to visit the Soviet Union to see what the people of his country were like. While she was in the Soviet Union, Samantha visited Moscow and Leningrad. She also traveled to the Artek Pioneer Camp where she met and talked with children her own age who were members of the Young Pioneers, a youth group similar to the Boy and Girl Scouts in the United States.

She stayed in a dormitory with nine other girls and spent time swimming, talking, and learning Russian songs and dances. She found that many of her new friends were also concerned about peace. Samantha realized, that in many ways, the Russian children were not all that different from Samantha and her friends in the United States.

By the time Samantha returned home, she had become an international celebrity. Over the next two years, she balanced schoolwork, swimming, and playing softball with television appearances, speeches and writing a book titled Journey to the Soviet Union. [14]

She also traveled with her mother to attend the Children's International Symposium in Kobe, Japan. There, she gave a speech in which she suggested that the Soviet and U.S. leaders exchange granddaughters for two weeks every year. She explained that a president "wouldn't want to send a bomb to a country his granddaughter would be visiting."

Gradually, Samantha Smith came to be recognized as a worldwide representative for peace. Tragically, in August 1985, Samantha and her father were killed in an airplane crash. The little girl who believed that "people can get along" was gone.

Long before her death, Samantha said, "Sometimes I still worry that the next day will be the last day of the Earth, but with more people thinking about the problems of the world, I hope that someday soon we will find the way to world peace. Maybe someone will show us the way."

---

[14] Samantha Smith, *Journey to the Soviet Union* (Little Brown & Co., 1984).

Samantha Smith was that someone who showed many the ways to create a more peaceful world.

Why Hannah and Samantha?

What's different about Hannah and Samantha? What made them POAs? Hannah and Samantha shared a lot in common. They both had supportive mothers. They both felt a strong sense of injustice and they both dealt with their perceived helplessness by finding people of power to help them out.

What they did was more than buy a lottery ticket and say, "I'll give the winnings to people who need it." They wrote a letter or made a phone call, actions that common sense would say were impractical and silly. The world around these girls would have scoffed at the mere idea that they could make any difference at all. But they did.

Where Does Motivation Come From?

Both Hannah and Samantha realized that they lacked the connections, ability, money, age and maturity to change something on such a grand scale. Have you ever felt helpless in your job? Have you ever wanted to take action but didn't because the solutions you created sound far-fetched? Many of us, when faced with extraordinary odds, understand our limitations and quickly calculate the odds of success. The conclusion we often draw is, "Why bother?" But not Hannah and Samantha. They took their helplessness and made it work. They asked themselves, "What can I do to motivate the powerful?" In asking the right question, they turned the table from helplessness to strong personal power.

We can learn from "the mouths of babes." This well-known phrase points to a truth, and yet many of us disregard the clarity of vision that children often have. Children don't complicate a situation with excuses or innuendo. They often see life as simple and straightforward. This leads us to one root cause of inaction—the tendency to overcomplicate things. As adults, we become adept at finding excuses for inaction—particularly when we are at the wrong end of the power scale. We say things like: "I shouldn't topple the apple cart." or "What if my efforts are scoffed at?" or "What if I'm looked at as a radical?" or "What if my friends find out, what if, what if, what if ...?"

The more we think, the more "what ifs" appear. With 500 television channels, unending access to information on CNN, and a world of knowledge at your fingertips through the Internet, anyone who attempts to analyze the pros and cons of taking action simply has too much information. Everyday decisions, such as should I approach a particular client, or how can I add more value to my customers, are equally as difficult as the big questions such as what to do about world peace.

There are 50 types of cereals, 15 different types of Aspirin, and more choices of diapers than you could possibly imagine from which to choose. Perhaps having lots of choices on the supermarket shelf creates the illusion of action and choice. But who cares which brand of toothpaste you use? At the same time, too much information about more important issues can be debilitating and create a sense of hopelessness. The world is a complicated place. The more technologically advanced we become, the greater the tendency for inaction. We can't make a major purchase or decision unless we check a Consumer Report, look it up on Google, or call our accountant, lawyer or homeopath. Many of us live in a world where we have a degree of control that our ancestors could not have dreamed of.

Competition in the marketplace brings choices of products our ancestors would have never thought possible. Restaurants serve foods from all corners of the globe. Cars are available in every imaginable size and color and with as many options as anyone could possibly want. If you are looking for an evening's entertainment, go no further than your local newspaper. In it you will find neighborhood multiplexes with dozens of movies to choose from. The average North American will change jobs seven times during his or her career. We can conduct our businesses in an office building, from our home office, or on our computer in a hotel room. Surely a society that provides so many choices to its citizens has opened the doors to action.

Through the media, we are inundated with information, and hear conflicting opinions through the grapevine. What we think is right may be wrong. What we think is healthy might be slowly killing us. What we think is safe might be hazardous. Too much information has left us feeling helpless.

Conversely, too little information can do the same. Picture Tom Hanks washed up on the shore of an uninhabited island in the movie Cast Away. [15]

---

[15] If you are one of the six people on the planet who did not see Cast Away, then rent it at your local video store. You are in for a real treat.

He was on his own with no help, no fire, no food and no shelter. After the crash, he spent the first few days staring at the ocean waiting for rescue. He assumed, like many of us, that there would be someone out there to help—social safety nets, governments, doctors and lawyers.

Tom Hank's character quickly understood that he had lost more than his personal belongings: He had lost everything. He was now on a high wire without a net. He would survive or die, depending on his actions alone. Being stranded on an uninhabited island is an extreme situation, but it makes a good point. Many of us feel stranded and helpless. Some of us roll up into a little ball and give up saying, "What's the point?" But another choice is to try the best you can with what you have. In one great scene, Hanks' character discovers fire. When he dances around on the beach, we all share his pride in his accomplishment.

Too much information can be stifling and too little can leave us paralyzed. There must be a connection between information and action. Technology and information play an integral part in our ability to do things. When we have a lot of information, we search for methods of organizing it into neat compartments. When we don't, we look for information to help us through one dilemma at a time with very little thought to other possibilities. In some cases, we simply do not have the power to achieve what we want, as we saw with Samantha and Hannah. Their choice was to mobilize those that do have power.

But what about the other side of the story? What if we have the power but lack the motivation to use it? Hannah and Samantha knew that on their own they were helpless, but by tapping into those with power, they were able to make great strides. A common assumption is that those who are helpless are very motivated to take action, while those who are powerful don't need additional motivation to act. In many ways, these are the same story from opposite points of view. But there are countless cases of people who possess power, talent and resources, yet fail to act. We will deal with this side of the story in the next chapter. For now, let's focus our attention on the problem of helplessness.

Perceived Power

Did Samantha and Hannah simply leave it to the powerful to solve the problems they saw? Certainly not! They each found the right person and asked that person, in their childish naiveté, to be part of the solution.

Perhaps Hannah and Samantha are extreme examples of how a little chutzpah and a whole lot of luck produces incredible results. What are the chances of you or me writing to the President of the United States about a problem we see and getting an answer directly from the President rather than one of many assistants? If you work for a large corporation, what are the chances of your CEO joining you at a local pub for an after work drink? You might come up with an idea and pooh-pooh it saying, "What's the use?" Indeed, this might seem like a reasonable response because the chances of success are remote.

You might equate them to your chance of winning a lottery, which is 17,000,000 to one. So what are your chances of the President of the United States, or your CEO, taking your request seriously? This all sounds reasonable, but playing the odds like this can put you in the backseat. When you do this, you give up your power to the perception that power is based on luck. You falsely conclude there is no way you can make a difference.

Every year, millions of new businesses are formed. Within five years, less than ten percent of them will still be active. There are thousands of restaurants opened each year and less than one in eight will survive their first year. It's easier to create lists of excuses than to find the one reason to act. So, the strategy to become a POA and take control of your career starts with understanding the root of your sense of helplessness. Once you've accomplished this, you can move beyond that point to find actions that are right for the situations where you feel helpless.

Helplessness is the perception of being out of control with no authority or status to affect how others will act towards you and no apparent solution to help you regain control. Helplessness is a sales person's greatest enemy. We live in a world of instant gratification. When we act, we expect instant results. But in many situations, that's not a reasonable expectation. When Samantha wrote to Andropov, it took months before she received an answer. She could have run home everyday to check the mail, but instead she simply went about her daily life.

That's what pro-activity is about. POAs activate the action and then let it do its work. Meteorologist Edward Lorenz found that convection currents and turbulence patters were chaotic--seemingly random but, in fact, exhibiting a pattern. From this observation he fathered what was to become known as Chaos Theory where he postulated that a butterfly that flaps its wings on one side of the world could cause a hurricane on the other. [16]

The winds don't build immediately. It takes time. When it comes to being proactive, like the butterfly, it's doing that counts. The results may or may not manifest themselves immediately, but results should not affect your decision to do something. It is the act of doing that makes you a POA. Sometimes it's just a matter of taking that last shot, of knowing you've left no stone unturned. It's knowing you did everything you could.

Perceived Helplessness

In the 1960s, Martin Seligman, a young psychologist, began work in an area later known throughout the psychological world as "learned helplessness." [17]

Like many significant scientific findings, he stumbled on this important area of human behavior by accident. In the mid '60s, he was working in the laboratory of Richard L. Solomon, another noted

---

[16] Much has been written about M.I.T Meteorologist Edward Lorenz and his Chaos theory and the so called Butterfly Effect. It appears in movies, books and of course, science. In human psychology "The Butterfly Effect" is reminiscent of Gestalt theory where the whole is greater than the sum of its parts.

[17] You could write a PHD thesis on Seligman and many have. Here are a few of the sources I found helpful:
Steven F Maier (University of Colorado), Christopher Peterson (University of Michigan), and Barry Schwartz (Strathmore College); *From Helplessness to Hope:: The Seminal Career of Martin Seligman*, www.strathmore.edu/socsci/bschwar/helplessness
Dr. Martin E.P. Seligman's Biography, Pennsylvania Gazette Profile, www.psych.upenn/seligman/bio.
Shibley Telhami, *Who is responsible?* (The Brookings Institute, August 2005).
Sam Vanknin, *Traumas as Social Interactions*, Nice2Know.com.
Barry Schwartz, *Pitfalls on the Road to Positive Psychology of Hope*, www.strathmore.edu/socsci/bschwar/pitfalls
Katherine Hahner, *Learned helplessness: A critique of Research and Theory*, www.curedisease.com/perspectives/vol_1_1989.
T. George Harris, *Psychology's New Handbook of Happiness, Spirituality and health*, (August 2004).
However, the best place to start is direct from the source, Martin E.P. Seligman, *Positive Psychology, Positive prevention, and Positive Therapy*, (University of Pennsylvania).

psychologist. Seligman was studying the relationship between fear and learning when he discovered an unexpected phenomenon.

Undoubtedly you are familiar with the work of Ivan Pavlov. [18]

The Russian psychologist found that when a dog is presented with food, it salivates. When presented with food along with the sound of a bell, the animal will also salivate. Eventually, when the food was withdrawn, the dog would salivate at the ring of the bell alone. Seligman took this one step further. Instead of pairing the ringing sound of the bell with a positive reward like food, he added a negative association with an escapable electric shock.

His thinking was that the dog, when shocked, would run away afraid. Therefore, when the dog associated the ring with the shock, the sound of the bell would instill fear and cause the dog to retreat. Seligman divided his dogs into three groups. Each group consisted of a pair of dogs. The first two groups were yoked with a shock device and one dog in each pair could terminate the shock by going for the food. The other dog in each pair had no control, which Seligman coined as, "inescapable shock." No matter what this second dog did, it could not affect the shock. The third group received no shock at all in this phase of the experiment.

Next, they put all the dogs into a shuttle box. This was a box with a low fence dividing it into two compartments. The dogs could easily see over the fence and jump over it at will. What they found was that the dogs who received escapable shocks and those that received nothing at all performed as expected. They would jump over the fence to get food. However, the dogs that were exposed to inescapable shock reacted in a surprising way. When the bell rang, these dogs did nothing.

Apparently the dogs had learned that trying to escape from the shock was futile. The outcomes of their actions were not related to their efforts. The result was not what you might expect. After all, food is food to a dog. But these dogs just gave up. The animals that had initially received escapable shocks learned that an action could stop the shock. Those that had initially received physically identical inescapable shocks learned that there was no action that could stop the shock.

---

[18] Your pet slobbering all over the kitchen floor when you open a can of dog food was explained by Pavlov. There is no reference in Pavlov's writing about cleaning up the mess - you are on your own.

The early human studies were similar, but rather than an electric shock, human subjects were exposed to bursts of white noise. And just as in the animal studies, the human subjects not able to control the bursts of light were slower at problem solving or creating productive strategies.

There are similar results from real-life situations. Those subjected to torture or extreme psychological pain often go through stages starting with denial through to helplessness, to rage, then to acceptance. Many children and adults learn helplessness through personal failure, embarrassment, peer pressure, lack of encouragement, and the constant bombardment of negative messages. In some cases, these conditions paralyze people; in others they motivate.

Seligman took his work one step further and created a model drawn from his work as well as the work of another body of literature known as "attribution theory." Attribution theory is concerned with the way we contribute to the causality of events. There are three main dimensions: internal, external and global.

The internal dimension is when a person assumes responsibility for an action, whether to give him or her credit for an outcome (positive) or to take the blame (negative). Those who have a negative self-image say things like: "I am stupid; if I had only noticed the signs earlier; if I only had the talent; I'm too short; I'm too tall; how could I have missed the obvious solution; if I had only been born with rich parents." They assume that something lacking in themselves caused the outcome and they continually beat themselves up over it. On the other hand, those who have a positive self-image say things like: "This challenge is perfect for me; I can let those negative comments roll off my back."

The external dimension is when individuals have the tendency to blame others. Often, more pessimistic people fall into this category. They may say: "If only they would stop picking on me; my boss won't let me do anything creative; the competition got there first."

The global dimension is when people are fatalistic and resigned, meaning that any situation is perceived as typical of what you can expect. Here are a couple of typical messages: "It's all you can expect; life's just a crap shoot; you can't fight city hall; we have been doing things this way forever."

There are advantages to both the optimistic and pessimistic outlooks. Certain jobs call for an optimistic and creative outlook. Successful salespeople need to be optimists, as do medical researchers. Pessimists consciously look for things that are wrong. They make negative assumptions about themselves, others and the world. Yet, without their outlook they would not be able to do their jobs well. Good law-enforcement officers come to mind, as do people who are responsible for quality control. Without their pessimistic outlook, they might miss important clues that would affect the quality of their work. By recognizing the origin of your behavior (internal, external or global) you can look at yourself, and the behaviors of others, and the way the world works.

Certainly the experimental dogs never worried about whether they were causing the shock, someone else was, or whether everyone on the planet was feeling the shock simultaneously. When you justify your circumstances using the internal, external or global dimensions as excuses, you lead a life of stagnation, frustration, and inactivity.

When you can look at the world around you in a healthy context, you can find different approaches which will lead to a greater level of satisfaction in your job. What about people who live on very little food and water as their only source of nourishment, or those whose only mode of transportation is their feet, and their evening entertainment is sitting around a fire to keep warm? What about people living under repressive political and economic systems with no personal freedoms? Surely these people are among the POA-challenged.

Yet, in every culture, and under every set of circumstances, there are POAs who do things to change their situations. Think about Mahatma Gandhi; Nelson Mandela, Oscar Schindler, and a host of others! Desperation can lead to action, too.

But just like the dogs in Seligman's experiments, a great many people have also learned that since the outcome was independent of the effort, it was useless to struggle. Learned helplessness affects people in all walks of life, in all cultures, and in all political and economic situations. But some people turn their helplessness into motivation for action.

Hannah and Samantha were not affected by any of the negative influences in their lives. Perhaps these two children are exceptional (although I personally do not believe this). Many books on child rearing and stories in the media deal with children affected negatively by their childhood "shocks." They experience symptoms ranging from anger, frustration, tantrums, and violence to withdrawal, complacency, and unfocused behavior. These tendencies become fodder for the Dr. Phils of the world. The children that manage to break through such difficulties use the advantage they have as kids and act as if there was no one to tell them they were wrong. There are countless examples of children rising out of poverty who have made positive choices. There are children adopted from Third World countries who have managed to refocus their past as a learning experience and continued to mature in a positive fashion.

The same is true of adults. The following is a great example of another POA who saw injustice in the innocent world of children. Like Hannah and Samantha, he bought his metaphysical lottery ticket – and won!

Paul's Story

One winter's day, a frustrated Toronto Police officer sat down to write an e-mail to a man that he had never met:

Mr. (Bill) Gates,

My name is Detective Sergeant Paul Gillespie[19] of the Toronto Police Service. I am in charge of the Child Exploitation Section of the Sex Crimes Unit. I have ten people assigned to me who are responsible for investigating online child pornography.

My staff is inundated with case files. They seized over two million movies and images of child abuse last year alone. Although the Internet is a wonderful tool, it has changed our lives forever. As the former director of the FBI so accurately observed, when you combine an age-old problem with modern technology, you create an insurmountable task for investigators.

By virtue of their age, intelligence and limited life experience, children are totally vulnerable as victims of sexual exploitation and abuse. Children are the "perfect" victims, and we are not very good at identifying their abusers.

I am frustrated and need your help.

Detective Sergeant Paul Gillespie

---

[19] Julian Sher, *Now, he's stepping up the fight* (The Globe and Mail, July 16, 2006).

Bill Gates receives millions of e-mails every year.[20] Paul never thought his would be among the few to grab Gate's attention. And then he got a call.

In the late 1990s, Paul was working in foot patrol in Toronto's Regent Park, a housing project notorious for its drugs and violent crimes, when his young son was diagnosed with leukemia. Paul's world suddenly changed. His son needed him. Paul took a leave from the force to help his son with his treatment. Going through this process changed Paul forever. Once the treatment was suitably underway, he knew he couldn't return to his job and perform the tasks that were required of him. Everything about him was different.

The Internet was still a relatively new phenomenon, and people had not even begun to think about its darker side—child pornography. A few examples of child pornography had been seized. The Toronto police had dealt with each occurrence as it came up, but there was no formal way to battle this crime. Paul got a call asking if he would consider taking a look at the problem. At the time, the feeling was that child exploitation on the Internet was probably going to go away in six months.

Child pornography on the Internet didn't go away; in fact, it got worse, and Paul quickly found himself heading a new department to combat it. Each day Paul would come to work thinking it couldn't get any worse. He said, "During 2001 and 2002, I saw more and learned more about Internet child pornography and how the computer facilitated and expanded the exploitation of children.

I had the opportunity to do some traveling and training around the world with Scotland Yard, the FBI, the Manchester police, and INTERPOL. I got a pretty good sense that law enforcement was not doing much, and what they were doing was certainly not in a coordinated fashion. No one was passing information on to anyone else. We weren't recognizing that there was so much that we could utilize the Internet, including newsgroups and instant communication or passing on intelligence to each other with massive amounts of storage at little cost."

---

[20] I have no actual proof that Bill Gates receives millions of e-mails. I can only surmise based on the amount of unsolicited stuff I receive.

Just when Paul thought it wouldn't be humanly possible to see anything more horrible than he had seen the day before, he inevitably would. Every single day, it got worse. The department was battling a technology that they didn't truly understand and that was making the sheer quantity of this kind of material more and more staggering. Rather than seizing 100 or 200 photographs in a typical raid, they were now seizing photographs in the tens of thousands. In one raid in 2003, they seized over one million images of child pornography on just one computer.

Paul described the problem as a cultural phenomenon, "We all think we own our own pieces of information. Nobody wants to share with anybody, not with our own division, the police department or the RCMP."

Paul's frustration was growing. While he was fighting the evils of child pornography, he was also still facing the very personal battle of his son's intense chemotherapy treatment. "On a personal level, I watched the horrors children with cancer have to go through and at the same time saw healthy children having their bodies tortured and hurt in much the same way. There was a real feeling of helplessness. While I really couldn't do much for my son, I sure as hell could do something for those other kids."

And Paul did. A week after his son's treatment ended with successful results, he returned to his office and looked up at one of the motivational quotes that adorned his office wall. It was from Albert Einstein. It read, "Significant problems we face cannot be solved by the same level of thinking that we were at when we created them." And then it struck Paul, "We didn't create this. I don't even understand it, but Bill Gates does." Paul sat down at his computer, opened up his e-mail program and began typing. "When I sent the e-mail, I was under no delusions that anything would come out of it."

A month later he got a response.

Bill Gates had read Paul's e-mail and picked up the phone and called Frank Clay, the president of Microsoft Canada. "About a month later," Paul recounts, "I was called out of the blue. It was a call from Microsoft Canada saying, "What do you want?"

"What I want is for you to tell me what I want," Paul answered.

"You're kidding, right?" Frank answered back.

"No," Paul replied.

A month later it became clear how they could work together. "Frank simply did not understand what we are dealing with, so I had to show him," Paul said.

During the presentation, Paul showed the executives from Microsoft five horrific images. There were pictures of babies being sodomized and three-year-olds being tortured. And Paul said, "This is what people are using the Internet for. As you know, 92 percent of all the software in the world is Microsoft. I'm not sure if you guys are aware of the bad things that are being done with your product."

The meeting was an eye-opener and Microsoft quickly assigned a team to come up with a solution to help this problem. The outcome is a powerful piece of software called the Child Exploitation Tracking System (CETS). [21]

For the first time, it gave officers locally, nationally, and internationally a way to store all of their information, share it with each other, and analyze it by using very sophisticated tools.

The program is now up and running in 22 police services in Canada. Paul has been showcasing the software to law-enforcement bodies all over the globe. The software has made links that, so far, have led to six arrests of people who either have been producing child pornography or distributing it in mass numbers. According to Paul, as the system continues to grow, there will be many more arrests to come.

The text from the e-mail he wrote to Bill Gates now hangs on a plaque on the wall of his office, a memento presented to him by Microsoft at the launch of the software. But for Paul, it's still not enough.

"Everybody asks 'how I can do this job'?" Paul states. "And it's a reasonable question. My response is 'how would you like to be on the other side of the camera'? Those kids need to know that someone is working for them. We've done our best to publicize the problem and get involved in coordinating forces around the world. Hopefully, there

---

[21] The Child Exploitation Tracking System evolved with the participation of Microsoft, The Royal Canadian Mounted Police and the Toronto Police Services.

are people reading the newspapers, seeing arrests being made, and victims are being found, identified, and rescued. It seems to me to be a worthy cause even though it is painful to work on it."

You can probably see how Paul could have easily fallen into a cycle of pessimism. His police training coupled with his experience with his son could have led to a state of hopelessness. We would have hardly blamed him. Paul had tried everything he could and simply felt he was now butting his head against a wall trying to solve a problem that was bigger than his budget, power, and intellect. But the lesson for all of us is similar to that of Hannah and Samantha. Helplessness, in many cases, is a matter of perception. But that perception is not universal. Reality shows that there are degrees of helplessness.

Think about something you are wrestling with - a problem with a stubborn customer perhaps. Let's say you work for a boss that simply makes your life miserable. His demands on your sales performance is sometimes unrealistic. The job is interesting and pays well. The company is located close to your home, which cuts down on commuting time. But each day you have to put up with the tirades of an overbearing, inconsiderate megalomaniac. Let's add one more ingredient: Your boss is also the son-in-law of the owner of the company. What do you do?

Perhaps you could quit and find another job. But, what if that wasn't an option? Job opportunities are not always readily available. You don't want to relocate your family. You don't want a reduction in your salary and you don't want to start all over again developing a new group of customer contacts. Just like Seligman's dogs, you give up. In terms of Seligman's dimensions, you may be faced with all three. Internally, you feel helpless in coming up with an answer that leads to a certain self-loathing. Externally, you say that the real problem is your jerk of a boss. And globally you feel powerless in looking elsewhere because on balance, if it weren't for the boss, it would be a pretty good place to work. What do you do?

A negative person might start taking out his or her frustrations at home. Others might internalize their powerlessness and turn to self-defeating behavior such as drugs or alcohol. Others might simply give up just like Seligman's dogs, saying, "What's the use?"

We all feel helpless at some time in our lives. However, when you recognize what is happening, you can find the courage to take steps, no matter how small, to find a solution.

An extreme case of helplessness became front-page headlines in August of 2005. [22]

Seven Russian submariners experienced a situation that would have left many of us without options. They were trapped 190 meters under the Pacific Ocean in a crippled mini-sub that was caught in a mass of underground antennas. Imagine their horror as their oxygen was slowly dwindling. The motors had ceased, leaving them in an eerie silence. The cold from the icy ocean was slowly permeating the shell of the craft, and was creeping into the marrow of their bones. The only word they later used to describe the feeling was "indescribable."

Their vehicle was stranded. Time was quickly running out. They were isolated with no contact with the rest of the world. They had no idea if the rescue plans would be successful. They must have reflected on another similar Russian submarine incident where 112 submariners lost their lives. In such circumstances, most of us might, like Seligman's dogs, simply give up. But not these well-trained sailors. Their only focus was on survival. They proactively decided to conserve as much oxygen and heat as possible until help arrived. So, huddled in the dark, these seven sailors had one option—to remain calm. They breathed slowly to conserve oxygen and limit the creation of deadly carbon dioxide. They put their trust in their comrades, themselves, and the men and women above who were trying to save them.

People often tell me, "It's not that simple," or "You couldn't possibly understand what I am going through." Often, we make things worse by over-complicating them. It's Occam's Razor, a principle that traces its roots to such philosophers as Thomas Aquinas, John Duns Scott, and even Aristotle that simply states, "One should not make more assumptions than the minimum needed." [23]

---

[22] This story had a happy ending and the sailors were rescued. See *USA Today* for two stories: "US Relief Crew on way to Russian Sub", (August 2005) and "Robotic Craft Rescues Russian Sub" (August 2005). "They are Pushing Down Panic", *The Toronto Star*, (August 2005).

[23] The principle of Occam's Razor is attributed to a Franciscan friar named William of Ockham in the 14th century. This principle is the source of the often quoted conclusion: if it looks like a duck and sounds like a duck – it must be a duck.

Chapter 1 - Lessons Learned

1. Overcome your helplessness and do not lose hope.
2. Do not overcomplicate your situation.
3. Find your keystone: it's the clue to what actions should you take.

We don't live in a safe and perfect world. When I walk my children to their car, after they've been home to visit, my parting words are always "have a safe trip," or "drive carefully." It's as if these words are a talisman that will protect my children.

Sales people understand the perils of living in an uncertain workplace. Even what appears to be positive can have a dark side in these uncertain times. You can get a great job with travel perks and end up spending far too much of your time in long security lines at airports.

You can get a great job with a chemical company only to find out that your work environment has been slowly poisoning you. A great job with a fast-moving, multi-national can fall apart when you learn that your top management has been looting the company's coffers for years. Customer's loyalties seem to change on a whim – one day they welcome you with open arms and the next visit is handled like an intrusion. What can you do in the face of such realities?

Rather than being defeated and giving up when your job gets tough, you can learn from Hannah, Samantha, and Paul, who put their helplessness to work. Knowing that they lacked the necessary ingredients to make changes, they found others who could help. No matter how slim their chances of success, they each gave it their best shot. This is a powerful lesson that you can apply when you find yourself in a difficult situation.

When you're overwhelmed by work situations, e.g. the number of sales calls you're expected to make, the number of departments that have to sign-off on an initiative, the degree of technological complexity your new IT systems seems to require, or having to choose between customer A or B, it is easy to overcomplicate situations to the point of feeling helpless. If you can step back and look at the situation through the innocent eyes of children like Hannah and Samantha, you'll often find positive, creative actions you can take in seemingly overwhelming situations. Paul was overwhelmed, so he reached out for help. What was his chance of success? In foresight, his chances of success were slim. In hindsight, he did the right thing. In many cases, the best you can do is what you learned from those Russian submariners who were put to the test — take one breath at a time.

Lessons into Action: Your Sales Action Plan

Step 1: Overcome your helplessness and do not lose hope:

a. Take a few moments and think of a recent sales-related predicament where you felt helpless and wanted to do something, but didn't because you didn't know what to do. Then, write a detailed description of this situation and your rationale for not taking action. In your rationale, list any ideas you came up with but didn't act on, and what happened. Just writing out the scenario will help you overcome the feeling of helplessness. Like all important things, this process takes time, so put your description away in a safe place for a few days. In the meantime, your subconscious will be working on the problem.

b. Establish a specific time in the next two or three days to re-read what you have written. Set aside this time by making an appointment with yourself. Put it in your calendar.

c. When you re-read and reconsider your problem, pretend that you have no restrictions of any kind, that there is no one looking over your shoulder who might criticize your ideas. See if you can come up with a few new suggestions and steps you can take to resolve the situation. Don't discard any ideas, no matter how seemingly absurd. The trick is not to stop in the middle of a sentence and say, "What a dumb idea," or "That will never work." Just let your ideas flow. You might have a few ideas immediately, but don't stop there.

d. Dig deeper. You may decide to put your work away for two or three days before looking at it again. Each time you scan what you have written, you will find fresh ideas that were there all the time, but you may have missed the first time. Scanning means quickly processing the same material. Each time you scan the material you see it with new eyes and a new perspective. Highlight or circle the newly relevant ideas as they pop out at you. You'll start to find solutions you missed at first.

Improve Your Scanning Skills

Solving Sudoku puzzles is a good way to learn the power of scanning. I was recently introduced to Sudoku; the wildly popular number game. The object is to arrange the numbers 1 through 9 in each square and on each horizontal and vertical line. When I first picked up the game, I quickly became overwhelmed. Even though I had been taught a few basic strategies, I often found myself at a dead end. More than once, the feeling of helplessness caused me to quit. Then I learned that there might be as many as 12 Sudoku strategies. What I learned, as I progressed, was that each of these strategies gave me a new way of scanning the game to find clues that were already there. What I also learned was that when I am really stuck, the best thing to do is to put the puzzle away for a while. I am often amazed, when I return to the puzzle, to see answers that were staring me in the face all along.

Step 2: Do Not Overcomplicate Your Situation

Start by listing your ideas from Step 1. You may be overcomplicating your situation because you're too close to it. You see all the problems, nuances, and quirks. You need to develop a sense of detachment from the issue. When you put your emotions on the back burner, you can see things differently. You will surprise yourself when you find solutions that were there all the time. Critically ask yourself, "Is there something I can do that's worth one last shot?" When you allow your thoughts time to percolate, ideas that might have initially seemed nonsensical can often reveal the beginning of a plan for action.

Unclutter your mind. Overcomplicating is indicative of a cluttered mind. This step will help you unclutter. You need to take all those ideas you gleaned in the first step and get you emotions out of the picture. You are dealing with your feeling of helplessness and you don't want it to get in the way of your progress. When I try to cool down my emotions I go to my workshop and build something. I find that when I refocus my energy from what I do every day to doing something manually, like carpentry, it does the trick for me. What works for you? Perhaps it's taking a walk, doing some yoga, practicing meditations, or exercising at the gym. Often, while I am puttering in my workroom, solutions clarify in my mind. Carpentry puts me in a relaxed, yet focused, state of mind. I am thinking about whether that board should be 7 and 1/8 inches or 7 and 1/16 inches. When I shift my focus from a problem that I am working on to something that is not related, ideas seem to flow. The trick is to write them down when they flow.

Step 3: Find Your Keystone

Throughout this book you'll learn steps to guide you through your sales career maze. Some of these steps can be accomplished quickly; others will take some time. The following falls into the latter category:

A keystone is a wedge-shaped stone that fits on the highest point of an architectural arch. Without the keystone, all other rocks that make up the arch over a doorway or ceiling would have no balance and therefore nothing to keep them in place. Your keystone is what holds up your beliefs about why you can or cannot take an action. Finding your keystone is crucial. Without a clear understanding, you run the risk of choosing sales solutions for all the wrong reasons. For example,

Paul Gillespie might have drowned in the complexity of Internet porn. Samantha Smith might have never reached President Andropov if she worried about layer upon layer of bureaucracy. Hannah Taylor might have succumbed to a grown-up world that told her she was too young and the problems of homelessness too complicated.

Your search begins with questions. Go back to the list you created in Step 2 and ask "Why," or "How," or "What" of each of your ideas for proactive action. These questions help you chip away at each stone until there is noting left between you and taking action. Be relentless until you run out of questions. When this happens, it is your clue that you are close to your keystone. What really matters most in this step is the asking, because if you don't ask, you will never know. When you have found your keystone you will say, "Aha!" as this truth will provide the answers you were looking for. You will have found the keystone that has held everything in place. Now you can decide if you want to keep the arch or start over again. It's your choice. It takes time to find your keystone, but it's worth the effort.

You have now taken the first steps towards overcoming your helplessness and restoring your sense of hope, simplifying your situation, and finding your keystone. Now you need to take a leap of faith. You are charting unknown waters. Go slowly; take small steps by first finding ways to make little changes. These changes can be found in ideas you have uncovered in simple everyday experiences. For example, the next time a customer asks you to do something and says, "Sorry, but something has come up; let's reschedule for 2:00 o'clock tomorrow"; rather than passively saying, "Sure, it's okay," tell this person, "That doesn't work for me. How soon do you have to leave?

Can we accomplish some of our agenda now?" Whether a simple request from a customer, a phone call that interrupts the flow of your work, or a sales call that goes on long after the agenda has been completed, the more times you stand up to your helplessness, the more you will be empowered. Every once in a while you will make the wrong decision. When this happens go back and analyze it and see what you can learn. A wise man once told me that the secret to success is to make more right decisions than wrong ones. I believe this wholeheartedly because it assumes that some of the actions you are about to undertake are going to be wrong. And that's okay. You can never lose when you choose: you lose when you stand passively by.

Not all of us feel a lack of power. Sometimes it's the lack of courage that puts our best-made plans on the back burner. In the next chapter we turn our attention to the issue of courage and learn the steps you need to follow to find the courage to act.

2
The Courage to Act

"Courage is grace under pressure."
- **Ernest Hemingway** [24]

When you think of courage, what comes to mind? I see a fire fighter running into a burning building or a police officer apprehending a violent criminal. I see someone starting his or her interior design firm or another becoming a concert pianist and succeeding in spite of overwhelming odds. I also see a new sales representative preparing to make his or her first cold call. Courage comes in many forms, in many situations.

I'm a child of the 40s. The post-war baby boom marked the beginning of an era filled with optimism. The world had fought its last Great War. Evil had been defeated and the troops were coming home. Courage was a virtue that was praised. War heroes were awarded medals, honors, and status. One such hero even became President of the United States. Physical courage was directly equated with the life-and-death struggle of protecting freedom. Men who went to war to defend their women, children, and homes were courageous. In the Nicomachean Ethics, Socrates defines courage as, "steadfastness in the face of death." [25]

This was what men in war faced when they came eyeball to eyeball with death. But our notion of courage has taken on new meanings.

In addition to physical courage, we now recognize moral courage. Injustice, or a lack of respect for human dignity, is what motivates people to be morally courageous. There are courageous people who

---

[24] Ernest Hemingway (1899–1961), U.S. author. This quote was actually an answer to Dorothy Parker during an interview as his definition of "guts." As a matter of interest, this quote may have inspired the title of John F. Kennedy's collection of essays, "Profiles of Courage", (1956).

[25] The Greek philosopher, 469 BC to 399 BC was perhaps responsible for more quotable quotes than anyone I can think of including, "One thing only I know and that is that I know nothing."

will stand squarely in the path of peer pressure, gang presence, clans, and prejudice.

Some respond courageously to direct and destructive attacks on a person's sense of worth, which can affect a person's social standing, acceptance by colleagues, or their financial well being, not to mention their self-esteem. Martin Luther King Jr., Nelson Mandela, or the unknown whistle blowers who inform about unethical activities in their work environments, or the sales person who refuses to sell a product to a customer that won't provide the needed solution are all examples of people who possess moral courage and are willing to face loss of income or even more dire consequences for their courageous actions.

There is a third kind of courage called psychological courage. This is the courage it takes for someone to face up to his or her internal demons, which are often packaged in fears, anxieties and phobias. The drug addict who has ruined a life who finds courage to change, the celebrity who uses their voice to bring attention to an issue, or an employee who takes a stand against an immoral or illegal act perpetrated by their employer are all examples of psychological courage. In this chapter we will explore courage as a motivator for proactivity. We will look at the underlying causes of courage and how some persons of action (POAs) have used their life's situations to find the courage to act.

What Is Courage?

Courage is not always easily recognizable. In some situations you will look at a person and admire his or her act of courage, whereas, in other situations, courageousness may be hidden behind a facade and only the courageous person knows what it took to act. Winston Churchill once said, "Courage is what it takes to stand up and speak; courage is also what it takes to sit down and listen." [26]

No profession understands the importance of courage better that that of a sales person. The online Wikipedia encyclopedia defines courage this way: "Courage is the ability to confront fear, pain, danger, uncertainty or intimidation." [27]

---

[26] If you search the web for the source of this quote, you find that some scholars don't recognize it as Churchill's and other say it was an antidotal comment made but fail to identify the recipient of Churchill's wit. In either case, I like the quote, so it stays.

[27] When I was a child, information like this came from one of my 24 volume set of the Encyclopedia Britannica.

The precise view of what constitutes courage not only varies among cultures, but among individuals. For instance, some define courage as lacking fear in a situation that would normally generate a fearful reaction. For most of us, jumping out of an airplane or off a high bridge would generate fear. However, for the parachutist or seasoned bungee jumper, his or her initial fear in such situations may have been replaced with exhilaration. Still, such individuals act courageously and jump. Others, in contrast, hold that courage requires one to first feel fear and then overcome it. According to this view, only when the parachutist experiences fear and still makes the jump, would we say he or she is courageous.

Some of us have the ability to see fear for what it is and tackle it head on. Others might require some reflection before they act. They might first experience fear, but common sense tells them to back away, and so they do. Then, with a change of heart, they make a U-turn and once again look fear straight in the eye. They are like the bumbling, yet shrewd television detective, Colombo, who asks all his questions and as he is about to leave, makes a final U-turn to the suspect and says, "Just one more question."

In the developed world we live relatively safe lives where the bottom rung on Maslow's hierarchy of needs — survival — is already well in place. [28]

We may think of ourselves as courageous, but we are rarely tested except for the exceptional circumstances of those who choose to put themselves in danger's way or battle illness. For some, courage is so deeply buried it is unknown to them, while for others, it is on the surface.

I believe that courage, whether physical, moral or psychological, comes in two distinct forms: deliberate and spontaneous.

Deliberate courage happens when there is time to assess and analyze a situation, and then act. By contrast, spontaneous courage happens on

---

[28] In 1943, Abraham Maslow wrote an academic paper titled "A Theory of Human Motivation", which included his observations of people. His Hierarchy of Needs has become the cornerstone for much of the work done in communications theory and training today.

the spur of the moment, as when someone suddenly jumps into a river to save a drowning child. We will examine both types of courage to determine what the underlying rationale is for each and to see if there are common threads between the two that can help us develop daily strategies for our own proactivity.

Deliberate Courage

History has seen many well-known men who have taken a stand in the face of mortal danger for a cause they believed in. Russia had Alexander Solzhenitsyn, Czechoslovakia had Václav Have, South Africa had Nelson Mandela, and in Albania, there was Fatos Lubonja.

Fatos Lubonja's Story [29]

Fatos Lubonja's story is similar to the others in that he stood up for what he believed and spent years imprisoned, faced with torture and death. Most of us would have difficulty imagining how we would act in similar circumstances.

Lubonja was born in 1951 in Tirana, Albania. His father, Todi, was the director general of Albanian Radio/television, and in 1973, was imprisoned following a clampdown on liberalism in the arts by leader Enver Hoxha. His mother, Liri, was ultimately interred in a remote village while her husband, and eventually, her son served their terms in prison. She later wrote of these times in her essay called Far Away Among People. [30]

At age 23, Lubonja was sentenced to seven years in prison for "agitation and propaganda." He began serving this sentence in the copper mines of Spac and in 1979, while still incarcerated; he faced a second and more serious charge of "counterrevolutionary organization." Along side nine other defendants, Lubjonja received an additional 25 years to his sentence. Three of his colleagues in the same trial were executed.

---

[29] You can read Lubonja's story in his own words in an article titled, "Courage and the Terror of Death", published by the *Journal of Social Research*, Volume 71, Number 1, (spring, 2004). There is also a good biographical sketch at www.wordswithoutborders.com and www.frosina.org.

[30] Calrissa de Waal, Albania Today: A Portrait of Post-Communist Turbulence, I.B. Tarus Publishing, 2005.

During his incarceration, Lubonja was placed in a hut at a prison camp in Ballsh with a Catholic priest, also a prisoner. The priest explained that the charge of espionage for which he was serving his time had been fabricated, but he had decided to confess to save his life. Upon hearing this, Lubonja wondered if the priest had acted out of courage or cowardice.

Other prisoners, like the priest, felt the threat of execution like a dense smoke choking their every breath. Some resisted the threat of "confess or die," while others broke early. "Fear," Lubonja wrote, "is like a terrible fire that arises from the depth of your stomach and heart and shakes and overwhelms your entire being, which melts at different temperatures, according to its capacity." Lubonja knew that even he had a melting point. Through the months and years of his incarceration, Lubonja questioned if he could achieve the level of courage needed to overcome his fear of death.

His road to courage was long and precarious. He described his journey as being accompanied by a wolf (his fear) that was always ready to attack. He learned that when the wolf attacks, he grabs at "our weaknesses and strengths simultaneously."

The battle Lubonja fought was the survival of life versus the acceptance of death. The life instinct is ruled by the primal, animal brain, which refuses to quit. Lubonja continued, "To humans death means leaving everything behind and to truly defy the world requires heroic courage." The courage to face death was where Lubonja's battle was fought. Lubonja wrote, "The courage that is nourished by the love of truth and justice cannot be imagined without the ability of the mind to distance itself from the self." Courage, according to Lubonja, is "the ability to perform with a cool head when fired by blood." By 'blood' he means the animal response and the need to survive.

Finding the quiet courage to face death was at the heart of Lubonja's internal struggle. French classical writer François La Rochefouchauld wrote, "Man's greatest courage lies in performing alone the kind of heroic act that some might usually accomplish in the presence of many witnesses." [31]

---

[31] François La Rochefouchauld, (1613 – 1680), *Reflections, Sentences and Moral Maxims*, (Montreal: Editions BD Simpson, 1946?) (Montmagny: Marquis Editions, Ltd., 1946)

The courageous, according to Lubonja, find strength in the belief that what causes their actions is the hope of something better for their spirit, family, life, and community.

Hope and Fear

For 17th century philosopher, Thomas Hobbs,32 the difference between hope and fear is this: Hope is the desire for something, while fear is an aversion from hurt, or in this case, death. Rather than confronting a fear, the fearful often invent the terror. They create some invisible power either to be avoided or appeased, and in doing so, fill the void with things that do not exist. The hopeful expects good things to come while the fearful do not.

If hope is the root of courage, then we can understand the innocent prisoner's decision to confess to crimes he did not commit—out of the hope of living. On this Lubonja wrote, "A victim is compelled to construct hope after he has fallen into danger, while a hero advances towards danger with the hope that he has already created."

After the fall of communism in 1991, Lubonja was released after serving 12 years in prison. Ultimately, with two fellow prisoners, he went on to establish the Forum of Democracy, in effect, the voice of the conscience of Albania. The slogan for their reform was "Flowers Instead of Stone." The priest with whom Lubonja shared the hut went on to become the Archbishop of the Albanian Catholic Church.

Hope, and in this case, courage, is kindled by beliefs that our efforts will succeed. Believing our efforts will fail arouses despair. Hope is what gives us a positive outlook on even the bleakest situations. It tells us there are businesses that need our product or service. Despair leads nowhere. Societies have understood this for ages. Religions, politics, and business all understand the power of hope and have built it into their very core. They provide hope for a glorious afterlife, hope for a peaceful and prosperous life, and potential for gains in our financial undertakings.

Therefore, we might assume that hope and despair are opposites. Not according to Randolph M. Nesse, psychiatrist and professor at the University of Michigan. "They (hope and despair) are intrinsically

---

[32] Thomas Hobbs, (1588 – 1679), His book, *Leviathan,* (1651) became the foundation for most western philosophies.

intertwined partners in a dance of desire, differing only in whether or not the object of desire is more or less likely to be reached." 33

This seeming conflict of opposites reflects on a basic truth that many of us face. We need both hope and despair in our lives. It seems to be nature's way of giving us the tools we need to survive. What Newton postulated, "That for every action there is an equal and opposite reaction," holds true for science is also quite true of human actions. 34

It goes back to our avoidance-of-pain and the movement-towards-pleasure principle. To know the difference, you have to experience both. If you have never experienced despair, then hope is only an illusion that is not based in reality. Feeling sad is all right because it allows you to understand happiness; experiencing failure in your career better prepares you for success. Experiencing these opposites gives you a firm grounding in reality.

If hope is the fuel of courage, then without a realistic understanding of the consequences of an action, you might logically assume courage to be nothing more than foolhardiness. For example, consider the actions of a naive businessperson who invests his or her entire savings in a venture without doing the necessary research.

It is a rare person who has not experienced hope at some time. Hope is more than a fertile landscape from which the poet finds inspiration. We have hope for our country, as we become concerned and active citizens. We hope for the planet and choose to work for companies that take an active role in environmental causes. We hope our sales careers will be rewarding and fulfilling.

As long as we have hope, we move forward. In his 2008 Democratic Party Presidential nomination race, Barack Obama said, "There has never been anything false about hope." 35

---

[33] Randolph M. Nesse, *The Evolution of Hope and Despair*, *Journal of Social Research*, Volume 66, Number 2, summer, 1999.
[34] Isaac Newton, 1643 – 1727, Physicist, mathematician, astronomer, philosopher, alchemists and theologian. His book, *Philosophiæ Naturalis Principia Mathematica*, is generally thought to be one of the most important scientific books ever written.

35. Remarks of Senator Barack Obama: Potomac Primary Night Madison, WI, February 12, 2008

When we lose hope, we experience despair. POAs are able to learn from despair's lessons and find hope—and ultimately courage. By contrast, when we wallow in despair we stagnate.

Hope is so crucial to our being that we often become prime customers to the people who market it. There are unscrupulous people who will take advantage of the naive hope of many when they tout stock market picks. Drug dealers push a drug-induced alternative to despair and legalized lotteries raise millions for governments that prey on the hopes of its citizens. We vote for politicians who stimulate our hope for a better future. We invest with businesspeople who present a compelling case for the future profitability of their corporations. We follow religious leaders who offer us hope and salvation. We choose to work for corporations whose mission statements and code of ethics are compatible with ours.

It is difficult for many to know if the hope that is being presented is realistic or not. Should a cancer patient, who has a 90 percent chance that surgery will fail, abandon hope? Or, should this same patient focus on the 10 percent chance of success? Should a sales person focus on their nine out of ten cold calls that leads to disappointment or the one in ten that is successful? Which course is right? Which more realistic? The difference between realistic and unrealistic hope is often in the eyes of the beholder.

Lionel Tiger, the Charles Darwin Professor of Anthropology at Rutgers University wrote, "People with hope often have the capacity to posit positive outcomes out of various situations that a directly realistic assessment might judge unpromising." [36]

There it is in a nutshell, that idea that the "experts" in the form of teachers, parents, trainers, IQ tests, etc, may not be accurate when telling someone what sales approach to pursue.

Hope Is Unique to All: A Tale of Two People

The next two profiles are about men who came from different times and different places a half a world and half a century apart. One was white and one was black. One was born in Europe and the other in

---

[36] Lionel Tiger, *The Decline of Males*, (Golden Books, St. Martins Press, 2000).

Africa. They were united in their belief in the power of the individual to do something for good in the midst of genocide and war. Each was able to find courage in the face of death. Each was motivated by the hope that their actions would make a difference.

Rudolf Vrba's Story [37]

Rudolf Vrba was born in 1924 in the Slovakian village of Topoicany. Vrba was a labourer who found himself caught up in the Nazi nightmare. This young Slovakian Jew, whose original name was Walter Rosenberg, was arrested by the Germans in 1942 and sent, along with thousands of his fellow Jews, to the Auschwitz death camps. Upon arrival, those that survived the trip were divided by sex into groups. The Nazi doctors, headed by Josef Mengele, decided with the flick of their thumbs who would live and be put to work, and who would be gassed. Vrba was assigned to perform the gruesome task of sorting the possessions confiscated from arriving prisoners and disposing of dead inmates.

While engaged in these duties, Vrba roamed the camps. He used his photographic memory to record the number of Jews that arrived at the camps and their place of origin. By the time he was ready for his historic escape, he estimated that 1,750,000 Jews had been killed during his time at Auschwitz. While on his rounds, he overheard the guards talking about the fate of the Hungarian Jews who were to be rounded up and sent to their deaths in a new section of the camp that was being built.

Vrba and a fellow inmate, Alfred Wetzler, knowing they would be tortured to death if caught, nevertheless resolved that they must attempt to escape so that they could bring news of the extermination camps to the outside world. With the help of the camp underground movement, they fashioned a hiding place inside a woodpile between the inner and outer perimeter of the camp. They poured gasoline soaked tobacco on the ground to throw the guard dogs off track. Having witnessed previous failed escape attempts, they knew that if they could remain undetected for three days, the search would be called off.

---

[37] Rudolph Vrba, (1924 – 2006), *I Escaped From Auschwitz*, (Robson Books, London, England, 2006). (This book also contains the Auschwitz Protocols). Also check Wikipedia and www.fpp.co.uk.

On April 7, 1944, they hid and three days later made their way south to the Polish border. Theirs was a desperate bid for freedom. They had only a page torn from a child's atlas as a guide.

After eight days of wandering and travelling mostly at night, they managed to contact units of the Slovakian Resistance. They were interviewed separately. The information they provided was used to compile a detailed 32-page report, which contained a precise description of the camps, the details of the mass murders taking place, and a history of what had happened there since April 1942.

The information in the Vrba-Wetzler Report was combined with that supplied by two other escaped Auschwitz prisoners, Arnost Rosin and Czesław Mordowicz, and became jointly known as the Auschwitz Protocols. Publication of information from these reports in June 1944 by the BBC and The New York Times is said to have contributed to the decision by Hungarian leader Admiral Miklos Horthy to halt the deportation of Jews out of Hungary. While Vrba's actions came too late to save many Hungarian Jews from the gas chambers, it is estimated that his actions directly saved the lives of over 100,000 people.

After the war, Vrba settled in British Columbia, Canada. On the news of Vrba's death from cancer in March 2006 at the age of 82, Ruth Linn, dean of education at Israel's Haifa University and author of Escaping Auschwitz: A Culture of Forgetting, a book about Vrba's experiences, called him an "exemplary courageous hero and warrior." She said, "We have lost a rare history maker that the history tellers are yet to find the right words to describe." [38]

Paul Rusesabagina's Story [39]

Half a century later, another man stood up to confront the forces of genocide that were sweeping his country. Paul Rusesabagina was an assistant manager of the Mille Collines, a luxury hotel owned by Sabena Airlines in Kigali, Rwanda. After the death of Hutu president Juvenal Habyarimana in 1994, the country descended into an orgy of violence, as Hutu extremists blamed Tutsi rebels for shooting down the president's plane. They began slaughtering the Tutsi minority and

---

[38] Ruth Linn, *Escaping Auschwitz: A Culture of Forgetting*, (Cornell University Press, 2004).
[39] Paul Rusesabagina, *An Ordinary Man*, (Viking, 2006). For movie buffs, I recommend *Hotel Rwanda*, staring Don Cheadle.

moderate Hutus. In a 100-day period over 800,000 people, out of a population of six million, were murdered.

As a Hutu, Rusesabagina and his family would have been relatively safe. But as neighbors and refugees began to seek the haven of the hotel, he risked his life to stay behind to save his self-appointed charges when he could have easily walked away. Over the course of a harrowing 76 days, while violence surged through Kigali and lapped at the walls of the Mille Collines, the hotel remained an oasis of safety. Using every means at his disposal, he kept the Hutu extremists at bay. Rusesabagina bribed and cajoled and appealed to generals and politicians, all the while making frantic long-distance phone calls to Washington, Paris, and Brussels for assistance. While the rest of the world looked away, not one person was murdered at the hotel. Rusesabagina is credited with saving over 1,200 refugees. For his courageous actions, Rusesabagina has become known as the African Schindler, in reference to another individual who put his life on the line to save others. [40]

You don't have to face a life-threatening situation in order to find courage. There are opportunities that confront us daily that require the courage to act. But what we need to know is whether courage is something we can acquire. In 1949, a group of psychologists led by Samuel A. Stouffer, conducted a groundbreaking study of 3,600 World War Two American soldiers. [41]

Fifty-six percent of the soldiers who expressed high self-confidence before combat also reported little or no fear during battle, while 62 percent of the soldiers who expressed little self-confidence reported a high degree of fear. This research suggests that self-confidence has a direct relationship to courage.

A similar conclusion was found in 1956 by Professor R. Walk,[42] who interviewed trainee parachutists to rate their fear before and after

---

[40] Oskar Shindler 1908-1974 a German industrialist credited with saving 1,200 Jews during World War 11.
[41] Samuel A. Stouffer, et al. *The American Soldier*, (Princeton University Press, 1949).
[42] R. Walk, *Self-rating of Fear in a Fear-Evoking Situation, Journal of Social and Abnormal Psychology*, 52, (1956), Stanley J. Rachman, *Fear and Courage:* A psychological Perspective, *Journal of Social Research,* (March 22, 2004).

jumping from a 34-foot practice tower. Most of the trainees reported a modest amount of fear, but their fear tended to subside after five jumps.

A third study by George Ruff and Sheldon Korchin, studied the original seven members of the Mercury Space Program. [43]

These astronauts were required to carry out extremely difficult and dangerous tasks with a maximum amount of uncertainty about their outcome. They had all grown up in middle-class families in small towns or farms. They were all married. They were intelligent (average IQ of 135) and held degrees in engineering. While they indicated that they had no willingness to face danger, similar to the studies of World War Two soldiers, they were willing to do so as part of their job.

Initially, there were 508 candidates for the program. Each candidate was given a battery of screening tests including physical, psychological, and mental examinations. The NASA committee narrowed down their choices to 32, then 16, and finally to seven.

These astronauts benefited greatly from their training and mastery of their skills. While they experienced both positive and negative emotions, they faced their tasks with courage. They unanimously agreed that as a result of their intensive training and past experience, they had the self-confidence to tackle any emergency. This ability to look potential disaster in the eye and deal with it falls squarely into our definition of courage.

The wartime observations, the parachute trainees, and the studies of the Mercury astronauts all suggest that the one road to courageousness is self-confidence. Self-confidence emerges when the individual has the appropriate skills and a high level of motivation or hope. Organizations, such as Outward Bound[44] have increased in their importance as they try to fill this need. They offer programs that enhance leadership, create high performance teams, and develop individual risk taking with activities such as mountain climbing, canoeing, and wilderness survival exercises.

---

[43] George Ruff and Sheldon Korchin, *Psychological Responses of the Mercury Astronauts to Stress*: The Threat if Impending Disaster, (Cambridge, MIT Press, 1964).

[44] Outward Bound was founded in 1941 in Wales. It has since expanded worldwide and offers individuals a chance to explore their personal boundaries. www.outwardboundwilderness.org.

Evelyn Personeus's Story [45]

Evelyn Personeus is a registered nurse. For 25 years she was a psychiatric nurse at Bergen Regional Medical Center in Paramus, New Jersey. Then, in 2002, she changed jobs to focus on patients suffering from substance abuse. Personeus is a woman who deals with hope and despair on a very real level every day.

Just after midnight on June 10, 2002, a sports car crashed in front of her home. Personeus's reactions were perfect. She called 911, and then ran to the scene. The driver was going into shock, so her triage assessment was to calm him first before helping the passenger. "The car was crushed and the rear was wedged on a pole," she said. "A transformer was at the top. I thanked God for its light — and that the transformer didn't fall."

The passenger door was damaged and couldn't be opened so she climbed through a broken window. In the car, Personeus saw fire flickering in the engine and a 19-year-old boy pinned under the dash. "I couldn't release the seat belt because the impact broke the back of the seat," she said. "His head was hyper extended and blood was pouring from his ears, mouth, and nose. Others had gathered around the scene and were encouraging her to get out of the car. "I couldn't leave this kid because if I did, he'd die," she said. "A strange peace came over me. He was in my hands."

As neighbors tried unsuccessfully to extinguish the fire, Personeus provided sternal rubs. "It looked like his neck was broken, so I couldn't do any worse if I picked up his head to breathe," she says. "I could hear blood deep in his chest, so I kept his head up the whole time.

The police arrived and ordered her out of the burning car. Personeus, afraid he'd drown in his own blood refused to go or let go of the boy's head until officers extricated him. They all made it out just before the car's interior caught fire.

---

[45] *In The News, American Red Cross*, (December 10, 2004), www.redcross.org, *You Don't Abandon Patients, Nurse Week*, (2005), www.nurseweek.com, *Red Cross and Nurse Spectrum Honor Nurse Hero's, USA,, Medical News Today*, (December 11, 2004), www.medicalnewstoday.com.

Days later, visiting the boy in the ICU, Personeus discovered his father was a high school classmate. "Eric had a long row to hoe, but he got his life back," Personeus says. "I would do it again. There's a proverb that says: if you know what to do when it's needed, woe to you if you don't act. This is what I went to nursing school for. I stepped in because I'm a nurse and am so thankful I had the knowledge and experience that kicked in during a crisis."

Courage can be learned, nurtured, and called upon in extraordinary times. The secret ingredient is hope. The courageous have hope, self-confidence in their abilities, and the belief that their actions will alter the future in a positive fashion. Now let's turn to another example:

Wayne Yetman—Marathon Man's Story

In the summer of 1976, 29-year-old Wayne Yetman was at the top of the world—signing autographs for adoring fans, lunching with the Queen, and chatting with the Prime Minister. Best of all, Yetman was representing Canada at the Montreal Olympics in the 42-kilometre Olympic marathon. A gold medal seemed well within his grasp. Then disaster struck. Felled hours before the race by a vicious flu bug, Yetman finished a disappointing 36th, eight minutes slower than his personal best.

His Olympic dreams were shattered. Fifteen years of running and training had all been for naught. "I was heartbroken," Yetman said. He felt that the world had conspired against him even though he had never thought of himself as a victim before. "I still frequently have flashbacks to that day and pangs of anxiety about what a wasted opportunity it was and how I wish I could do it again." In fact, after the Olympics, Yetman sought psychiatric help for a time because the disappointment had been so traumatic. "In my mind," he later wrote, "I had squandered the greatest opportunity of my entire life."

But though his quest for an Olympic medal had been dashed, his marathon dreams had only been shelved. "I always wanted to try to redeem myself in some way." Yetman added. "I always had it in the back of my mind." The chance for redemption came in 1995, when an early retirement opportunity enabled him to concentrate on his dream: to run — and win — a marathon for his 50th birthday. That was easier said than done.

To undertake such a task required a great deal of physical, moral, and psychological courage. "I had run so hard for so long," Yetman says, "that my body just wouldn't take it anymore. I couldn't train properly and I was injury-prone."

He tried to push his body as he always had, but by April 1996, he was in no better shape than when he had started his training regimen. At that point, Yetman stopped to take stock of the situation. He assembled his own personal team, which included his wife, his old Olympic coach (who had gone on to build a professional coaching business), his doctor, and other specialists.

Together, they were able to figure out a way to maximize Yetman's strengths, while playing down his weaknesses. Yetman's days passed in an exhausting blur of training, massage sessions, and doctor's visits, but soon, Yetman felt he was ready to tackle his dream.

Yetman decided to aim for the California International Marathon in Sacramento on December 8, 1996, two months after his 50th birthday. Yetman prepared for the event as well as he could. Even so, he still felt he wasn't in any better shape than other people in that race. "You can't let your limitations stop you or define you," Wayne Yetman believes.

"We've all got limitations. Every person on the planet has his strengths and weaknesses, but I think the people who really achieve significant things in life learn to use these limitations like signposts on the highway that tell you when you can drive fast and, conversely, when you need to back off and bide your time or maybe even choose another route." "Your limitations, merely require you to think a little bit more and plan and create a more imaginative route to your goal." Yetman reflects, "The early retirement was the climax of a long period of scheming, planning and manipulating in order to arrive at that end. I think the same sort of scheming, planning and manipulating fell into place with the decision to enter the run in Sacramento."

As the autumn passed, Yetman was burning out. He hadn't trained nearly at the level that he should have to successfully run the marathon. But at the same time he had driven over the full course six times in order to be more familiar with it and take advantage of areas where other runners didn't know the course. Yetman goes on to say, "I think I was in a frame of mind to best deal with the situation and on the day of the race, everything clicked."

It was a grueling run, but Yetman finished first in his age class! "The joy I found in Sacramento—and missed in Montreal—was more valuable than any worldly accomplishment," Yetman mused years later. "It was simply the thrill of doing my best. Not measured by someone else – but by me."

Success, Yetman thinks, doesn't just come from some really strong desire to achieve something and then working flat out at it. Granted, a great dream and hard work are essential parts of the equation, but there's a lot more to it. "It seems to me that this goes back to what I was saying about limitations. Every person who has a great dream has to figure just how he or she is going to get there within the context of that person's own weaknesses and strengths."

"You've got to take failures in stride and turn them into opportunities," Yetman explains. "And life offers endless opportunities!" Yetman continues. "In order to be a success in running, and I suspect, successful in a number of things, you've got to start with good genes and add a lot of hard work and smart thinking. But then, on top of all that, you need a good dollop of luck," he sums up.

While that implies something beyond one's control, Yetman's feeling is you can manage your luck. While you can't control luck, you can make yourself available and open to luck when it comes your way.

Bolster your courage

There are countless ways to bolster your courage. Taking a non-job related course in something such as administering CPR, or learning basic auto mechanics can be helpful. You can learn how to swim or to tie a knot. The greater your personal diversity, the more likely you are to have the knowledge that if you can handle small tasks you will also be able to handle the big challenges that life will throw across your path.

There is no training that will prepare you for everything, but that's not the goal. Becoming proficient at a skill will help boast your confidence. You will feel secure in the knowledge that if you were needed, you would be there, ready and able to help.

The courage of these POAs is based on training, self-confidence, and a high level of motivation to do something. Each of them had time on their side to focus on finding their own courage to act. Each has demonstrated deliberate courage. However, there are circumstances where time for reflection and deliberation is non-existent and you will have to rely on your ability to react quickly and courageously in the moment.

Spontaneous Acts of Courage

It's the morning of September 11, 2001. United Airlines Flight 93 was preparing to leave from Newark, New Jersey, destined for San Francisco. [46]

There was a delay, which many travellers had grown to expect. Some were probably grumbling about missed appointments. The 40 passengers on board included a lawyer, public relations specialist, university student, corporate executive, salesperson, manager, and an arborist. It was a normal day at the airport. Once in the air however, things turned for the worse. By 9:35 both of the World Trade Centre Towers in New York were in flames. Flight 77 was bearing down on the Pentagon and Flight 93's passengers were aware that their airplane had changed direction. According to calls made by some of the passengers on their cellular phones, the airplane had been taken over by three men. There was bedlam in the passenger cabin.

Passenger Deena Burnett called 911 and reported, "We've been hijacked." Passenger Jeremy Glick called his wife to report the same news. Tom Beamer used the on-board Airfone service to report the incident. The passengers learned of the World Trade Center crashes. America was under attack. The plane plunged from its assigned altitude. The passengers quickly grasped the situation. The last words heard by those on the ground were, "Are you ready, guys?" Let's roll."

The rest is history: None of the passengers aboard United 93, except for the hijackers, could have prepared themselves for this situation. Yet, 40 people needed to respond immediately to the worse kind of emergency that anyone could image.

Spontaneous courage is the second form of courage, which is precipitated by the immediacy of the situation. These acts of courage happen without warning. You never know when circumstances will challenge you to respond. It could be today or it could be never. Yet, you would like to believe, that if called upon, you would step up to the challenge. It is not necessary to be a courageous person to carry out a

---

[46] *United Airlines 93*, A complete account can be found at www.flight93crash.com, also stories at CNN.com and Newsweek.com are helpful. If you would rather see the movie than read the stories then rent "Flight 93," at your local Blockbusters.

courageous act. Acts of courage like this can be prompted in people who are regarded by themselves and others as timid.

Penny Gonzalez-Green's Call to Action

On October 24, 2004, Penny Gonzalez-Green, 47 an EMT with Care Ambulance Service, was working the last day of her rotation when she responded to a 911 call from of a diabetic woman. Penny, and her partner Dave DuFerene, arrived on the scene along with fire and police authorities. While Penny and Dave were treating the patient, they suddenly heard, "Stop, Get Back, Put it down!" A man with a weapon hiding in the bushes nearby began to attack the police and fire responders at the scene.

Uncertain of what was unfolding a few feet away, Penny's main concern was to continue to assist her diabetic patient. While the police were trying to apprehend the suspect, Penny felt a burning pain in her back and when she touched the area, there was blood on her hands. This was Penny's moment of spontaneous courage. In the face of danger and despite her own injury, she single-mindedly focused on the job to be done — caring for her patient.

It might be argued that Penny's demonstration of spontaneous courage came from the confidence she had gained from helping people in emergency situations. While Penny's career did present many horrific situations, being shot at was without precedent. Yet she soldiered on and saved her patient.

Our next example is of someone facing a dangerous situation, but without the experience of life-and-death situations like Penny had:

Cathy Charaba's Moment of Courage

June 22, 2004 was Tacoma Public Utilities (TPU) employee Cathy Charaba's call to action. [48]

Tacoma Public Utilities is a busy place full of clients, building employees, and visitors. On this particular day, a dozen firefighters and their guests happened to be in the building attending a meeting in a conference room just off the main lobby. From the conference room, Administrative Battalion Chief Twyla Bryant, with the Tacoma Fire

---

[47] Penny Gonzalez-Green, www.oc-redcross.org. – 2005.
[48] To read about other hero's like Cathy Charaba, visit www.carnegiehero.org.

Department, heard a commotion. Twyla marched into the lobby expecting to find the culprits. But there was nobody around, so she returned to her meeting. Moments later a second commotion erupted, but this time the shouting from the lobby was louder. When she tried to exit the conference room, Twyla heard someone yell for her to get down. She backed up to take cover and heard the sound of gunshots.

The woman, outside the building was threatening the safety of the firefighters and the lobby full of people. Cathy Charaba, the swing shift janitor, was quick to assess the situation. She took immediate action to physically block the main door to the TPU lobby. Selflessly putting herself in front of the glass doors, Cathy prevented anyone in the lobby from exiting the building. She shouted instructions to the firefighters and anyone else in harms way to get down and take cover.

Cathy's razor sharp instincts and selfless courage kept countless people from harm that day by preventing them from exiting the building into a barrage of gunfire which had begun as a domestic dispute. Cathy was credited with saving several lives that day.

These courageous POAs had three ingredients necessary for deliberate courage: self-confidence, skills, and hope. However, spontaneous courage is different. There seems to be no rational way of developing self-confidence through practice or learning skills that will help in these unique, once-in-a-life-time situations. We cannot lean heavily on hope to motivate us because, in many of these situations, hope is illusive. We may logically conclude that motivation for these people must come from some other source.

Theodore Roosevelt wrote, "It is not the critic who counts, not the man who points out how the strong man stumbled, or where the doer of deeds could have done better. The credit belongs to the man who is actually in the arena, whose face is marred by dust and sweat and blood, who strives valiantly, who errs and comes up short again and again, who knows the great enthusiasms, the great devotions, and spends himself in a worthy cause, who at best knows achievement and who at the worst, if he fails, at least fails while daring greatly so that his place shall never be with those cold and timid souls who know neither victory nor defeat." [49]

---

[49] Theodore Roosevelt, (1858 – 1919), 26th President of the United States, Speech at the Sorbonne, Paris, April 23, 1910

What is it about spontaneous acts of courage that so captures our attention? Perhaps we don't believe we'd have the wherewithal to act in these situations. Or, perhaps we have been given the opportunity to act and did not, and so justified our inaction by saying, "If I had only thought of that, I would have jumped headfirst into the problem."

What would you do if you knew a competitor was stealing customers from your company? What would you do if you saw a colleague being harassed? What would you do if a colleague had a stroke at their desk? Every day we are faced with opportunities where our courage to act is put to the test. We are drawn to courageous acts like groupies are drawn to a rock concert. So, before we examine the cause of spontaneous actions, it is prudent to take one step back and see what is so appealing about reading stories of courageous people.

Jonathan Haidt, a professor of psychology at the University of Virginia, is a pioneer in studying the effects that people's deeds have on those who witness them. [50]

He is one of the psychologists, like Martin Seligman, whom you met in Chapter 1, who is a member of the school of positive psychology, a group of professionals who have moved away from the study of what's wrong to the study of what's right. Haidt's studies found that participants, when exposed to stories about people who performed good deeds or acts of heroism, were more likely to report pleasant physical feelings in their chests, especially warm, pleasant or tingling feelings. He labeled this feeling "elation." It's no wonder we gravitate to stories of people who perform remarkable acts. They make us feel good.

But my contention is that each of us has opportunities throughout our working lives to mount the stage. Rather than sitting in the audience with our warm, tingly feelings, we can each become the performers.

Kant on Spontaneous Courage

Emmanuel Kant, the 18th century philosopher, addresses the subject of courage in Critique of Pure Reason. [51]

---

[50] Arthur Danto, *The Abuse of Beauty*: Aesthetics and the Concept of Art, (Corus Publishing, 2003).

Kant argues that there are three steps to action: knowledge, judgement, and reason. Kant's arguments take the discussion of courage away from the field of science and mathematics to a more moralistic arena where free choice lives and breaths.

Knowledge

Knowledge, according to Kant, is a "dualism" of appearance and reality. That is, there is a difference between the way things are and the way they appear to us. Knowledge of a situation, therefore, is a person's interpretation of reality, but is not reality itself. For example, how do we judge a smoker who finds the courage to kick the habit? We may see someone quit and say, "Good for her, she finally has taken her life in her own hands and is doing something positive for herself." In this case, we are interpreting the smoker's actions to mean she has taken a positive step towards a healthier life. If we are quick to react, we are not balancing our interpretation with alternative truths. The real truth of the situation depends on the standpoint of the individual who is doing the interpreting. In this case, a friend's view of the smoker's quitting may be positive, but a long-frustrated spouse or an employer may see it negatively. Perhaps she has "given up" smoking in the past only to return to it again.

Judgement

Judgement is the result of what we do with our knowledge or interpretation of reality. We often attribute cause and effect to our judgement of a situation. In the case of the smoker, we might assume that the constant bombardment of anti-smoking hype finally made an impact, which, in turn, caused her to reassess her smoking and decide to quit. The effect is the cessation of smoking.

We can see from this example that, according to Kant, we interpret the situation (our reality) and act accordingly. In our example, we might respect our friend's courage and offer her our moral support or we might research and give our friend some literature on how to permanently kick the smoking habit. But in so doing, we won't understand that we may have read the situation incorrectly. Not

---

[51] Emmanuel Kant, (1724-1804), German Philosopher. His books are still available. The three to look at are: *Critique of Pure Reason*, (Dover Publications, 2003), *Critique of practical Reason*, (Cambridge University Press, 1997), and *Critique of Judgment*, (Dilireads.com, 2006).

everyone quits smoking for the same reason. Or, as Ralph Waldo Emerson wrote, "The courage of the tiger is one, and of the horse another." [52]

Kant goes on to explain that "it is presumptuous to believe that thinking something makes it exist." For instance, if you were a smoker and you saw this person's action, you might mistakenly conclude that if you read enough anti-smoking literature you could convince yourself to take the same action. That's the fallacy; some people are motivated by what they read while others are not.

Reason

For Kant, the human mind sees situations through its senses and interprets the situation through the same senses. Kant goes on to say that humans have a capacity called reason. Reason is what motivates and stimulates the pursuit of knowledge. Reason brings unity to the experience. The purpose of reason, according to Kant, "is to dream and to believe in the dream." This is the core of what Kant was referring to when he spoke about human actions. All human beings possess the same equipment for sensing and understanding. They understand that all events have a cause and an effect. When looking at an action, one might ask: Does this person act without some reason, or is he or she motivated by some unseen force? Understanding Kant let's us know that human beings can act spontaneously, but these behaviors are interpreted and constructed by perception and understanding.

So what can we learn from Kant? Merely looking at POAs like Penny Gonzalez-Green, and Cathy Charaba, and wishing we had behaved as courageously as they in similar circumstances is misleading. It is important to understand that the actions taken by others, although admirable, are not always appropriate actions for each one of us. We each must find our own motivation. One way to find our motivation is to understand why other people do what they do. This often provides insight that will help us on our own personal journey of discovery. Eleanor Roosevelt said, "You gain strength, courage, and confidence by every experience in which you really stop to look fear in the face. You must do the thing, which you think you cannot do." [53]

---

[52] Ralph Waldo Emerson, (1803 – 1882), US Essayist and poet.
[53] Eleanor Roosevelt, (1884 – 1963), wife of US President Franklin D. Roosevelt.

There is a special allure to stories of courage. Particularly where an ordinary person tackles a foe much larger than him or herself and wins. It triggers, inside each of us, the admiration and the hope that, if we were put to the test, we could perform equally. There was the mythical little boy who saved Amsterdam by putting his finger in the dyke. There was another little boy who, armed only with a slingshot, was able to save a nation from the giant of the Philistines. Then there is the real story of Rosa Parks. 54

Rosa Parks' Story

Rosa was a seamstress for a department store in Montgomery, Alabama. Her life was typical of many black women of that time. She lived in an atmosphere of bigotry and prejudice that affected every part of her life; which water fountain she could drink from, who her friends could be, and which seat she could sit in on the bus. Then on December 1, 1955, everything changed for Rosa, and ultimately, for every black citizen in the United States. Rosa said "no."

Riding public transit, which many of us take for granted, was a complex issue for African Americans in the 1950s. They were required to pay their fare to the driver, then get off the bus and re-board again through the back door. Sometimes the bus would pull away before they were able to get on again. If they were able to board, there was a "Blacks Only" section at the back of the bus. But having a seat in the "Blacks only" section wasn't secure. If a white passenger got on board and the "Whites Only" section was filled, a black passenger was required to give up his or her seat.

That's what happened to Rosa. She was asked to give up her seat, and she said no. Legend has it that she was just tired. She had been standing on her feet all day and didn't have the energy to get up. But according to Rosa in her autobiography, Quiet Strength, she said that she was tired, but it had nothing to do with her feet. She was tired of being humiliated. When the young civil rights leader, Martin Luther

---

[54] Rosa Parks, My sources for this remarkable story include "Rosa was Tired," The Writing Company, www.writingco.com, (April 12, 2006); Kira Albin, "Rosa Parks: The Woman Who Changed Everything, grandtimes.com, (April, 2006); E.R. Shipp, Rosa Parks, 92, "Founding Symbol of Civil Rights Movement, Dies", *The New York Times*, (October, 2005).

King Jr., heard her story, he mobilized the black community, which precipitated the 382-day-long Montgomery Bus Boycott. [55]

Rosa's simple act of courage was credited for being the spark that changed American culture forever. King wrote, "No one can understand the action of Mrs. Parks unless he realizes, that eventually, the cup of endurance runs over and the human personality cries out, "I can take it no longer'." Why don't more of us have the courage to act?

Perhaps it's all too easy to find vicarious courage in the acts of others. Perhaps it's easier to find courage in our X-box or admire raw courage in books, television, and movies. Getting involved in a heroic fantasy world satisfies a need that people often feel they can't live up to in the real world. It's tough to find the courage to stand up to an overbearing boss or an abusive spouse. However, taking out a laser gun and zapping away the enemy in a fantasy game is not only easy; it's safe. When it's over, you shut the game down and go back to your life.

There are advantages to daydreaming. It allows you to get your frustrations out in a reasonably healthy way without harm to anyone; it helps you verbalize situations that are troublesome; and it gives you an outlet that helps you contemplate future possibilities.

In his book, The Mystery of Courage, author William Ian Miller spells out four components to isolating courage; timing, training, nature, and luck. [56]

1. Timing: Most of us are not tested daily. We can fantasize how we might act, but rarely will we be put to the big test. It took Rosa years of frustration until the timing and players were all in place, that she found her courage. The bus driver who asked her to give up her seat was the same driver who sent her to the back of the bus 12 years earlier.

2. Training: You can train yourself to be proactive and consciously look for situations where you can exercise your courage daily. Aristotle

---

[55] Montgomery Bus Boycott, for 382 days (between December 5, 1955 to December 21, 1956), nearly 90% of the black community (nearly 40,000 people) in Montgomery Alabama honored Martin Luther King's plea to boycott the public transportation service.

[56] William Ian Miller, *The Mystery of Courage* (Harvard University Press, 2002).

believed that we have to train ourselves to be ready when the call comes. 57

There are countless opportunities to exercise courage on a daily basis. You can help a homeless person asking for money when your friends or colleagues might pass by and ignore the person. You can volunteer for activities in your community, or at work, or simply show up at your child's recital when it is difficult to get there. You can say no to your kids rather than giving into their every whim. You can offer to stay late at work to finish a task when everyone else is leaving. These are small steps that are often contradictory to your nature.

Writings in Kaballah refer to "restriction." It simply means that rather than going about your life playing the same song over and over again because you know all the words, you stretch a bit and seek new experiences that might challenge you. 58

It's like downloading a new song on your I-pod. It might be uncomfortable at first, but the more you do it, the more you will crave a wider range of music. This step becomes habit forming, and before long, you will find your workplace looks different. It is no longer a place with desks and computers, it is a living, breathing entity and you are a vital part of its existence. In terms of courage, when the day comes that you are called upon, your courage will be well honed and ready to do its magic.

3. Nature: Some people are courageous by nature. We see some people who don't seem to scare easily and assume that their courage comes from lack of fear. The flaw in this thinking is that ultimately, everyone is afraid of something. There is a difference between courage and fearlessness. Courage is feeling the fear and facing it. Acting with no fear is not courage at all. It is simply acting. Is walking out your front door in the morning and act of courage? Hardly. But for the agoraphobic with an overwhelming fear of leaving his or her home,

---

[57] Aristotle, (384 BC to 322 BC), Greek philosopher. I found a terrific article on an unlikely site called allfreeessays.com.

[58] Kaballah, Wikipedia defines Kaballah as "the mystical aspect of Judaism." Some Jews view its doctrine as the true meaning behind Judaism. Until recently the study was restricted to a handful of rabbinical scholars. Recently the teachings of Kaballah have found a larger audience attracting celebrities such as Madonna.

taking that step onto their front porch is an act of heroic proportions. Facing the fear is often a greater sign of courage than acting in a foolhardy manner devoid of fear. There is a difference between the headline-grabbing acts of courage and the acts of courage that happen everyday. Quiet acts of courage are simple things like owning up to a mistake on a report or accepting responsibility for the failure of an initiative.

4. Luck: Luck can create confidence and fuel courage. There are times when you create your own luck. You may be lucky when you buy a lottery ticket and win millions of dollars, but that's blind luck. I'm referring to the kind of luck that emerges when you are ready and approach life with your eyes wide open.

You don't wait for the day when you need courage; you take a proactive approach and look for opportunities that let you exercise courage every day. By exercising your courage and facing your fears, the universe will put opportunities in your path.

Many of us struggle with the everyday routine of a job, family, and relationships. Courage, on the scale of saving lives, never seems attainable. But that doesn't make the everyday quests less important.

Helen Keller wrote, "I long to accomplish great and noble tasks, but it is my chief duty to accomplish humble tasks as though they were great and noble." [59]

It's as simple as that.

---

[59] Helen Keller, (1880 – 1968), American author and educator. Movie buffs will remember her portrayal by Patty Duke in *The Miracle Worker*.

Lessons Learned

Learn to tackle new and interesting issues with an open mind.

Learn new skills and practice them as the opportunities for quiet acts of courage present themselves.

Be primed, that at any moment, you may be called upon to perform an act of courage.

Courage is a learned trait. Often, in our naiveté, we assume that if the situation warrants it, we would act. While it's true in some cases, it is not in others. Former United Nations Secretary General Dag Hammarskjöld aptly said, "Life only demands from you the strength you possess. Only one feat is possible — not to run away." 60

Courage is something that hides in a locked room, outside your everyday experience and often never gets put to the test. There are times your sales career will demand that you exercise courage. Being prepared for these moments is your best offensive move. There are two types of courage: deliberate and spontaneous. You read about acts of deliberate courage in Fatos Lubonja, Rudolf Vrba, Paul Rusesabagina, Evelyn Personeus, and Wayne Yetman. Time and hope are what each of these brave people had in common—the time to examine their inner self and the hope that their actions would create a positive outcome.

You also read about spontaneous courage in the stories of Penny Gonzalez-Green, Cathy Charba, Rosa Park, and the passengers of United 93. These ordinary people were forced to make a decision based on circumstances that appeared out of nowhere and demanded action. So what motivates spontaneous acts of courage? Mortal danger, boredom, being tired, feeling repulsed, looking for something better? There is no simple answer. But as you have learned, even small acts of courage have enormous consequences.

While the two types of courage may seem different, there is one thread that runs through both: people who had the self-confidence to tackle the situation at hand. Rabbi Shmuley Botech, in his book, Face Your Fear—Living with Courage in an Age of Caution, writes, "Don't be pushed by fear; be pulled by promise." 61

---

[60] Dag Hammarskjöld, (1905 – 1961). Swedish diplomat and Former United Nations Secretary General.
[61] Rabbi Shmuley Botech, *Face Your Fear*: Living with Courage in an Age of Caution (St Martins Press, 2004).

Lessons into Action: Your Sales Action Plan

Step 1: Learn to tackle new and interesting issues

Tackling new and interesting issues with an open mind is easier said than done. This step guides you through a process that helps you to look at your career through a child's eyes and see everything as a new adventure. Children are great teachers. When they see something new they want to touch it. If they don't understand, they ask. That's the way we begin life, but as we grow older we develop fears and avoid difficult situations. Now is the time to unlearn these behaviors.

a. Take a piece of paper and divide it into five columns.

b. In the first column, list things that threaten your physical, moral, and psychological well being. For example, a fear of flying, rejection by customers, losing your job, success or criticism by your boss.

c. In column 2, list the methods you use to avoid dealing with each of your fears. For example, if you have a fear of flying then you travel only by train or automobile. If you fear rejection, perhaps you sit meekly in meetings and don't voice your opinion. If you are worried about losing your job, you may avoid controversial decisions. If you fear success, then you might give up too soon. If you fear criticism you may find that you make up a lot of excuses for shoddy work.

d. In the third column, categorize your list of fears from easiest (the one that poses the least amount of threat to you) to the most difficult (the one that feels most threatening). Rank the degree to which you feel threatened from one to five, with one being the least and five the most threatened. Here's an example below of how your content might look:

Column 1	Column 2	Column 3	Col. 4	Col. 5
Career Fears	Avoidance techniques	Perceived Difficulty overcoming Fear		
Flying	Take trains or automobile	4		
Rejection	Will not voice opinions	3		
Losing your job	Avoid making decisions	3		
Success	Give up too soon	2		
Criticism	Make excuses	5		

e. Transform fear into an opportunity:

The best way to do this is to take baby steps, one at a time. Go back to your list and look at the fear that is lowest on your scale of difficulty. Now write into Column 4 a list of things you can do to transform it from a fear into an opportunity for personal and professional growth.

Step 2: Learn and practice

As the opportunities for quiet acts of courage present themselves, you can learn new skills and practice them so you can become more courageous. For example, take the fear of giving an opinion in front of peers. You need to slowly build your confidence.

Start with something innocuous like seconding a motion in a meeting. Once you're comfortable with that, move on to more difficult tasks. List all the situations in which you're afraid to express yourself.

Column 1	Column 2	Column 3	Column 4	Column 5
Career Fears	Avoidance techniques	Perceived Difficulty overcoming Fear	Action Steps	
Flying	Take trains or automobile	4		
Rejection	Will not voice opinions	3	Second a motion Volunteer for committee work Invite key personnel for a drink Make a presentation	
Losing your job	Avoid making decisions	3		
Success	Give up too soon	2		
Criticism	Make excuses	5		

As you conquer each fear, you will build the confidence to take the ultimate risk and stand up in a board meeting and clearly articulate how you feel in any situation. Start with your least threatening fear. Once you have a plan to tackle it, you can move on to your next fear.

Take one step at a time, each time moving yourself closer to the ultimate goal of having the courage to express your opinions in any situation. You can't rush the process. The trick is to get comfortable at one level of difficulty before moving on to the next. Each action step will require learning new skills.

Make a list of the skills you want to acquire and those you need to hone. Learn the skill first, and then tackle the fear. For example, before you second a motion, you will want to understand the background and ramifications of the issue being presented for a vote. This requires research skills. You can use the same approach for all the action steps to overcome other fears that are holding you back.

Column 1	Column 2	Column 3	Column 4	Column 5
Career fears	Avoidance Techniques	Perceived difficulty overcoming fear	Action Steps	New Skills
Flying	Take trains and autos.	4		
Rejection	Will not voice opinions	3	Second a motion. Volunteer for committee work. Invite key personnel for a drink. Write a report. Make a presentation.	Research into issues and procedures organizational Skills Networking skills Writing skills Presentation skills
Losing your job	Avoid making decisions	3		
Success	Give up too soon	2		
Criticism	Make excuses	5		

Step 3: Be Primed to Perform an Act of Courage

I call this step "Adopt a Hero." Everyday you learn of an act of heroism in the newspaper, on TV, or while surfing the Internet. These acts are not limited to the firemen who run into burning buildings. They can also include someone with a debilitating handicap who has taken steps to lead an independent life, employees who blew the whistle on unfair or illegal practices they witnessed at work, a person who took the time out of his or her busy life to coach a children's sports team, or the sales person who makes a difficult presentation.

Heroes are everywhere. Author Tanis Helliwell wrote, "True heroism is not found in reality TV shows where people eat worms. True heroism is becoming the best human being that we are capable of becoming." [62] Some of your heroes might have found fame and fortune, while others may have not. You be the judge.

The following exercise will help you understand, firsthand, how acts of courage are born. Courage is like a muscle that needs exercise to remain strong. It reinforces your internal strength. Practice it long enough and inaction will no longer be a viable option.

Clip or copy an article or photograph of your favorite hero and put it in easy view of your desk. Pin it up on your bulletin board or use it as a screensaver on your computer

a. Imagine that your hero isn't just in your bulletin board or computer, he/she sits on your right shoulder and goes everywhere with you.

b. Look for opportunities to exercise your courage at work, at home, at the gym; wherever you are. Once you open your eyes and ears, you'll be amazed at how many opportunities there are, and how many you avoided in the past. Example: when you're in a meeting and reluctant to voice your opinion, ask yourself "What would my hero do?" If you're unsure, listen to your hero whisper a solution to you – and take action!

In chapter one, you learned steps to proactivity through your helplessness. In chapter two, you learned how to find the courage to act. The next chapter focuses on persistence, which for many POAs, is the trait they point to most often when asked, "To what do you attribute your success?"

---

[62] Tanis Helliwell, *International Institute for Transformation* newsletter, (spring 2007), www.tanishelliwell.com.

Grab Success by the Horns

3
Stay in the Game

"Most of the important things in the world have been accomplished by people who have kept on trying when there seemed to be no hope at all."
Dale Carnegie [63]

There are people who keep going long after the competition has stopped. Like the "Energizer Bunny", they just keep ongoing. Something deep in their psyche causes them to turn their back on age, health, money, or common sense to do what they do. The one constant among successful sales people is their desire to stay in the game. Picking up all of their marbles and going home is not an option. This chapter is about Persons of Action (POAs) whose motivation can be directly linked to their desire to remain a player. Everyone has his or her own game. Some people want to build a business, some want to pursue the arts, while others want to have a successful career in sales. It comes down to finding and pursuing your work and then finding the power in you to stay in the game for the long run.

Albert White's Story

One man who immediately comes to mind is Albert White. His is a rag-to-riches story completely devoid of luck. He once said to me, as we sat at the dinner table (Albert was also my father-in-law), "I like the challenge of coming up with new ideas and seeing them through." Here was a man of wealth and accomplishment who wanted nothing more than the stimulation and excitement of coming up with a new idea and seeing it to fruition. But I am ahead of myself.

Albert, one of five children, was born in Kitchener, Ontario, Canada. Growing up, he was considerably influenced by a strong willed mother with good business sense. In the early twentieth century, life was difficult for Jewish immigrant families in Canada. They had difficulty dealing with a new language and culture and finding work.

---

[63] Dale Carnegie, (1888 – 1955), US Lecturer and author of *How to Win Friends and Influence People* first published in 1936 and has sold millions of copies worldwide.

When the family moved to Toronto, Albert was eight years old. He acquired an after-school job selling the Toronto Telegraph newspaper at a corner near the King Edward Hotel. His net profit was 25 cents each day, which went to help his family's finances. He bought papers from a distributor who had a number of boys like Albert working for him. Albert liked making money and seized an opportunity to make more.

One day, Albert approached the distributor and said, "I'm not making enough money; I want 50 cents." The distributor laughed and said 'no', so Albert bought papers directly from The Telegraph and sold them himself. Quickly, the distributor approached Albert, who was working his prime corner in downtown Toronto, and offered him the 50-cent raise. Months later, using the same tactic, Albert was able to shrewdly negotiate a further raise to 75 cents. Everyday he went to school and afterwards ran to his corner to sell papers. In the winter months he would walk by construction sites on the way home and scrounge for bits of wood to burn in his family's stove.

After completing grade 10, Albert, like his other siblings, had to quit school to help the family. Being the youngest didn't protect him from the harsh world of survival. He did his best at various jobs. Life was a struggle, yet he looked back on this time with fondness. "We had a boys' club where we could meet and talk about things that were important to us," he said. Among his acquaintances was the young Johnny Wayne, who as an adult became half of the famous Canadian comedy team of Wayne and Schuster.

When he was twenty-three, Albert married a woman who understood his struggle. She even offered to make sandwiches when they went on their first date. Factory work was plentiful at that time. But that wasn't for Albert; he chose to go into business for himself. At first, he bought rubber bands in bulk, repackaged them into smaller bundles at night and sold them door to door. He took his profits and expanded into pencils. Soon, he had enough money to open a storefront. This was a humble beginning, yet Albert's hard work and persistence formed the groundwork for Albert White and Company, one of the oldest and largest office supply companies in Toronto. He eventually bought the building his store was in, and with one manager and a secretary, went on to make history. He hired a team of eight commissioned salesmen who went on the road.

He purchased his second building, a foreclosure, from the bank. Both his real estate and office supply business grew. At some point he moved from office supplies to furniture. He opened his showroom and was one of the first merchants to display complete model office suites. From there, he sold prints and posters to decorate office walls. This led to his love of the art business and ultimately his own gallery.

Nothing came easily. There was no stroke of luck that can account for Albert's success. He saw opportunities and tackled them proactively. His was a life built on pure persistence. He networked feverishly. He was the President of the Canadian Art Dealers Association, Chairman of the Forest Hill Library Board and a lifetime member of the Y.M.H.A. Board of Directors in Toronto. He counted, among his acquaintance, artists such as Henri Moore, Pablo Piccasso, Fernando Botero, and David Hockney.

I remember talking to him when he was in his 70s and attempting to create a gift mart in one of his downtown buildings. With brochures under his arm he walked the Toronto Gift Show talking to companies about joining his mart. "Why are you doing this?" I asked. "Surely you can hire someone to do all this leg work for you."

"This isn't about money," he said. "I get tremendous satisfaction by doing things myself and seeing the result of my work."

As I read biographies and talk to people, I have found many examples of people who, like Albert White, do what they do — just to stay in the game. The option of quitting does not ever cross their minds. In the previous chapter, you read about Hannah and Samantha who proactively set out to right a wrong. But, doing something once does not necessarily lead to a lifetime of proactivity. Those who stay involved and proactive seem to possess something others do not. Is it superior intellect, a special talent, or a matter of hard work and determination? Each of these qualities is worth examining.

Intelligence

On first blush, you would expect that those who manage to fulfil their career goals might possess superior intelligence. But, if that were the necessary ingredient, when we hold up a mirror, most of us might be too discouraged to act. We might not try if we believe we don't have the necessary brainpower. I recently met a woman who asked me what it takes to write a book. One of the qualities she was curious about was education. "Do I need a Ph.D. in English?" she asked.

I was surprised by her question. Most of the writers whom I admire do not have PhDs, although many have received honorary degrees. The woman's question, however, was symptomatic of a deeper concern. I would guess that for this woman to actually sit down and write something, while comparing herself to accomplished writers with PhD's like A.S. Byatt, Robert Lowell and J.N. Coetzee, would be intimidating. I know it would hold me at bay if I were to assume that the only way I could be taken seriously as a writer was to have several postgraduate degrees. The reality of writing is that there is no magic formula—writing is as individual as the writers themselves.

I think back to things I have read and ask myself what had the most impact on me. I think about the spellbinding works of Stephen King. I like the Baroque style of Anne Rice. I like the lyrical writing of Edgar Allen Poe. I also recall letters from my kids at camp, memos hastily written by business colleagues, and notes of appreciation from clients. The woman who worried about a university degree was doing herself an injustice. Holding on to this mindset limited her potential and the possibility of being proactive. Such thinking can lead to a life of saying, "I was never good enough." What I told this woman was to focus on the work. The rest will take care of itself.

IQ Tests [64]

When I went to school, the test most quoted as an indicator of intelligence was the IQ test. At the age of 15, I was having problems at school, so my worried parents sent me to a vocational counselor to determine what I was most suited for in life. I remember the counselor. Her name was Mrs. Black. She took me through a battery of tests, and to this day, I remember her final comments:

"You are about five points too low on the IQ scale to be a successful university candidate," she said. The conclusion was that I should consider looking to the trades for employment. If I wanted to be a doctor, lawyer, or writer, I couldn't cut it. However, being a plumber, electrician, or salesman would best fit my intelligence. I guess her assumption was that people who work in the trades do not have the academic chops that medical school students have. Yet trades people are often brilliant.

My counselor didn't understand what intelligence really is. To understand the importance of intelligence, it's worth examining the work of Robert Sternberg. [65]

---

[64] I.Q. Tests. Abbreviation for "Intelligence Quotient," see some interesting facts at www.ig-testing-online.com

Sternberg's story begins in the sixth grade when he did so poorly on his IQ test he was told to retake it with classmates in the grade below his. This experience was the beginning of his lifetime of interest in the field of intelligence. Sternberg recovered from this initial experience and ultimately became a professor of psychology at Yale. His Triarchic Theory of Intelligence examines three aspects of intelligence that we are all governed by: componential, experiential, and contextual. [66]

1. Componential

This is a measurement of how people decide what to do. It relates to the speed in which people solve problems. Sternberg said that instead of just measuring speed, you also want to measure the person's knowing when to be fast and when to be slow.

There is an old adage that good cabinetmakers live by: "Measure twice and cut once." Instinctively, the cabinetmaker knows what he's doing, but he also knows to take the time to be sure. This is the componential part of Sternberg's work. You wouldn't expect anything less from your neurosurgeon. However, you would not want police officers in the face of danger to take out all the crime scene photos and examine all the pros and cons before taking action. By the time they did that, they would be dead. Here is a case where time is of the essence. Fast decisions might be the difference between life and death.

The componential person is one who looks and acts smart according to the conventional theories of intelligence. They are able to make good decisions and are often top of their class in the first year of university, but by the time they finish, they might have slipped to the lower 50 percent. You will be able to identify these people easily at work. They look like the perfect candidate – on paper. When they are first hired, there are great expectations, then as time passes, their results fall short.

2. Experiential

The experiential aspect is about insight—the ability to find unique solutions to problems. While there is no clear definition as to what insight really is, Sternberg found it to consist of three distinct things: encoding, selective combination, and selective comparison.

---

[65] Robert Sternberg, Professor of Psychology and Education at Yale University, Visit his homepage at www.yale.edu/rjsternberg.com
[66] Robert J Trotter ,Triarchic Theory of Intelligence, *Three Heads are Better Than One*, Psychology Today, (August 1986), Volume 20.

Encoding is the ability to focus on critical information. There are all sorts of clues to problems and the insightful person senses which clues are important and which are not. When gathering evidence from a crime scene, the detective needs to decide what information is important and what isn't relevant. Doctors have to decide which bits of evidence are crucial to their diagnosis and which are not.

Selective combination happens when you put all the pieces together to create the big picture. I am doing this with this book. I have found a number of reasons that people are proactive and can conceptualize where I am going by selectively looking at the clues that I think are relevant to my thesis. There is nothing terribly original. All the bits and pieces are already out there. It is my way of putting them all together that will make this book unique.

Selective comparison involves being able to see things in a new light. This is the process of discovery. It was at work when Einstein was looking at the rays of sun and realized that they were bent, or when Newton saw the falling apple and asked why, or when Professor Alzheimer realized that what people were calling the natural aging process was really a disease.

The experientially intelligent person might score below average on intelligence tests, but might have superlative letters of recommendation from employers, friends and teachers. Such people are often extremely creative, have good ideas, and do exceptional research. These people are the workers we attribute to working at their maximum potential. They take on tasks eagerly, and through their sheer willingness to find a solution, apply all they have.

3. Adaptation

Adaptation is the third leg of Sternberg's Triarchic Theory. Here, intelligence is viewed as a person's ability to adapt to the environment. It's what we might call practical intelligence. Here, you capitalize on your strengths and minimize your weaknesses. POAs understand this. They don't let their weaknesses get in the way; they simply work around them. Adaptive people might have an average IQ score, but Sternberg found them the most employable. They learn how to play the game and do the kind of work that is valued by employers. They have "street-smarts."

This book is a good example of adaptation in action. My strengths lie in my ability to find simple answers to somewhat complicated issues and present them in a way that is helpful. The problem, or my weakness, is that I write like I talk. That's fine in a classroom or in front of a live audience, but in a book it simply doesn't work. So, I capitalize on my strengths to develop ideas and overcome my weakness by soliciting the help of experts. This book has gone through the careful hands of several editors who have helped me mold my words into information that works for my readers.

Sternberg's conclusion is that there are three ways to be smart. What you need to do—and our POAs seem to have done just that— is to take the three components of intelligence, apply them to your experience, and use them to adapt to, select. and shape your environment. That, in a nutshell, is the Triarchic Theory of Intelligence. Sternberg's findings go beyond the traditional findings in an IQ test and show us that we all have different strengths when it comes to intelligence, yet a whole generation grew up believing, that without a high IQ, their life options were limited. They probably didn't know that when Einstein (with a reported IQ score of 160) took the entrance exams to attend Zurich's Electrical Engineering School, he failed. So much for IQ tests. [67]

Experts concur the smartest person ever was Leonardo Da Vinci. Based on his works and writings, his IQ was calculated to be 220. [68]

Millionaire oilman T. Boone Pickens once said about his intelligence: "I used to say my IQ swings with the price of gas. When gas is at three dollars, I'm a genius; when it hits about one dollar, I'm a moron." [69]

It seems that society has a need to classify its members. One such classification is the measurement of intelligence. The first IQ testing began in 1905 with the Stanford-Bine test. [70]

Today, the next generation of testing is based on the WISC-IV, which was established in 1974, and is used as a method of determining

---

[67] Einstein, Just to be clear, apparently excelled in science and physics, but his downfall was the non-science subjects such as History, French, Music and Geography. See www.abc.net.au/science/k2/moments.
[68] If you want other interesting bits of trivia check www.wiki.answer.com.
[69] T Boone Pickens, born in 1927 he is now the CEO of BP Capital. As I am writing this oil is edging up to $ 150.00 per barrel which I suppose using Boone's rational would send his IQ score off the chart.
[70] In 1866 psychologist Alfred Binet, at the request of the French Government, attempted to create a method of identifying intellectually challenged children. The test was revised in 1916 by Stanford psychologist Lewis Terron. (Wikipedia)

strengths and weaknesses in a person's intellectual abilities, and as an indicator of future performance. Perhaps the assumption is that if one has a high enough IQ level, then he or she is in a superior position to achieve career success. 71

Nobel Laureates

If society is putting all its eggs into the IQ basket, then with 40 years of experience, you would expect to see some pretty compelling evidence that this type of testing produced dependable results. Yet POAs don't act simply because they are smart. Take a random look at some of the smartest people in the world. Finding them is easy: Simply check the list of Nobel Laureates. Here are 10 chosen at random: Wilhelm Roentgen, Neils Bohrs, Marie Curie, Alfred Werner, Max Plank, Albert Einstein, Fredrick Banting, Robert Koch, Charles Richet, and Ivan Pavlov. Not one on this list is a slouch in the brains department. 72

Here are some of my findings. The average age of my Nobel winners was 52.9 — not exactly young. But, what about the gap between their discoveries and winning the Nobel Prize? Here, I found the average age of their major discovery was 39.8 years. It took the world 13.1 years between the times they made their mark until they were recognized with a Noble prize. These people were smart from the get-go, but it took time to develop their abilities. Assuming that they joined the scientific work force at age 28 (four years undergraduate work, two years for a Masters Degree and four to six years for a Doctorate.), there was an average of 11.8 years where they focused their genius in their respective fields of physics, medicine, and chemistry, while tackling questions that they couldn't resist.

So, in addition to their intelligence and formal education, they also needed to commit to a dozen years of research before they made their groundbreaking discoveries. Nobody handed these people fame and glory; rather, it was the result of years of painstaking work.

Since 1901, there have been a total of 646 Nobel prizes awarded - only five people and organizations received two Nobel prizes and only one went on to get three. This is interesting. You would assume that if

---

[71] WISC – IV – "The Wechsler Intelligence Scale for Children" developed in 1949 by David Wechsler to test IQ of children from ages 6 to 16.
[72] There are lots of cool bits of information about the Nobel Laureates at the foundations official site, www.Nobelprize.org.

intelligence were the prime ingredient in success, then if someone won one Nobel Prize, theoretically he or she should have been able to win another. Not so.

Winning the Nobel Prize is not an end, but a milestone; a stop along the way. The average life span for Nobel Laureates is 77.8 years. This means that after their moment in the spotlight they all had another quarter of a century to quit, go on the lecture circuit, or stay in the research game. Most of them chose the latter. While they never achieved the pinnacle of Nobel glory again, they continued researching, writing, and teaching. If society recognized these high-IQ individuals at roughly the halfway point in their lives, there must be more than sheer brilliance that kept them in the game — both before and after their prize. There must be more to proactivity than intelligence.

American Presidents

Another group of proactive people is politicians. Does it take a high IQ to become the President of the United States? Putting your political beliefs aside, you might expect the answer to be yes and you would be right. Which one do you think had the highest IQ? Here's the surprise: It's Richard Nixon with a score of 143. Between 90 and 100 is considered average, so 143 is pretty smart. There are lots of American presidents with high IQs — Abraham Lincoln's IQ was estimated to be 128, Bill Clinton's 137 (Hillary is 140), and George W. Bush's is 125. However, IQ isn't the only indicator of someone's chance of becoming an American president. [73]

George Washington had an estimated IQ of 118, JFK 121, and Ulysses S. Grant an estimated paltry 110. Yet none of these people became the president without years of political involvement. They often worked up from one political office to the next, each time honing their political skills, increasing their contacts, and developing a clear understanding of how the game of politics is played. Once again, you might conclude that there is something more than straight-up intelligence that kept these people in the game of politics.

SATs

IQ is not the only method of categorizing intelligence. Another method is the Scholastic Assessment Test (SAT). The SAT is the most widely taken college entrance exam in the U.S. It's deemed the most

---

[73] US President IQ, www.my-iqtest.com. Also visit www.kids-iq-test.com.

accurate method of predicting a student's ability to perform in college. [74]

SAT tests decide the fate of millions of high school students by either allowing or preventing them from attending their desired universities. SAT testing dates back to the First World War when Robert Yerkes persuaded the U.S. army to let him test recruits for intelligence. This test, the Army Alpha test, was the first mass-administered IQ test. [75]

One of Yerkes' assistants was a Princeton-based psychologist named Carl Brighman. After the war, Brigham adapted the Army Alpha test for use as a college admissions test. It was first administered experimentally to a few thousand college applicants in 1926. [76]

In 1933, Harvard President James Bryant Conant[77] used the test as a method of finding candidates for his new scholarship program for gifted boys. Conant liked Brigham's test because it measured pure intelligence, regardless of the quality of the candidate's high school education. In 1938, all College Board schools began using the SAT.

Today, between 1.5 and 2 million college-ready students try the SATs. A perfect score is 1600. Time Magazine reports scores from some recognizable people such as Senator Paul Wellstorm, 800; author Amy Tan, 1100; U.S. President George W. Bush, 1206; Television personality Meredith Vieria, 1300; author Stephen King, 1300; former Vice President Al Gore, 1355; Sun Microsystems' founder Scott McNealy, 1420 and TV personality Ben Stein, 1573. [78]

---

[74] SAT, there is a terrific article written by Jon Blackwell in the *Trentonian* called *1947*: America's tester-in-chief. You can read it at www.capitalcentury.com/1947.html. Another was written by University of Wisconsin Professor Steven Dutch called "Killing the Messenger: Attacks on the SAT." You can read it at www.uwgb.edu/dutchs/pseudosc/denysat.htm. Also, an article by Reggie Ross in 2003 called "Whim's Place," www.whimsplace.com/011504/technosociety.htm.
[75] Robert Yerkes, (1876 – 1956). At one time, he was the President of the American Psychological Association.
[76] The first SAT was developed by Carl Campbell Brighman in 1926 for the College Entrance Examination Board.
[77] James Bryant Conant, (1893 – 1978) was President of Harvard U. 1933-53.
[78] Time Magazine, "How They Scored on the Test", (March 4, 2001).

SAT's have come under much scrutiny during the past few years. Consumer advocate Ralph Nader was quoted as saying, "... SAT did no better than a pair of dice in predicting college performance. [79]

Inventor Robert Williams accused the SAT of bias against Blacks, yet it's still the most common testing tool for college entrance. [80]

The assumption is that those with the highest SAT scores will likely be the best candidates to successfully complete their university education.
The University of Iowa conducted an interesting study of student retention rates starting in 1988 and running to 2002. [81]

Of all the students enrolled during the course of the study, 30 percent never made it to year four. After 70 years of SAT testing, universities are still showing a 30-percent failure rate. The University of Iowa took a proactive step to try and correct the problem. They were able to report a significant increase in graduation rates, which grew from 64.6 percent in 2003 to 66.4 percent in 2004, by looking beyond the SAT scores as their only criteria for entrance. While a mere 2 percent may not sound like much, and it is still a long way away from the 30 percent in all SAT-tested students, it is a positive first step towards reversing a trend that has cost universities millions of dollars each year.

This is only the beginning for the University of Iowa. In 1995, they initiated their "Four Year Graduation Plan." The plan was designed with three "interventions" to help students reach their goals.

The first was to provide students with a set of benchmarks that would help them plan their schedules and keep on track. The second was a "college transition" experience course, which enabled students to better adjust to the differences between high school and university life. The third was a determination of students who were best suited for

---

[79] Ralph Nader born in 1934, an outspoken critic of almost everything. Nader holds a record for running the most number of times for the office of President of the United States (5 times.)
[80] Robert Williams, (1886 – 1965), born in India and the son of Baptist Missionaries. He was no stranger to hunger and disease. He is noted as the inventor of a method of synthesizing vitamins to help fight malnutrition and vitamin deficiency diseases.
[81] University of Iowa, "Persistence and Graduation Report", (Fall 2004), uiowa.com/dg/h/grad-ret04.

university life. This intervention was based on the principles of enforcing rules and deadlines. For example, the university did not accept late applications because "students who apply late tend not to persist." They taught their students the way to play the game.

West Point's dropout rate of new cadets is 5 per cent – staggering when you equate this to the cost of training them. Predicting attrition clearly is an important factor in controlling spending. A questionnaire given to 1223 cadets entering the class of 2008, showed that persistence – over athleticism, SATs or faculty appraisal scores – is the best yardstick for predicting who will survive the first few weeks of basic training. [82]

POAs like Albert White, with his grade 10 education and well-honed street smarts, stayed in the game long after he had accomplished his financial goals. Nobel Prize winners and presidents have learned it takes more than intelligence to remain an active player in their respective games. We have also seen that IQ and SAT testing can be misleading as predictors of academic success.

High attrition rates at universities that base admission to their programs based only on test scores offer more evidence that these methods don't always work. The only rational conclusion is that while intelligence is helpful, it's not the primary ingredient for POAs who want to stay in the game; which brings our discussion to the issue of talent.

Talent

Now that we understand intelligence is not the prime ingredient to action, it's time to explore talent. Is talent the secret ingredient one needs to become a POA? Certainly POAs possess a natural-born talent in their fields. Talent is defined as "a natural ability to do something well," whereas intelligence is defined as "the ability to learn." [83]

Talent is often confused with intelligence. People with extreme talents are often labeled "geniuses," a term usually reserved for those who are highly intelligent. We hear about the genius of Mozart or Van Gogh. Robin Williams and Jim Carrey are often labeled comedic geniuses. The genius label is found in all disciplines. Think of Andy

---

[82] Angela L. Duckworth, Christopher Peterson, Michael D. Mathews, Dennis R. Kelly, *Perseverance and Passion for Long Term Goals, Journal of Personality and Social Responsibility*, (February, 2007).
[83] Microsoft Encarta Dictionary, (St. Martin's press, 2001).

Warhol, Pablo Piccasso, Alexander Graham Bell, Virginia Woolf, Luciano Pavaratti, Ernest Hemingway, Frederick Banting, Marie Curie, Charles Edison, Frank Gehry, Sigmund Freud, Carl Jung, and Paul McCartney.

All of the above were credited with the label of genius, but in reality, what they demonstrate is an extraordinary talent in a certain area.

Mozart

Wolfgang Amadeus Mozart was credited with musical genius because of his extraordinary musical talents. Mozart is said to have performed on the piano at the age of five, and throughout his life, created dozens of symphonies that have engraved his name in the hearts and minds of music lovers. [84]

Many of us are familiar with Mozart's accomplishments — over 600 works, including 21 stage and opera works, 15 masses, 41 symphonies, 25 piano concertos, 12 violin concertos, 27 concert arias, 17 piano sonatas, and 26 string quartets — and he died at 35!

Mozart started learning music at the age of three from his father. Leopold Mozart was a famous musician in his own right and received an appointment as violinist in the orchestra of the Archbishop of Salzburg. He recognized his son Wolfgang's natural talents and his "ear" for music. (It is said that Mozart possessed "perfect pitch.") Leopold Mozart was Wolfgang's "stage father." History is filled with stories about parents who mentor their children. Mozart's story is the equivalent of Earl Wood's work with his son Tiger. [85]

Under Leopold's tutelage, this father-and-son team took to the road to perform for kings and emperors throughout Europe. Their grueling schedule kept them away from home for four years. During this time, Amadeus honed his craft and harnessed his talent.

Show biz seemed a natural vocation for the young Mozart. His natural talent on the piano and violin was the foundation of his remarkable career. While his reputation as a composer grew, it was

---

[84] Charles K. Moss, Wolfgang Amadeus Mozart, www.carolinaclassical.com/articles/mozart.html. John Terauds, *Modern Maestro*, *The Toronto Star*, (January 14, 2006).
[85] Earl Woods, *Training a Tiger*: A Father's Guide to Raising a Winner in Both Golf and Life (Thorndike Press), 1999.

performing that gave him "star" status. Yet, there was more to Mozart than pure talent.

Initially, Mozart was quite successful. But, life was not easy. He was a poor businessman, liked to play billiards and was constantly in debt.

He was continuously moving his family to increasingly more modest housing. He needed to get back in the public eye. In 1790, when Leopold II was crowned German Emperor in Frankfurt, Mozart saw a public relations opportunity. Although he was not formally invited to participate in the festivities, in a desperate attempt to gain public recognition, Mozart journeyed to Frankfurt at his own expense and arranged a concert at which he performed two piano concertos.

The performance caught the attention of the right people, and once again, Mozart was back in the spotlight.

Was it his talent that immortalized his reputation or his persistence as he agonized over each new musical piece? If he hadn't taken one last chance and gone to Frankfurt, would his name have disappeared into history? Mozart did what was necessary to stay in the only game he knew how to play.

Paul McCartney

Paul McCartney tells about waking up early in the morning with a new tune playing in his head. When asked about his inspiration for writing one of the Beatles'' most popular tunes, "Yesterday," McCartney said the tune "just appeared." [86]

I assume many of us find ourselves humming a tune. I do it while working out on my treadmill. The difference between Paul McCartney and me is that the tune I am humming is probably one that he wrote. But there is more to proactivity than thinking up a catchy tune. Songwriters know that it takes hours of work to bring the tune to life. It needs writing and re-writing. It requires arranging and orchestration. Then it needs many hours in a studio. Thomas Edison once said that genius is "one percent inspiration and 99 percent perspiration." [87]

---

[86] Paul McCartney, John G. Sutton, "Inspiration VS Perspiration", *Physic World*, (2006).
[87] Thomas Edison, one of the most prolific inventors ever. held 1093 patents.

Inspiration

Carl Jung suggests that there exists a collective, unconscious body of knowledge that is available to anyone who knows how to open the door. Talent is what focuses you on one door versus another. [88]

Hemingway's writing door was open and he heard a great story through his writer's focus. Leonard Cohen is able to look at the world through his poet's eyes and Donald Trump through the eyes of a real estate developer. However, it takes more than an inspired idea to write a book or build a skyscraper.

Paul McCartney's talent is as a songwriter and entertainer. He spent years honing his craft. His inspirations are in music while yours and mine relate to our careers. Does Paul McCartney wake up in the morning saying, "I have a great idea for a sales presentation?" Probably not, but many sales people do.

In 1994, K. Anders Ericsson and Neil Charness authored a paper which was published in American Psychologist titled "Expert Performance: Its Structure and Acquisition." [89]

The paper examined intelligence and talent. Participants in their studies were tested on their abilities in mathematics, vocabulary, grammar, and problem solving. Their conclusion was that IQ does not reliably discriminate the best adult performers from the less accomplished.

They also suggested innate talent is not the prime determinant of one's ability to acquire proficiency. Ericsson and Charness wrote: "There has been a bias toward attributing abilities to gifts rather than experience." They concluded it takes at least a decade of hard work or practice and overcoming obstacles to become highly successful in most endeavors. Yet, we live in a fast-moving world that business in short-term economic cycles. With advancing technology being updated every 60 to 90 days, 10 years seems unrealistic.

Many of us have moments of inspiration. On long car rides my wife and I play a game called "Let's invent a new business." During our car

---

[88] Carl Gustav Jung, *The Archetypes and the Collective Unconscious*, (Princeton University Press, 1969).
[89] K Anders Ericsson and Neil Charness, *Expert Performance*: Its Structure and Acquisition (American Psychologist, 1994).

trips we spend right-brain time strategizing new and wonderful things our clients can do to solve their dilemmas. Often, these id eas involve new businesses. Our talent is our intellectual ability to look at a problem and be able to get through the clutter and see the heart of the issue. From this vantage point, solutions often roll off our tongues. The question we often ask ourselves is, "If we are so talented, why aren't we rich?" The answer is simple. Anyone can come up with a brilliant idea. The more familiar you are with a subject, the easier it becomes. Perhaps you have a talent for fixing cars, flying airplanes, or climbing mountains. The doors you open will often relate to cars, airplanes, or mountains. When a door to nuclear medicine opens, you look bewildered, scratch your head, and slam it shut.

Hard Work and Self-Discipline

The difference between talent and being a POA is your ability to walk through the door and do something with the newfound insight. Talent helps, but it takes more than talent to be a POA. So, if it isn't simply intelligence or talent that lead people to proactivity, then there must be something else underlying their reasons for getting things done. Many studies point in the same direction - persistence.

A series of studies undertaken at the University of Pennsylvania found that persistence, not intelligence or talent, might be the secret ingredient. [90]

Persistence enables POAs to develop their stick-to-it-ness. And, what is encouraging for most of us is that persistence, unlike intelligence and talent, is a learned skill.

Is persistence just another word for self-discipline? Much has been written about self-discipline in self-help books, diet books, how-to-raise-your-kids books, and books on selling. The Microsoft Encarta Dictionary defines persistence as "a tenacity to continue despite problems or difficulties." [91]

The difference between persistence and self-discipline is that persistence implies the ability to keep doing something, while self-discipline is often short term and sometimes implies the ability to refrain from doing something. Have you ever set a New Year's resolution? Many of us have. Your resolution may be to find a new job

---

[90] University of Pennsylvania, Strategic Study Group, Second Year Persistence Study, Presidents Executive Council, (April 26, 2005).
[91] Microsoft Encarta Dictionary, (St. Martin's Press, 2001).

or sell more than you did last year. Both are ambitious goals and both require a sacrifice to succeed. The action you take requires self-discipline. While self-discipline is an important factor, it is not sufficient, by itself, to create a climate for persistence. Yet, the more you practice self-discipline, the more you get into the habit required to spark persistence.

In many ways the approach taken by the persistent person is one of optimism. While the self-disciplined also hope for a positive result, refraining from an activity is short term. For example, when smokers quit smoking, it is their self-discipline that helps them initially. They also call upon optimism in the hope, that in time, it will be less difficult to maintain a non-smoking lifestyle.

Optimism is what helps persistent people hang in when the road is difficult and filled with obstacles. Self-disciplined people occasionally cheat. They take a day off work or extend a deadline. The road to persistence is never ending—it is a way of life. Stories abound concerning Edison and the thousands of experiments he performed before actually inventing the light bulb.   [92]

Medical researchers have spent decades looking for a cure for cancer. For over a century, physicists have been searching for the TOE (Theory of Everything), the one unifying theory that will unite all the rules of the cosmos.   [93]

Writers can spend years honing, molding and perfecting their manuscript. Successful sales people spend years developing their skills and confidence. It is the persistence of the inventor, researcher, physicist, and the sales person that keeps them in the game.

---

[92] Thomas Edison is often considered as history's most prolific inventor. But the reality was that many of his inventions were improvements of products invented by others. The light bulb is a good example. Edison bought the patent from Henry Woodward who was the true inventor. Then as the story unfolds, Edison applied his real genius by making the light bulb commercially viable.

[93] Theory of Everything. This is a hypothetical theory that would link two of the fundamental theories in physics: quantum theory (really little things), and general relativity (really big things). In the 1990's scientists hit upon something called "String Theory" but whether it will be the TOE – well, the jury's still out.

Christopher Reeves stands out in my mind as a man of persistence. Everything I have read points to a man of tremendous self-discipline. He acted; he was involved in sports and was passionate about the world he lived in. Then tragedy struck, and a moment later, his body was forever immobilized. His path was temporarily derailed.

But he got back on track. His years of self-discipline had taught him a deeper skill — persistence. Once again, he rejoined the human race, and in spite of overwhelming odds, until his death, he was a POA. Self-discipline allowed him to do what he did. Persistence fueled his discipline.

Hard Work

How does hard work fit into the equation? We often confuse hard work with persistence. Recently, I was at a banquet where the speaker was thanking her colleague for a job well done. Her exact words: "I'd like to thank Annette for her persistence and hard work." They are separate things. They are not mutually exclusive. Hard work is the process while persistence is the commitment. Hard work is the result of self-discipline. When you say, "I'll just plod along and do my job day by day," you're tackling the hard work. However, when you do the hard work with a bigger goal in mind, and are prepared for the work involved, that's persistence. Hard work implies something more immediate. It's action you take today. But, as a motivator, it's seldom the cause of action. If you ask successful sales people their secret they rarely point to hard work, but instead talk about their commitment to staying in the game through persistence. Yes, hard work is part of the process, but it alone does not motivate people to action.

Understand that hard work really connotes something that is difficult as well as short term. We "get to work." We can hardly wait until "work's done." We take a breath of relief when it temporarily ends and say, "Thank goodness it's Friday."

When we refer to hard work, we often connect it to labor: hard labor, labor-intensive, the job is laborious, labor pains.

Labor is a struggle to do something that is difficult. Samuel Johnson wrote, "He that never labors may know the pain of idleness, but not the pleasure." [94]

---

[94] Samuel Johnson, (1709 – 1784) English poet.

In the 13th century, King John of England took this one step further when he decreed people must use surnames that pertain to their trades. So, we had names like Cartwright, Goldsmith, and Shepherd. [95]

Today, we even have organizations like the Department of Labor and labor unions whose mandate is to help us make the most of hard work. There is a profession built around labor relations. We have Labor Day, a day to honor laborers. There is even a time to stop your labor; it is called retirement. The middle syllable in retirement is "tire." Tired of what? Obviously, all that hard labor.

Which leads us to the scoreboard: Labor and hard work's reward is tallied up in what the effort returns to us financially. The harder we work, the more things we can buy. While the cost of goods between 1995 and 2005 increased by 27 per cent, the amount of debt carried by American families during the same time rose from 65 Billion in 1995 to almost 1 trillion in 2005, a huge increase of nearly 1,500 per cent. [96]

Labor once satisfied the lowest rung on Maslow's hierarchy of needs, but survival has changed for the majority of people. It is now something they need to do in order to keep up with credit card payments, or the Joneses, or both, and the majority of people caught in this web of deceit aren't able to keep up at all. When 43 percent of Americans report less than $1,000 in liquid savings, and the average credit card balance is $10,000, there is something seriously wrong.

Labor refers to the task at hand. What is hard one day may become easy the next. When you approach a task and find some aspect of it difficult, it is labeled hard work. If other elements of the work are easier, the task is viewed as something nice or fun to do, and therefore, is not work. If it weren't such a chore to do hard work, then perhaps labor itself would be an action motivator. But it is not. It seems that people approach hard work as something to get beyond. It is short term. Who wants to do hard work forever? In the past, criminals were punished to a lifetime of hard labor. Why would a sane person choose this same punishment if there's an option? It's an option that many of

---

[95] King John (1167 – 1216), was the younger brother of Richard 1 (The Lionhearted) signer of the Magna Carta and immortalized in fiction as the nemesis of Robin Hood.

[96] See consumer debt statistics at www.consolidate-credit-card.net and www.trinity.edu/mkearl/time-4.html.

us impose on ourselves, and the term of our sentence ends when we retire. Many look to retirement as a time when hard work ends and life begins. Or, does it?

Persistence Is Key

Calvin Coolidge wrote, "Nothing in the world can take the place of persistence. Talent will not. Genius will not. Education will not. Persistence and determination alone are omnipotent." [97]

One occupation where persistence is a must is the job of President of the United States. During the 250 years of the existence of the United States, we have seen only 43 (soon to be 44) men take on this precarious job. [98]

When you read their biographies, the one constant in 70 percent of these men is that they had military experience. The military demands discipline of its members. They learn to think, to act and to perform in a strict and unrelenting environment. Discipline and hard work seem to have set the groundwork for persistence in American presidents. But, you do not need to spend time in the military to learn persistence. Discipline that teaches persistence is a common theme for many POAs. Take, for example, the story of Dr. Mike Ackerman.

Dr. Mike Ackerman

Mike Ackerman was a promising young high-school student in Montreal during the late 1970s, effortlessly pulling in marks in the 90s. But then, like so many, he joined the drug culture. His marks took a nosedive. When he graduated high school, he barely squeaked by. "I don't want to make any excuses for my behaviour," Mike maintains, "but the fact is that for me the '70s were a wasted decade. There were a lot of people into that kind of activity and I was one of them."

While he went on to do post secondary studies, at his parents' insistence, Mike bombed out the first semester. "Basically, I withdrew from most of the courses. Those I kept, I failed at," he says.

Thoroughly disillusioned with school and life, Mike headed up to the wilds of Northern Ontario for a couple of years, winding up at a pulp mill in Terrace Bay. "My job in the mill was at the lowest end of

---

[97] Calvin Coolidge, (1872 – 1933) 30th US President.
[98] See www.neptune.com and learn more about which Presidents served in the military. Also check out www.factmonster.com/ipd/A0584623.html.

the food chain," he recalls, "pushing a broom and shovelling slop." He'd work days and spend his pay check partying the nights away.

Mike did that for about a year, but soon, the seeds of dissatisfaction were beginning to bear fruit. He had innovative ideas on how to make the mill operations smoother and more efficient, but nobody wanted to hear from him because "I was the dirty kid pushing the broom." He realized this really wasn't what he wanted to do for the rest of his life.

"It started to dawn on me that if I wanted things to improve, there was only one person that could make that happen – me, " Mike said.

One day, an old Montreal friend of Mike's came up for a visit. "I was waiting for him at the local pub," he recalls. "I had a beer in front of me, a beer sitting out for him, and a pack of cigarettes on the table."

His friend walked in, sat down and said: "Long time no see. I see you're still smoking." He then proceeded to snap the cigarette Mike was smoking in two.

Mike was enraged. He jumped up, knocked over the table and grabbed his buddy by the shirt, ready to beat him up.

"All of a sudden," says Mike, "I had an epiphany. Here was a guy that I used to hang around with, we were like brothers, and I'm about to pound him out over a stupid cigarette? What's wrong with this picture?"

Mike sat down, gathered up all the wreckage, threw down his pack of cigarettes and said to his startled friend: "You know, you're right. I'm never going to touch one of these things again." Shortly thereafter, Mike realized that if he was going to quit smoking, he might as well divest himself of the rest of the bad habits he had acquired, and get on with his life.

"I'll never make excuses for the poor decisions that I made," continues Mike. "I'm the one who made them. And once I realized that I was the one who was making them, then it was a pretty straightforward decision to go on and do something about it."

Soon after, Mike left Terrace Bay and returned to Montreal, where he got a job as a stock boy at Canadian Marconi. "I was basically stocking shelves and putting little parts in bins and then taking other parts out of bins and sending them up to the assembly line where they were making radios."

Mike confessed that he really didn't mind the work; it was the work environment that was the problem. "It was winter and my work station was down in the basement. "I didn't see the sun from Sunday night until Saturday morning. It was dark when I got to work and dark when I got off work, so I was starting to feel a bit like a vampire."

In the fall, he went back to school with a newfound positive attitude and straightaway began pulling high marks again. "It's amazing when you stop poisoning your brain with psychoactive substances, how smart you can get," Mike chuckles.

Mike enrolled in the health sciences program. "I was getting some pretty good marks but not in the 90s, not where I thought I should be. To me, brilliant people who deserve all the goods of the earth falling on them should be pulling high 90s," Mike said. From there he went on to Acadia University in Wolfville, Nova Scotia. Postgraduate studies at Dalhousie University followed.

One of Mike's favorite subjects was biology. Fourth-year students working on their thesis were given a key to the laboratory and were allowed to work on whatever they wanted, just as long as they "didn't blow the place up." Mike had found his passion and spent many nights in the lab. "I'd be sitting there putting things under the electron microscope just to see what they looked like."

While at Acadia, Mike joined the Canadian Armed Forces Reserves. In the summer of 1982, he volunteered to undergo the infantry-training program. "Successfully completing that course was the biggest challenge in my life. It also gave me the discipline I needed to entertain the idea of enrolling in medical school." Mike enrolled in the Armed Forces as a medical student and went through the Medical Officer Training Program, (MOTP), coming out the other end as a military medical officer. He was in the military for 10 years, (there's that 10 year rule which is the amount of time to develop career proficiency again), serving at bases in Germany and Cyprus before becoming the Base Surgeon at CFB Shilo.

After leaving the military, Mike took up private practice back in the Maritimes, where he resides today with his wife and two daughters. A pillar of the community, Dr. Michael Ackermann has come a long way from his days as a troubled youth: "The big thing that I took away from my experience through the '70s and with my later life, is that the people that care about you, don't give up on you. They persist. They saw I was doing something to turn my life around, and were willing to give me a second and third and fourth and tenth chance. It's a very lucky person who gets a second chance and a luckier person who can find what he likes, do the hard work and learn the stick-to-it-ness necessary to overcome anything. I really haven't done anything remarkable, The world is full of people who pulled themselves up by the boot straps and got the job done. All I did was wake up one day and realize I was the author of my own misfortunes and that if I wanted to get ahead, waiting for life to give me a break was not the way to do it."

Studies in the Roots of Persistence

Let's turn our attention to an interesting group of studies conducted by Gershon Tenenbaum of the University of Florida; Ronnie Lidor and Noah Lavyan from the Wingate Institute at Haifa University in Israel; Keiran Morrow and Shirley Tonnel of the University of Queensland, Australia, and Aaron Gershgoren of the Israel Institute of Technology in Israel. In their academic paper titled, "Dispositional and Task-Specific Social-Cognitive Determinants of Physical Effort Persistence," they attempt to create a series of experiments to uncover the determinants that are indicators of a person's ability to persist in tasks that pose difficult demands. [99]

Traditional motivational thinking states that the main determinant of commitment, and therefore persistence, is either task-oriented or ego-oriented. Task orientation involves an individual focusing on the task at hand. People who are task-oriented perceive their competency will increase through their ability and effort. Therefore, the increase in competency motivates them and increases the likelihood of their adapting persistence behavior.

In contrast, ego-oriented people are less concerned about long-term efforts; they concentrate on their existing competence and self-image.

People who are ego-oriented, the theory says, might opt out if they perceive they do not have the competence now and are not motivated by the prospect of developing that competence in the future. For example, a friend of mine took years before she agreed to take a computer course. Her concern was how she would be perceived because she knew that for the first few months, her computer skills would be less than spectacular. She is an intelligent woman, but lacks

---

[99] Tanenbaum et al. Gershon Tanebaum, Ronnie Lidor, Noah Lavyan, Kieran Morrow, Shirley Tonnel, and Aaron Gershgoren, "Dispositional and Task-Specific Social-Cognitive Determinants of Physical Effort Perserverance", *The Journal of Psychology*, (2005).

the motivation to learn a new skill, which in her opinion, might make her look foolish. And yet, this same woman will undertake strenuous hiking trips, because in this sport, she perceives that she has some control of her abilities.

Ego-oriented people will only adopt persistence behavior if it fits what they perceive as their present competencies. The theory concludes that task-oriented people will have a greater tendency to adopt persistent behavior skills than ego-oriented people.

The study also discusses another trait; self-efficacy and its role in adopting persistence behavior. When people develop a belief in their ability to accomplish a desired result, this self-efficacy might lead a person to an increased feeling of control and a reduction in stress.

The Tanenbaum Group conducted three separate experiments. The first involved 15 Australian men, ages 18 to 35, who ran once or twice per week and had no health or disability problems. They were first asked a series of questions about their general health and level of fitness, task and ego orientation, and self-efficacy. Then, they each were asked to perform a single task and were told, "You are now requested to run as long as you can. This is a very difficult task." They were asked about their confidence in their ability to complete the task. Then, they were sent to the treadmills to begin running.

In the second study were 15 Israeli students at the Zinman Education College, 18 to 25 years old, who were active in a variety of sports, but not competitively. They went through the same process as those in the first study. The third study involved 25 Israeli students ages 20 to 26. All participants had to bring a certificate from their doctor saying they could participate in moderate to vigorous physical activity. They were then tested in the same manner as the other two groups. The results were that neither task nor ego was a predictor of the subjects' performance. The authors noted that readiness to invest effort, commitment, and determination were also important indicators of a successful career. When POAs are asked, "What made you think you could succeed?" Many will reply that failure was not an option.

Dorothy and Jack

A good example of persistence is the poignant story of Dorothy and Jack Babcock. They didn't change the world; they just fell in love—but not right away. It took some persistence. When Dorothy finally agreed to marry Jack she was 47 and Jack was 76.

Grab Success by the Horns

Jack's story actually begins in 1900. Born in Kingston, Ontario, Canada. his life was ordinary in many respects. He joined the army at 15-and-a-half years old because "he thought it would be a good idea." Although he was physically fit, he was underage, so his Commanding Officer sent him to Quebec rather than to the front of World War One. Ultimately, he was stationed in London, England, where he got involved in "rounding up" underage kids who could help in the war effort. "They drilled us eight hours a day," Jack remembers. "Then, they moved us to Wales."

After the war, Jack got a job at an electrical power plant working on the generator. In the summer of 1920, he went to Saskatchewan to work on the harvest. He earned $250 that summer. But according to Jack, "By the time I got home I had nearly spent it all." For the next 14 years he had miscellaneous jobs until he opened up his own business supplying and maintaining oil burners. He recalls, "My friend Pete said 'all you need to be in business is buy three oil burners and the bank will take care of the financing'." Jack thought it over, took the plunge and within the first year sold 100 burners.

For the next 26 years, Jack worked at his business, married, and started his family. Jack met Dorothy in 1975, when Jack's first wife had cancer and Dorothy was her nurse. During her illness, his first wife talked about Dorothy's kindness. But, neither Jack nor his wife was quite sure what the prefix "Ms." meant on her name badge. When Elise died, the couple had been married 44 years. Jack was lonely, but not ready to pack it in. He wanted companionship. After checking with some of his friends and finding out Dorothy was widowed, he asked her out. She declined. "He was too old," Dorothy said.

So, Jack tried another approach. He invited her to play golf. Then, they started going for walks and he took her out to dinner a few times. In Dorothy's mind this wasn't dating. Jack persisted for six months. "He just kept hanging around," Dorothy remembers. Then, Jack wanted to take their relationship to the next step. Dorothy, while she liked Jack, wasn't sure. A friend of Dorothy's finally made a remark that changed the course of their history. "Dorothy," she said, "If a man can live past 70 and still be active then maybe there is a chance." She took this to heart and made a pact with Jack. She made Jack promise to give her at least 10 years. That was 29 years ago. When I visited them, Jack, now 105, was sitting in his favorite chair, and Dorothy (who had just returned from an aerobics class) was sitting lovingly by his side. It is a reminder to us all that the game isn't over — until it's over.

Lessons learned

- Understand your strengths.
- Develop an approach to your career that is rooted in self-awareness, hard work, and self-discipline.

Persistence doesn't require a superior level of intelligence or talent, only a commitment to hard work and self-discipline. In your sales career, the challenge is to create the job you want and never give up. Persistence is the tool you need to stay in your game.

As we've seen, persistence is the common element among our POAs.

We saw it in Albert White, a man who built an empire from nothing, one brick at a time. We also saw how Nobel Prize winners managed to stay in the game long after they had received fame, and sometimes, fortune. We saw Wolfgang Amadeus Mozart, one of the most talented musicians ever draw on his persistence when his talent alone wasn't cutting it. Your ability to play for the long run is a key element to success. That's what Mike Ackerman learned as he pulled himself up by the bootstraps in pursuit of a meaningful career and life. Persistence is deeply rooted, and once implanted, hard to shake no matter what the circumstances. When you work hard and long enough, you form the persistence habit. You decide how you want to live your life and accept that only you can make it happen.

The context of persistence varies from individual to individual. You can start a business like Albert White, pursue a profession like Mike Ackerman, or win the heart of your companion like Jack Babcock.

Lessons into Action: Your Career Action Plan

Step 1: Understand Your Strengths

The first step is to determine your strengths. I have often heard people say, "I have no special talent." My answer to this assertion is, "rubbish." When you say this, you are lying to yourself. Everyone is good at something.

a. Start by developing a career description based on your own career

A career description is similar to a job description in that it includes all the duties and competencies needed to perform the job. But, your career description offers a much bigger picture. It starts the day you had your first inclination of how you wanted to spend your working life, that first moment when you proudly said, "I want to be a fireman," or "I want to be a doctor," or "I want to be a sales person." It unfolds as your life progresses. There are twists and turns, but you keep moving forward. Whether those initial childhood fantasies stayed with you or changed, they are important issues to include in your career description.

Your career description will have three parts: the past, the present, and the future. The first two parts will chronicle what you have done and the steps you have taken to get where you are today. Part three will answer some of the following questions:

How would I like to see my career in sales progress?
What do I want to accomplish?
How do I want to be regarded?
What legacy do I want to leave?
What kind of people do I want to associate with?

Devote some quiet reflective time to this step. Don't get caught up in the unknowns about the future. Don't say, "How do I know what is going to happen tomorrow?" You don't. Now is your chance to mold your future the way you would like to see it unfold.

b. Go back to your career description and complete the chart below:

In column one list the talents, skills, or strengths that brought you to where you are today. Beside each strength, note whether they were acquired, or were natural talents (innate). If it falls into the first category, list those things you did to acquire these special skills. If they are innate, list those things you did to nurture your talent. Here is a partial analysis of my career description. My analysis looks like this:

Column 1	Column 2	Column 3
Strength/talents	Acquired (A) Innate (I)	Action step
Writing	Acquired	Attend writer's workshop Develop a writer's discipline Write short articles Work with editors Stay open to feedback
Speaking	Innate	Take a presentation course Study good speakers Practice Fight complacency

My acquired skill is writing. I write well, but it has taken a long time to get comfortable with this skill. Many years ago, I wanted to write a letter to the editor of a local newspaper, but didn't think I had the talent, so I enrolled in an evening writing course. One of the lessons I learned was, that to take writing seriously, I had to develop the habit of writing every day. I progressed, and began writing that letter to the editor along with several short articles. Along the way, I have worked with excellent editors and have stayed open to feedback.

My presentation skills are strong. I have a natural talent for speaking. Early in my career, I attended a workshop where I learned the mechanics of developing a presentation. I studied good speakers and modeled their techniques, and then I did what all good speakers must do: practice. I looked for opportunities to speak. I spoke at community gatherings, libraries, and business clubs. I took advantage of every opportunity to hone my craft. I fought complacency and never took my speaking talent for granted. I am always looking for techniques to continuously improve myself.

Column 1	Column 2	Column 3
Strength	Acquired (A) Innate (I)	Action step

c. As you develop the future of your sales career ask yourself, "What talents or skills do I need to complete my career description?"

Add these skills to the second column of the chart. If you believe, that in order to complete the next chapter of your career description you need some natural gifts that you don't think you have, then it's time to get some feedback. Ask three or four of your colleagues, friends, or manager for honest feedback. Ask about your strengths and talents and listen to their feedback. This feedback will help you complete your career description.

d. Now it's time to lay out a plan for the future.
List those steps you can take to acquire or nurture special skills or talents in the third column of your chart.

Step 2: Develop an approach that is rooted in self-awareness, hard work and self-discipline. You work because you love the job, the environment, the focus, the challenge, and the product, but sometimes love is not always a factor. Not everyone has the luxury of choosing where they work or what work they do. It's easy to congregate around the water cooler and complain about your boss, your customers, or your working conditions. But, all this does is reinforce the negative. You need to break away from this routine and focus on what you like.

This requires a concerted effort on your part to find the parts of your work that are best for you and integrate them into your everyday activities. It's going to take a lifetime of hard work to get where you want to go. There will be some aspects of your career that are exciting, challenging, and fun, and others that are tedious, frustrating, and uninteresting. In this step you, will learn to use those aspects you like as a motivator to get you through the parts of your day that are not as thrilling. It's like eating a piece of chocolate cake and saving the icing for last.

Refocus your energies

Make a list of the things you really like about selling. Be as detailed as possible: Explain exactly what it is you like and why you like it. For example, what I really like about writing is the ability to meet interesting people, explore new topics, and ultimately see what I have created in print. What I don't like: Editing and rewriting.

Find a balance.

When you feel tired, overwhelmed, and ready to throw in the towel, focus on those things at work that are most interesting to you. Go back through your career description and identify those things that you find most interesting and joyful. Then, schedule specific times to take a break from your tasks to do something you like. I write books one chapter at a time. Then, while I am rewriting a chapter and going through the editing process, I can be working on a new chapter at the same time. You can be creative about short-term rewards. Take a walk, have a cappuccino, talk to colleagues, or catch up on your reading. All that matters is that you like the reward.

Use the parts of your work that you enjoy the most as your motivator to continue the hard work. Think of each moment as a deposit in your persistence bank account. After a while, you will have sufficient funds in the account so you can live off the interest. But, what's really interesting is that you won't. Rather, you will continue to make additional deposits. That's what persistence is all about.

Persistence comes with time and patience. In the next chapter, we will look at proactivity in the face of opportunities, whether you create them or they just happen.

Grab Success by the Horns

4
When Opportunity Knocks – Answer

"The great secret in life is for every man to be ready when opportunity comes."
— **Benjamin Disraeli**   100

Have you ever thought about financial independence? Are you looking for the perfect job? How does the thought of making money while you sleep sound? Do you want to find the secret formula to creating the perfect life?

Sound familiar? These are a sampling of the messages we are inundated with daily. Pick up a newspaper, browse through your junk mail, or turn on your computer, and there is someone hawking an opportunity that promises to be that big break that will change your life forever.

While some of us might shake our head and wonder how anyone would be gullible enough to jump at these opportunities, many people do. The "snake oil" sales approach has been around since the beginning of time.

You might feel discouraged when a prospective customer doesn't return your calls or seems to be stalling their decision after you have made a pitch. Maybe you feel the burden of your ever-increasing debt. There are problems we all face and sometimes you just can't see a way out. This is when you would love to have opportunity come knocking at your door.

An article in Canada's Globe and Mail reported an incident with famed architect Daniel Libskind. Libskind had just created his crystal designed rebuild of the classical Royal Ontario Museum in Toronto, Ontario, Canada. Libskind's design was a one-of-a-kind project with few precedents.   101

---

[100] Benjamin Disraeli, (1804-1881) served as Britain's Prime minister. While baptized in the Anglican Church, Disraeli was really Jewish – interesting!
[101] William Thorsell, When In Doubt: Say Yes, Globe and Mail, May 8, 2006.

The architect was at a meeting with engineers who were developing the schematic designs for the building. As the engineers focused on "loads, drains, and steel," Libskind sat quietly. After about an hour he said, "We've sat here all afternoon hearing nothing but problems. There are no problems." He had the engineers' attention, "People hate problems; they avoid and reject them. On the other hand, people love puzzles ... Solving puzzles often creates surprising solutions. We have no problems here. We have solutions." Libskind's words are a perfect reframe for our task at hand — finding surprise solutions.

Recognize or find opportunities: a five-step process:
There are five basics you need to explore that will make the balance of what you will learn in this chapter more realistic.

1. Be Open to the idea that you have a choice
You can wallow around in your despair and uncertainty and say, "poor me," or open yourself up to the possibility that there is a solution, even though it might not be evident. This first step is incredibly easy to say and often difficult to invoke. When you are overwhelmed with the problems and challenges you face everyday in your job, it is often difficult to believe that there are solutions, and as long as you hold onto this belief you will never move to step two.

The reality is that the same opportunities are available to everyone. The universe isn't giving some people more opportunities than others. Although, on the surface, it may seem that others have an unfair advantage; the opposite is true. Opportunity is equally divided and there is enough for all of us.

2. Recognize opportunities
There's no shortage of opportunities. They're everywhere. They're part of living. Every day you choose one path over another. Often with very little knowledge of where that choice will lead. Many of these choices are the mundane stuff of living: which brand of butter to buy, what bus to take, or which movie to see.

Other decisions have greater consequences: Should you take a job in your home town or move away, give up the luxury and certainty of one job for another, or become vocalized about an issue that will affect your workplace?

Each decision is triggered by the presence of an opportunity. Sometimes opportunities fall across your path and you have no choice but to come face to face with them. Other times they hide in the bushes and you have to beat the branches with a stick to knock them free.

Regardless of where your opportunities come from, taking advantage of them involves a risk. Your job is to assess that risk and make sure taking the opportunity gives you the best chance of success.

3. Understand the factors.

Many decisions people make today are complex and multi-disciplinary. We often need to draw upon our knowledge of psychology, political science, economics, and commerce to make informed decisions.

4. Have confidence in yourself.

The trick, as you will learn in this chapter, is knowing which opportunities are comfortable to act upon and which are not. When you are too far outside your comfort zone, pursuing new opportunities can have a deleterious effect on your confidence level. When opportunities fit nicely with your personal values and lifestyle, then finding the confidence to act is easier. For example, it's more comfortable working in an environment where you have affinity to your industry or customers than feeling alienated because you neither understand nor like them. In the former scenario you might be more likely to take risks.

5. Take action.

To act or not to act — that is the question. That's what this book is all about, taking action by working through the obstacles in your way.

Throughout this book, you have the opportunity to learn by example. Our next POA is no exception. Jon West's story is insightful and a reminder of what can happen when we open the door to opportunity.

Jon West's Leap of Faith   [102]

How did a respected molecular biologist become an award-winning butcher? "It's a bit of a long story," 39-year-old Jon West replies. "When I was young, my parents divorced. I didn't really enjoy school. This was a difficult period in my life." Jon dropped out of school, but soon realized he could do more with more qualifications.

Jon went on to a university and completed a four-year degree course in applied biology, which entailed a year's industrial experience.

---

[102] Jon West. Check out Jon's mouthwatering home page at www.localsecrets-art of meat- west and son.com.

"I worked for a year in a laboratory in Kew Gardens, which spurred my enthusiasm for plant sciences," says Jon. "My field of research was working on the molecular biology of plants, first on ornamental flowers and then on tea leaves where I continued for most of my scientific career. While I was at Kew Gardens, I managed to publish three scientific papers, which stood me in good stead when I applied to attend Cambridge." Jon ended up with a Masters of Science and worked in the laboratories at Cambridge for the next 12 years. And that's where matters stood. "My wife and I were quite happy," reflects Jon. "Neither of us was earning a huge amount, but we were enjoying what we were doing. She worked as an administrator for a charity and I was following the career that I loved in the field of research."

While science was the vocation of his dreams, it wasn't financially rewarding. "I didn't feel my career was progressing the way that I wanted it to." The irony was, to actually earn any sort of reasonable salary, he would have to give up what attracted him to the job in the first place. Matters came to a head after the couple returned from a joint sabbatical. After a year and a half back on the job, Jon was convinced that it was time for a change.

"My wife and I discussed it," Jon says, "And we decided that our current career track wasn't something that was going to be a benefit to us in the long run. You reach a certain stage in science where you can either become essentially a manager, where you don't get to do the lab-work that I actually love, the actual research side of things, or you stay at the same pay level. To actually earn any sort of reasonable livable wage, I would have to give up all the things that attracted me to the job."

But what to do? One evening, Jon was chatting with a friend who used to run a small butcher shop in Cambridge. He mentioned that his old shop, which he had sold, was up for sale again. According to his friend, "There was a gold mine going to waste there."

Jon had nine months experience working as a butcher when he was in his early teens, a quarter-century ago. While he loved cooking, working in the kitchen, and entertaining, these could hardly be called solid qualifications on which to base a new career in the food industry.

But Jon did have some cards up his sleeve. The friend who had recommended the shop wanted to work for Jon, as did the butcher already working there. "So part of the reason why I knew the business would work was I had this wealth of experience to draw on," says Jon.

But Jon's most important advantage was his confidence in himself and his abilities. "I've never been afraid to try something new," he asserts. "And I've always been a people person. I knew that I could do the job, or I could learn the job within a reasonably short amount of time, and I knew that I could make a success of it."

His self-confidence was matched by his savvy business sense. In the United Kingdom, where there were once approximately 60,000 butcher shops; only about 8,000 are currently in business.

Large supermarkets, with their huge purchasing power, have rendered many small shops obsolete. We have experienced the same phenomenon in North America where "big box" and superstores have substituted individual service and quality for convenience, lower prices, and greater selection. However, a backlash developed against the big grocery stores in the U.K. There are a significant number of people willing to pay a premium for personal service and interesting, innovative products, organic products, and free-range meats, which the superstores don't offer. This is the niche market that Jon hoped to tap into and capture.

Jon's idea was to use traditional skills to bring in people who loved gourmet food, but wanted something better than they could buy in a big supermarket. He called his new enterprise "The Art of Meat."

His effort succeeded beyond his most optimistic dreams. In eight-and-a half months, Jon took a failing business and increased its value by 50 percent. As a marketing ploy, Jon entered two different sausages and cured bacon at the prestigious East of England sausage-making competition. He won two gold medals and one silver, but more important, he got the attention of the media, which brought The Art of Meat much needed exposure in the United Kingdom and abroad.

"Coupled with the birth of our first child during this period, all in all, the past eight-and-a-half months have been a bit of a whirlwind," says the proud father and business owner. "But, everything's going really well." Jon's long-term plans are to open a chain of shops specializing in high-quality traditional butchery.

Asked if he misses the scientific world that was such a large part of his life for almost two decades, Jon replies, that while he still keeps in touch with the research in his field through scientific journals, the Internet and former colleagues who are now his customers, he is getting the same amount of satisfaction and enjoyment out of his butcher shop. Jon says, "It appeals to a different aspect of my personality."

Reflecting on his leap of faith, Jon said, "It was a mixture of applying myself and realizing that this a was a great chance for me to try to do something different. I was fortunate that the opportunity involved a subject that I loved as well."

Some readers may look at Jon West's story as a smart entrepreneur's dalliance with an opportunity. Others may view Jon's risk as a distraction from his real work. That's the problem with opportunity and risk — it's subjective. Why some of us jump at opportunities and others ignore them is a matter of personal perception. What is right for some is wrong for others. The trick is in knowing how to recognize the opportunity and process it to decide if it is best for you. POAs don't jump at every opportunity; they are selective.

Jon West's opportunity arose when he was busy and engaged as a molecular biologist. Opportunities can also arise when you are at your lowest point. Example: Walt Disney, in the ashes of personal bankruptcy, went on to found a giant entertainment company. [103]

Bankruptcy is something many people have faced; going to prison is not. Being convicted and sentenced to pay for a crime can be a blow to one's esteem, self-confidence, and social standing. When you look at the number of people who have come face to face with the law you see an astonishing number who can't seem to break the downward spiral that being a convicted felon sets in motion. Then there are exceptions.

John Myatt's Genuine Turnaround [104]

John Myatt was born in 1945. And in 1980, he was living in Staffordshire, England, a full-time dad with two children, separated

---

[103] Denise Corcoran, Walt Disney, "The Disney Difference: How One Man Rose Above Bankruptcy & Failure to Build a Multi-Billion $ Empire", *The American Chronicle*, (November 3, 2006).

[104] John Myatt, , Sandro Contenta, "Portrait of the Artist as Reformed Con Man", *The Toronto Star*, (May 7, 2006); Beth Houghton, Art Libraries as a source of false provenance, World Library and Information Congress, 69th conference and Council, August, 2003 – Berlin; "The Master Forger", *The Guardian*, (December 8, 2005).

from his wife and the living the life of a "starving artist." While looking for work, he placed an advertisement in a magazine offering to paint 19th and 20th century replicas of famous paintings. For a mere £240, anyone could have a Matisse hanging over his or her mantle. These were not forgeries; they were replicas. John was the art world's answer to what the music industry calls "tribute bands," individuals and groups who perform in the same style as the original artist.

He was contacted by John Drewe, who claimed to be a nuclear scientist and wanted Myatt's paintings for his home. Later, Drewe reported to John that Christies auction house had paid £25,000 for a replica of an Albert Gleizes painting that they certified as genuine. He convinced John to move from replicas to forgeries. From the mid-80s to the mid-90s, John produced 200 Master and Impressionist paintings, including works by such artists as Roger Bissiere, Marc Chagall, Le Corbusier, Jean Dubuffet, Alberto Giamcometti, and Matisse, for which he earned a grand total of £90,000. Drewe, on the other hand, earned a reported £1,500,000.

Each member of this lucrative partnership had his job. John painted and Drewe faked the source of ownership and history of the forgery. Ultimately, the pair's work came to the attention of Scotland Yard's antique and arts squad. By providing information to authorities about Drewe's involvement on what was labeled "the biggest art fraud of the 20th century," John Myatt received a reduced 12-month sentence. He served only one-third of that time.

John's legitimate opportunity came after his release. With a potential feature movie about his story in the works, he realized there was still a market for reproductions. This time, his efforts were legitimate. John now calls his paintings "Genuine fakes." He sells them for £400 to £4,000. On the back of each painting there is an embedded microchip along with the legend "genuine fake" written in indelible ink. According to John, he now earns more money in his legitimate enterprise than he did from his forgeries.

How we decide

We have seen two POAs, Jon West who found an opportunity which required he abandon his training and profession, and John Myatt, who stuck with his talent and found a legitimate opportunity to reverse the course of his life. While on the surface each decision seems to be a product of timing, luck, and necessity, there is in fact a sophisticated mental process at work.

Dr. Daniel Kahneman and Dr. Amos Tversky, professors of psychology at Princeton University, studied intuition, thought, and perception. [105]

One of their key hypotheses was that intuition, or snap decisions, occupy a mental position somewhere between the automatic operation of perceptions and the deliberate operation of reason. In Chapter 2, we learned about Kant's interpretation of knowledge and reason. Kant argues that knowledge is a person's interpretation of reality. Reason, on the other hand, is what "motivates and stimulates the pursuit of knowledge." Reason looks at situations and assigns cause and effect.

While Kant sees decision making as a continuum, Kahneman and Tversky hypothesize there are really two systems of decision making in play at all times. The first system involves processes that are typically fast, automatic, and effortless. The second are slower and more deliberate (based on reason). Kahneman and Tversky assume that the second system monitors the activities of the first. Their model assumes that there are two types of people: those who react on intuition and those who think problems through.

In Barry Siskind's book, *Bumblebees Can't Fly*, he equates these different approaches to an inner motivation to action, that he calls "voices." [106]

This is not a new idea. Indeed, Jean-Jacques Rousseau wrote: "This voice is an extremely complex mechanism, and for that reason demands a more detailed examination. The inner voice makes the world's movements so apparent to me that I cannot watch the course of the sun without imagining a force which drives it." [107]

---

[105] Kahneman and Tversky, "A Perspective on Judgement and Choice: Mapping Bounded Rationality, Daniel Kahneman", *American Psychologist*, (September 2003), Volume 58, Number 9, P 697-720; Kahneman and Tversky's Prospect Theory, Thayer Watkins, www2.sjsu,edu.htm; Interview with Amos Tversky, Decision Science News, July 2005; Ruth Bennett, "Risky Business – "New Subjectivism in Risk-Assessment Theory", *Science News*, (September, 2000).

[106] Barry Siskind, *Bumblebees Can't Fly* (John Wiley and Sons, 2004).
[107] Jean-Jacques Rousseau, (1712-1778) French philosopher composer and author.

Let's now consider the process of writing, which is crucial to many careers, to help us understand how this inner voice works.

Many writers, whether they write as their profession or to create a report, memo, or proposal, first create work on paper without editing it.
This frees them to explore new possibilities and ultimately create more powerful and insightful writing.

But this type of writing is not ready for publication the moment it's done. First, it must be edited substantively for content, flow, and continuity. Then it must be checked line-by-line, for grammar, syntax, and spelling. Once this part of the process is complete, the article, story, or presentation is ready for submission. To get to this point, we need three things: 1) an interesting idea, 2) the words that make this idea a reality, and 3) the detailed examination of the whole work that makes it publishable.

Likewise, our internal voice that guides this process also has three parts: the thinker, the doer, and the critic. All three are important and in an ideal world must work in harmony.

The thinker is the part of the voice that develops new ideas or provides new opportunities to the challenges we face. It is the innovative component that creates new, unrefined ideas. The thinker focuses exclusively on solutions, without paying any attention to their implementation. For many writers, the thinking component works overtime. In fact, most writers carry a pen and paper around at all times to record their moments of inspiration. But, they have to guard against over-inspiration, jumping around from project to project and never seeing anything through.

The doer turns the ideas conjured by the thinker into reality. Many writers keep files of ideas, and when they have a quiet spell, they scour them, looking for something interesting to write about. The doer then assesses each idea for its feasibility and the amount of research needed to bring it off.

Let me illustrate this with another example. Say you wake up one day and your thinker tells you, "I have a great idea for a new business!" The doer, concerned about how you will finance this idea, says, "I could cash in my retirement plan and mortgage the house, or see if Aunt Harriet will loan me the money." The doer takes the thinker's ideas and finds ways of making them happen. Our two voices must work together before you can accomplish anything. But there is one more voice. What you are missing in this dialogue between the thinker and the doer are the logical consequences, which are directly tied to cause and effect. Uncovering these is the job of the third voice — the critic.

The critic balances the thinker and the doer. It watches from the wings with impartial eyes. Like a true critic, it is honest and relentless. You can ignore it or disobey it, but it will not go away. The critic adds its wisdom to the work of the thinker and the doer, refining the decision or even quashing it. When you're thinking about a new sales approach, the critic might say, "Maybe I should do a bit of market research to find out what other solutions are already being offered," or "That idea is dated. You should think of something else." Often, what looked like a great idea in the beginning doesn't seems so clever in the cold, hard light of day. The critic enables you to take a look at the impact of the idea that the thinker thought up and that the doer is itching to act on.

The thinker, the doer, and the critic have separate voices, each with a distinct message and are integral to the success of any endeavor. The thinker and the doer could destroy the whole process if left unchecked by the critic. But what good are ideas (the voice of the thinker) if they remain unexplored? And what good is planning (the voice of the doer) if there is nothing to plan?

Now let's relate this to Kahneman and Tversky's model: The thinker is using system one (spontaneous), the critic is accessing system two (reason) and the doer lies somewhere in between. With Kahneman and Tversky's model, system two is triggered by doubt. In some cases doubt is desirable; in others it is not. Take the example of a surgeon.

Prior to a complicated surgery he will tune into his thinker and will examine the patient's history, medical tests, x-rays, and other relevant data. Then, he will access his critic, mentally playing through in his head the consequences of each step of the procedure he is about to embark upon.

Finally, when he is actually in the surgery, he will activate his doer. His critic has no part to play here. The surgeon must act and trust his intuition. When a crisis, or some unforeseen problem occurs, the surgeon works on instinct.

Years of intensive training have prepared his thinker and doer for such a moment. At this stage there can be no room (or time) for doubt.

The same holds true for opportunities. In some cases they seem to appear spontaneously and we, without thinking, jump at the chance. In other cases we need to process the opportunity to balance the pros and cons of taking action. There is good rationale for both approaches.

People who create opportunities

An opportunity is not an opportunity unless it satisfies some need. But who is to say there is a need? It is easy to go along and work day after day accepting things the way they are. We can get caught in our own complacency and create blinkers that stop us from seeing alternative paths. When we question something, we often find the seeds from which opportunity will sprout. Here are a few people who did just that.

Sonora Louise Smart Dodd

In 1882, Sonora Louise Smart Dodd was one of six children born to William Jackson Smart and his wife. When Sonora was 16, her mother died giving birth to her sixth child. The widowed William Jackson Smart shouldered the burden for his newborn and five siblings.

William Smart was a veteran of the Civil War, in which he was part of the First Arkansas Light Artillery and fought in the battle of Pea Ridge in 1862. Being a single parent has its difficulties today, but at the turn of the 20th century it was more difficult. Sonora grew up with a strong, caring father. She knew the sacrifices he had to make for his family. According to her story, in 1909, at 27 years of age, Sonora was sitting in church when she was struck by the idea of celebrating fatherhood. Everyone honored motherhood, but fathers were often neglected. Sonora persuaded the Spokane Ministerial Association and the local YMCA to pass a resolution in support of Father's Day. The idea then took off and Woodrow Wilson approved the idea. In 1924, President Calvin Coolidge made Father's Day a national event. [108]

You might be thinking "that is a nice story and very touching," and leave it at that. But what if Sonoma worked for Hallmark and was charged with finding new markets to sell greeting cards? Then you might read this story and conclude that the creation of Father's Day was an act of brilliance. The next POA did have a brilliant idea; the problem was that initially, no one recognized it.

---

[108] Sonora Louise Smart Dobb. For the whole story check, www.fumchallsville.org.

Sylvan N. Goldman [109]

Try to buy a book on Amazon.com. You search by category until you find the book you want. Then you add it to your shopping cart. When you are finished, the touch of a button moves your electronic shopping cart to the checkout. It is simple enough and you are used to this model of shopping. Why? It is exactly what you do at your favorite supermarket or big-box store. But, there was a time when shopping was different. If you wanted to buy food, you either arranged for home delivery or, if you had a car, you went to the grocery store. There you picked up a small wire basket that got heavier and heavier as you added products. Once your cart was filled, you proceeded to checkout.

Sylvan N. Goldman, the son of a Jewish immigrant from Latvia, was an owner of Standard Food Markets and Humpty Dumpty Supermarkets in Oklahoma City, Oklahoma. Goldman was a savvy businessman. He came through the ranks and understood the challenge of looking for opportunities to make his stores more profitable. In 1921, Oklahoma oil prices plunged and he and his brother lost everything. They went to California where they studied new methods of retailing groceries and returned to Oklahoma to establish a chain of supermarkets. The business was eventually sold to Safeway. Then, the depression wiped them out again, when their Safeway stock plunged in value. Steadfast in their belief in food retailing, the Goldman brothers tried again.

Goldman observed that customers would add to their baskets until they were filled and then go to the checkout. Goldman wondered if they would buy more if they didn't have to lug around the heavy baskets, so he hired a runner to approach shoppers with nearly filled baskets. The runner would take their basket to the checkout and give the shoppers an empty basket ready for more purchases.

The idea worked, but the cost of the runner, and the space needed at the checkout for customers' groceries while they were still shopping, was considerable. One day as he was sitting in his office, Goldman noticed two folding wooden chairs and had an idea. He could build a

---

[109] Sylvan N Goldman, (1898 – 1984) Realcart University, www.realcartuniversity.com, 1995, Sylvan Nathan Goldman; "History of the Shopping Cart", www.realcartuniversity.com; "Shopping Carts", John H Lienhard, www.uh.edu/engines/epi995.htm.

shopping cart using the basic structure of the chairs — but with wheels. He hired an assistant to help him develop his idea, and the first shopping cart was invented.

While the first carts were clumsier than the streamlined ones we see today, they did make the shopping experience easier, and they eliminated the cost of runners and space at the checkout. The problem was this: Customers wouldn't use them. Some younger shoppers thought it insulting to suggest that they couldn't handle a basket. Mothers who were tired of pushing strollers objected to pushing shopping carts, which they perceived as a stroller of another kind.

Despite the objections, Goldman persisted and was convinced that he could change customers' attitudes. He hired shoppers in different demographic groups to walk around pushing carts. There were young singles, middle-aged couples and seniors participating. These "shills" gave the regular shoppers the message that it was okay to use the cart. From the unsuspecting shoppers' point of view, "everyone was using them" and this perception made them more willing to try.

Goldman went on to create the Folding Carrier Co., and by 1940, he had a seven-year waiting list for new shopping carts. The folding cart was ultimately replaced with a nesting cart, similar to what we see at supermarkets today. It is estimated that there are between 30 and 35 million carts in use in the United States, and each year another 1.25 million new carts are added.

What we take for granted — pushing a cart around our local grocery store, and immediately understanding the virtual concept at Amazon.com, and other internet sites — is the result of one man who reframed a problem into an opportunity.

Perhaps the easiest method of examining how we view opportunity and decide on how to proceed is to continue with our shopping example. Shopping is something we all do. Sometimes we go shopping with a list and rigidly adhere to it, never deviating or succumbing to impulse. At other times, we may be attracted by new products or attractive packaging and impulsively add items to our shopping cart. The product represents an opportunity to satisfy some inner need, to add to our sense of power, prestige, or affiliation.

Our analogy is complete when we also look at a shopping experience where we incorporate both Kahneman and Tversky's stage-two cerebral approach with a stage-one impulsive approach. We may begin by saying something like: "I need a new suit." The overall objective of buying the suit is clear, but which suit you ultimately buy is left to chance unless your objective is more specific. Is the suit for a formal event, for work, or for a party? Once your parameters are set, you go shopping. You get to the clothing store and see racks filled with suits that fit your criteria. Which do you choose?

Is your decision based on brand, price and the look, or that an eager salesperson was smart enough to make the right suggestions? You can use the same thought process when you are looking for a job. Why would you jump at some opportunities and ignore others?

Paco Underhill, founder of the New York-based consulting firm Envrosell is also the author of the book, *Why We Buy, the Science of Shopping.* [110]

He examines how and why people make retail purchasing decisions. His observations of buyers have uncovered a number of interesting truths, that once revealed to his clients, were the basis for sound business decisions on how to display, position, and promote products in a retail environment. Here are some of his findings:

The "Butt-Brush Effect." Underhill's team, through hours of observation, found that people who found interesting products near the front of a busy store might abandon their interest if they were bumped, pushed, or shoved by traffic coming into and out of the store.

People treat their pets like children, and yet, retailers used to put doggy treats on top shelves out of the reach of children and seniors.

Products for persons with disabilities were not displayed in a manner that made them easily assessable. People had to stoop and bend in order to get what they wanted.

Ceiling-hung signs should be facing the front door of the store rather than in the opposite direction.

People need to rest occasionally, so well positioned benches make their shopping experience easier.

The longer a person remains in the store, the more he or she will buy.

---

[110] Paco Underhill, *Why We Buy; The Science of Shopping* (Simon and Schuster, 1999); Leslie Scrivener, "The Scientist in Aisle 3". *The Toronto Star*, (May 7, 2006).

These are just a smattering of Underhill's findings. Underhill uses his research to advise retailers on how to arrange merchandise so stores will sell more products, but as shoppers for career and business opportunities, we are at a disadvantage. There is rarely someone like Underhill who can make our search easier. If we want to find those hidden gems, we may have to bend and stoop a bit.

Let's take a look at how you typically react when confronted with an opportunity.

Have you ever found an interesting idea, only to abandon it because people looking over your shoulder offering "helpful" advice that was not helpful at all?

Have you ever missed a sales opportunity because you simply didn't see it first?

Have you ever failed to make the connection between an opportunity and its benefit to you or your customer?

Have you ever given up on a stubborn customer because you simply lacked the energy to continue?

If you answered yes to any of these questions, then you are a typical "opportunity shopper" in the selling market. Finding the right sales approach is like finding the perfect suit. We get used to smart retailers who make shopping easy, but in our search for solutions, we need to look past the distractions and learn to focus.

Real opportunities are out there. Carolyn Kepcher knows this well.

Carolyn Kepcher's Rise to the Top

If you have a television, you probably know Carolyn Kepchler. She is the perky blond who sat on Donald Trump's left-hand side on the first few years of The Apprentice. It's quite an accomplishment for this 38-year-old to have grabbed hold of opportunities that led her to this prime spot in America's most celebrated boardroom. [111]

Carolyn Kepcher was born in 1968 in Westchester, New York. At age 12, she sold Avon products to women in New York's New

---

[111] *The Apprentice*, This popular TV reality show features Donald J. Trump as executive producer and host. While Carolyn Kepcher participated in the first few years she has since been trumped (sorry about the pun but I couldn't resist) by Ivanka Trump who now sits in Carolyn's seat at the board table

Rochelle Hotel. In her junior and senior years she captained her high school volleyball team, leading them to undefeated seasons and state championships. This led her to a full college scholarship. During her undergraduate work at Mercy College, she worked part-time as a waitress at John Richard, a restaurant in Dobbs Ferry. The work provided funds for tuition — and more. It also provided the cornerstone for her business ethics. Throughout her life Carolyn has recognized and acted on opportunity. In her book, *Carolyn 101, Business Lessons from The Apprentice's Straight Shooter*, she talks about her time waiting on tables, where she realized: "Every time you approach a new table, you are greeting an entirely new set of customers to whom you are obliged to sell yourself, close the deal, and move on." [112]

After graduation she went to work as an assistant manager for a Manhattan restaurant, The Zephyr Grill. Within six months, at the age of 22, she was managing it. The restaurant was profitable and Carolyn did well, but she was looking for a change.

One day, an advertisement in a New York newspaper caught her attention: Briar Hall Country Club, an old and well-established golf club, had gone into receivership. The bank had foreclosed and handed over the operation to the Florida-based Summit Corporation, which manages premium resort properties across the United States. The ad was for someone to run membership sales at Briar Hall, while it was being prepared for sale. Carolyn knew that at best, the job would be temporary, but she saw an opportunity to catch the eye of the Summit decision makers and perhaps leverage good performance at Briar Hall into something better at Summit.

Carolyn had no experience selling golf or country club memberships, but she presented her experience in the hospitality industry as her strongest asset. She was offered the a job of selling club memberships.

Some people might look at Carolyn's decision as foolish. Why leave the Zephyr Grill where she achieved status, money, and a respected job? But, Carolyn weighed the risks against the potential benefits and took the plunge. During her time at Briar Hall, she had the opportunity to show perspective buyers the property. One such buyer was Donald

---

[112] Carolyn Kepcher, ***Carolyn 101: Lessons from The Apprentice's Straight Shooter*** (Foreside Books, 2005); Wallace Immen, "She Knows a Good Hire When She Sees One", *The Globe and Mail*, (April 27, 2006).

Trump. During the months that followed, Trump relied on Carolyn to provide solid information, which he needed to prepare his bid.

What was once a run-down and outdated country club was destined to become The Trump National. At the age of 25, Carolyn was ultimately promoted to general manager. Was Carolyn lucky? Was her sense of timing dead on? Perhaps. It can be argued that she was in the right place at the right time. But when you read her story you quickly realize she was not the only contender. There were countless managers and colleagues who had the same exposure to opportunities. What made Carolyn different? Was her belief that luck only comes around every once in a while? Carolyn writes that "everything depends on what you do with it." Carolyn had the ability to see an opportunity, to analyze the best way to proceed, and then to go forward. Carolyn's approach seems to echo the three voices of the thinker, the doer, and the critic.

In Carolyn Kepcher's situation, working at The Zephyr Grill provided a good income, lots of responsibility, and a certain amount of status; Carolyn did the job well. She was comfortable with her surroundings and was part of a well-honed team. You might rightfully ask why she would risk a good situation to seek employment with a company for a job that seemed temporary. Why would she gamble that she could make a good enough impression to find a job with Summit Corporation? Even if they were impressed with her, did they even have a place for another good employee? So many unanswered questions and yet, Carolyn seized the opportunity and went for it.

What is your risk tolerance?

What would you have done in a similar situation? There are times when we all feel unhappy with our present job, standard of living, level of stress, our spouse or partner, even our friends. Yet, how many of us are willing to gamble with what we have and look for something better?

The answer to this question is unique to us all. We all possess what the financial world calls "risk tolerance."

Your tolerance for risk is intertwined with your willingness to invest money, time, prestige, or whatever it takes to get what you want. Your tolerance is directly related to the concept of "risk reward." In financial terms, the greater the risk the higher the potential reward, and conversely, the lower the risk the lower the reward. If you invest your retirement savings in guaranteed investments such as government bonds or investment certificates that are offered by many of the major banks, you will be able to calculate, with a reasonable amount of assurance, the amount of money you will have at retirement. However, if you choose to invest your savings in the stock market, there is the potential, that upon retirement, you will have a larger nest egg — but there is also a chance you won't. The risks here are higher, but if you are right, so is the payoff.

The decisions you make as a sales person are analogous to your investment strategies. How much we are willing to invest in an opportunity is directly related to how we view the risk–reward ratio and our personal comfort level. More often than not, we automatically fall back on our risk–reward comfort level when we assess any opportunity.

For example, if I told you that for an investment of $2 you had a chance to win $10,000,000, would you take the chance? Maybe yes, maybe no. But it's a risk our lottery culture keeps waving in our faces. Many of us have succumbed to the trap and purchased a ticket. After all, what's $2 when the reward is so great?

Here is another proposition. What if I offered you a chance to win $10,000,000 for an investment of $100,000? Would you invest? Rationally, it seems that it's a better deal. You will increase your odds considerably by purchasing 50,000 two-dollar tickets. What if the scenario was different and you had an opportunity to invest $100,000 in a business? Would your decision differ? Yet, this decision goes beyond the impulse to put down two dollars and takes the risk–reward factor discussion to another level. What circumstances would make you risk, as Carolyn did, an established job for a chance at something better?

What would it take for you to go back to school to earn a degree? What would it take for you to walk into your boss's office and present a new idea that had the potential of saving your company valuable resources? Every day you are faced with risk, and how you act depends on how much risk you can live with.

There are different types of risk. Mary Rowland is a personal finance expert and the author of *A Common Sense Guide to Mutual Funds and Best Practices for Financial Advisors.* [113]

In her article, *How to Assess Risk Tolerance,* she writes about four types of risk that go beyond the realm of finance: inflation risk,

---

[113] Mary Rowlands, *A Common Sense Guide to Mutual Funds and Best Practices for Financial Advisors,* (Bloomberg Press, 1998).

opportunity risk, concentration risk, and interest-rate risk. Inflation risk is the risk that your money will not be worth as much in the future. It is also the risk that your present job skills or marketability will lose value if you stay in a dead-end job in the same company. [114]

Opportunity risk is when you tie your investments into a low-risk instrument and lose the opportunity of investing in something that has real growth potential. In the 1980s we all would have been smart to have sold all our possessions and invested in Microsoft; we would all be millionaires today. But, that insight has the benefit of hindsight.

People have said to me, "If I had taken that job, my life wouldn't be what it is today. I would have never met my wife and had this great kid." We are constantly weighing risk and reward with opportunities that face us daily. There is no point going back and rehashing history.

Concentration risk is when you put all your eggs into one basket — one investment, one opportunity. While your financial portfolio might benefit from diversification, there is a strong argument for personal specialization. The marketplace puts a real value on people who are experts in certain areas.

Interest rate risk is the risk interest rates will move up or down. If you tied your interest rate to a fixed percentage, then you're protected if the rates go up and lose if they go down. If you choose a floating rate, then you're gambling rates will go down and you can benefit from the drop.

Life is all about risk of one sort or another. Financial planners categorize our tolerance of risk in five categories. Think of your risk tolerance on a horizontal line. At the low-risk end you have the conservative and moderately conservative investors, and as you move toward the high-risk point of the line, you have moderately aggressive, aggressive, and very aggressive investors.

Where you are on this risk line depends on your situation. Sometimes we become aggressive risk takers and go whitewater rafting or jump off a bridge with a bungee cord tied around our ankles. In other situations we're like pussycats curling up by the fireplace within our comfortable limits. Some of us take certain risks while others avoid them. The trick to taking action when opportunity strikes, is knowing

---

[114] Mary Rowlands, *How to Access Risk Tolerance* http://moneycentral.msn.com.

what risks are acceptable to you. An opportunity is only an opportunity if it provides value for you. The calculation of value versus cost is at the heart of your decision and is key in determining your risk tolerance.

For ages, mathematicians have tried to express our propensity to take risk in mathematical models. The 18th century mathematician, Daniel Bernoulli, was among the first to develop a theory around this issue. Bernoulli was born in Holland into a family who had carved a solid reputation in the academic world as distinguished mathematicians. By the time he was 24, he was a professor of mathematics in St. Petersburg. And at age 38, he wrote *Exposition of a New Theory on the Management of Risk*. This was his answer to what later came to be known as the St. Petersburg Paradox. It goes like this: [115]

Suppose I tossed a coin in the air and paid you two dollars if it lands heads up on the first throw, four dollars if it lands heads up on the second throw, eight dollars if it lands heads up on the third throw, and so on. With each throw the potential payout doubles. Each flip has a 50–50 chance of landing heads up. But if it lands tails-up, you have to pay me at the same levels. The question the St. Petersburg Paradox tries to answer is how much are you willing to pay to join the game?

The answer is that it depends on how much money you have. If you're a multimillionaire, you might deem $1,000 as "chump-change," and part with the money just to see where the game goes. Perhaps you view the game as mild entertainment. But if your $1,000 rent is due tomorrow, choosing between meeting rent obligations and placing a $1,000 bet takes on a different perspective. [116]

Conversely, what if the multimillionaire doesn't feel he has enough and is afraid of losing what he has and the renter feels he's living so close to the wire he has nothing to lose? Perception for many of us defines our reality.

---

[115] Daniel Bernoulli (1700-1782,) and the "St. Petersburg Paradox", www.bun.kyoto-u.ac.jp Wikipedia; J. Davis Hands and U. Maki, *Handbook of Economic Methodology* (London, 1997). "Determining Risk and the Risk Pyramid", *Investopedia*, (May, 2003)

[116] There is a lot written about game theory. A great primer was written by Avinash Dixit, www.pbs.org; **What is Game Theory**, David K. Levine, Department of Economics, UCLA, http//Levine.sscnet.ucla.edu.

Bernoulli was attempting to understand the dynamics of financial decisions. But, what's true for money can also be true for other areas of our lives. During the past decade, I have seen a dramatic rise in real estate prices, particularly in major centers such as New York, Los Angeles, London, Tokyo, and Toronto. I know people who have speculated and won large returns by investing in houses and quickly flipping them for a profit. For someone with a large amount of money in the bank, buying a million-dollar piece of real estate with the intention of quickly earning a 10 or 20 per cent return is an easier decision than for someone who has to borrow against everything they own for the possibility of the same reward.

How about changing jobs? How much risk are you willing to take? If you have a job and are doing well, have advanced through the ranks and developed a strong reputation within your industry, then changing jobs is less of a risk to you than to someone who works hard but has a different view of his or her employability. Perhaps he or she does not have a strong network of colleagues or has fallen behind in keeping up with new skills and technologies. For such an employee, the perceived risk of changing jobs is greater.

In economics, the measure of happiness or satisfaction you get when you consume a product or service or weigh an opportunity is called "utility." Think of utility as the amount of money, time, or reputation you are willing to risk to increase your happiness and satisfaction.

Your unique situation determines how much cost you will bear to improve your personal situation and the amount of risk you will take to obtain the satisfaction from the product, service, or job that you desire.

Let's go back to the example of the real estate investor. Investing in real estate requires a tremendous amount of capital. The risk of carrying one investment property plus your own home can put a difficult strain on people. Some may conclude it's too risky, while others may conclude that the risk and inconvenience to their family is not as great a cost as the lack of money. Therefore, they find a compromise to minimize their risk. They might buy one house at a time, live in it, fix it up and then sell it. Then, with the profits from the first property, they buy another property and move their family into it and start the process all over again. Your risk tolerance is dependent on the potential of the opportunity and your perception of the cost. If you perceive it as jeopardizing everything you have, you might have a low-risk tolerance.

On the other hand, if you thrive on all-or-nothing chances of a lifetime, you probably have a high-risk tolerance. However, that's not to say that people with fewer assets never risk everything. If you were stranded in the desert and hadn't had any water in days, I could demand whatever I wanted from you for a cup of water and you would probably pay, regardless of how much you had or didn't have. Before you traded for the water, would you ask me for a certificate from a chemist attesting to the water's purity? Not likely. However, if you live in the heart of a city, you probably run water from your tap without thinking. The bottom line is this: The perception of risk is individual to all of us.

Knowing your risk tolerance is a good place to start when looking at sales opportunities. If you understand your reasons for taking or not taking advantage of an opportunity, then you can decide whether to stretch your risk tolerance a bit or leave it as it is. It's important to be able to take advantage of opportunities and still be able to sleep at night. Understanding your risk tolerance allows you to approach your sales career choices consciously rather than going through on automatic pilot. It also can motivate you to look for opportunities that you may have never imagined existed. Brian Scudamore's story is a good example of someone who did just that.

Brian Scudamore — Turning Junk into Gold

"The idea hit me out of the blue," says Brian Scudamore, founder and CEO of 1-800-GOT-JUNK? the most successful junk removal operation in the world. [118]

The year was 1989 and Brian Scudamore was a commerce student at the University of British Columbia who needed to find work in a tight job market. While waiting in a McDonald's drive-through, he saw a beat-up old pickup with plywood side panels with the words "Mark's Hauling" emblazoned on the side. Brian said to himself, "I can do that." All he needed was a cheap truck to start hauling junk. "Instead of going out to find a job," says Brian, "I decided to create one."

That very week, Brian used his last $700 to buy a second-hand pickup truck, spray-painted his phone number and the name of his company on the sides, and started hauling junk. 1-800-GOT-JUNK? was born.

---

[118] 1-800-GOT-JUNK.com

The story might have ended there: just another case of a young enterprising university student paying his own way through school.

Brian recounts, "Ironically, though, I was learning much more about business by actually running one than I was [learning] in school. And so in 1993, I made the decision to drop out and pursue junk full time."

Unknowingly, Brian had discovered his niche, an untapped gold mine in junk. Brian likes to compare the situation in his industry to the world of coffee. Before Starbucks really got into the market in a big way, the world of coffee consisted of mom-and-pop corner coffee shops. Then Starbucks came into the industry and created a brand and an "experience." "And we've done the same thing," Brian continues, "just in a different industry."

By 1997, 1-800-GOT-JUNK? was established in Vancouver and Victoria and had a presence in Seattle. "I've always talked about building the FedEx of junk removal," says Brian. "Clean, shiny trucks, friendly and fun drivers, on-time service and fair rates." By 1997, the company had reached a million dollars in sales, and Brian knew he was on the right track.

At that point, he said to himself, "Okay, I've got a business model that works. Let's see if we can duplicate it across North America."

Brian approached "a ton" of different backers and investors, saying, "Listen I want to franchise 1-800-GOT-JUNK?." He approached mentors, people who'd built successful franchise companies themselves as well as franchise consultants, and every single expert told him that his company could not be franchised. They all claimed that franchising the junk industry was impossible. Their basic objection was that there was nothing to stop others from getting out there and buying their own trucks to haul junk. "Why would they want to join your company and become part of your system?" the experts asked Brian.

Brian listened to the why-nots, but rather than abandon his dream, Brian regrouped and took stock. "Everyone told me why I couldn't franchise this business," Brian relates. "I had to find a way to answer those concerns, and, not so much [to] prove them wrong, but [to] use those concerns as leverage to figure out how to make it work."

Brian realized that he had to add something to his business model that would make it more compelling to join 1-800-GOT-JUNK? than to start a rival business. What Brian brought to the mix was a turnkey system, including a call center that handles the booking and dispatching. "Rather than start a junk company from scratch, we make it easy," says Brian. "It makes more sense for people to partner with the 1-800-GOT-JUNK? brand than to build a Frank's Hauling on one's own. All the franchise partners have to do is build a team of outstanding people, acquire a fleet of trucks, and then get out there, pound the pavement, and drive sales."

Brian's philosophy: They're building something much bigger together than any of them could ever have built alone. "We're really building an exciting brand that provides a great service in a niche market!"

Today, 1-800-GOT-JUNK? has over 250 locations across Canada and the United States, Australia, and United Kingdom. The company boasts over 2,500 people across the globe with a fleet of over 1,000 trucks.

Brian's aim is to build a billion-dollar industry by the end of 2012, in 10 countries. "And we're well on our way there," says Brian. "It's all about building a brand as big as I can and as well as I can."

Brian's advice to anyone with a dream is this: "If you have a great idea that you truly believe in 100 percent, then hold on to your faith in that idea and stick with it and you will find a way to make it happen." Brian's story mirrors many others who have seen an opportunity and built a business. Brian is unique in that he hasn't lost the entrepreneurial spirit that often is put aside as corporations grow and the need for conservative management steps in.

According to an article in *Profit Magazine*, Brian's marketing manager, Andrea Baxter, approached him with an idea. Starbucks was accepting submissions for its series, "The Way I See It," which would appear on coffee cups throughout the chain. Andrea saw the value of having 1-800-GOT-JUNK? on 10 million cups. [119]

Initially, Brian was skeptical, but Baxter persisted. Eventually they won Starbucks "The Way I See It" coffee cup message number 70. Their message read: "It's difficult for people to get rid of junk. They get attached to things and let them define who they are. If there is one thing I've learned in this business, it's that you are what you can't let go of." —Brian Scudamore, founder and CEO of 1-800-GOT-JUNK?.

---

[119] *Profit Magazine*, Brian Scudmore, "Make-Believe Magic", (May 2006).

Brian concludes, "Stay focused. Just take one thing, and do it well. I will always run this business; I will never sell it or take it public. Just stay focused on one niche."

Lessons Learned

- Understand your propensity for risk.
- Develop a methodology for evaluating opportunities.
- Understand your action framework.

Taking action in the face of opportunity will definitely have a positive impact on your sales career. You have learned that opportunities don't always fall into your lap; sometimes you have to go out and find them.

For POAs like Jon West, a career-change opportunity was there when he needed it. Jon's brilliance was in recognizing and acting on it.

John Myatt initially had a poor business opportunity thrust upon him, but with time he was able to redirect his talent and energies in a lawful direction.

We saw how Sonora Louise Smart Dodd, Sylvan Goldman, Carolyn Kepcher, and Brian Scudamore all actively searched for opportunities and found the strength and ability to act on them. Each of these POAs could have remained nameless people, save for their willingness to take action.

Lessons into Action: Your Career Action Plan

In the introduction to this chapter, I said that the first step to change is opening yourself up to possibilities. It starts with an awareness of where you are now and what you are willing to risk taking your sales career where you want it to go.

Step 1: Understand your propensity for risk; Propensity to risk is unique to all of us.

Some of us have an appetite for risk, while others do not. Knowing where you lie on the risk continuum starts with an understanding of your propensity for risk.

a. Check the response that best describes your actions:

My Actions	Always	When I can	Occasionally	Avoid when possible	Never
	1	2	3	4	5
1. I'm prepared to take a stand when I see things that I don't agree with.					
2. I'm willing to accept some risk to advance my sales goals.					
3. I am eager to get involved in issues that affect my community.					
4. I'm willing to voice my opinion when I think a family member is making a mistake.					
5. I am willing to do what it takes to get ahead.					
6. I often try to resolve conflicts with co-workers.					
7. I'm prepared to sacrifice financial security for higher financial return.					
8. I choose to eat foods I like; not just healthy ones.					
9. When traveling, I prefer new adventures rather than returning to the same place.					
Total					
Weight	5	4	3	2	1
Weighted score					

b. Calculate your results:
Calculate your score by adding up the number of checks in each column.

c. Calculate weighted results:
Multiply each column score by its weight. For example, column 1 has a weighted score of 5; therefore, if you checked two boxes in column 1, your score for that column would be 10, and so on.)

d. Calculate your overall propensity for risk.
Add up the weighted total for each column.

e. Interpret your propensity for risk:
Using the guidelines below, determine what kind of risk taker you are:

0–9   Conservative
10–18 Moderately conservative
19–29 Moderately aggressive
30–38 Aggressive
39–45 Very aggressive

Note that in some areas of your life you are more averse to risk than in others. That's quite normal.

Step 2: Develop a methodology for evaluating opportunities:
Your Opportunities Evaluation Grid:

a. Develop your metrics.
When faced with an opportunity, ask, "What are the benefits to following this opportunity?" Limit your answers to no more than five items. For example your list may include:

1. I will be happier.
2. I will have more status.
3. I will have a better opportunity to use my creative talents.
4. I can get in on the ground floor.
5. I will make more money.

Put your metric in order of priority.

We are all different in what we value most about our work. A helpful method is to classify your metrics into three categories:

Priority #1 — Have to's
These things are crucial in helping you achieve what you want. These are non-negotiable; without them you will not pursue this opportunity.

Priority #2 — Want to's
These are things that are not crucial, but are things you want in order to make the opportunity more rewarding, fun, interesting, and fulfilling.

Priority #3 — Nice to's
These are things that are nice to have, but the reasons why are difficult to articulate. Items that fall into this category are those that you cannot rationally articulate; they are simply nice to have.

Weight your metrics:
Assign weighting to your metrics:
Have to's = 3
Want to's = 2
Nice to's = 1

Develop performance indicators:
In order to determine if the opportunity gives you what you want, you need to define how you will measure it.

Performance indicators are specific actions that will help you know when your metrics have been met. Create a detailed list of related activities, offers, or other potentials that will give you a concrete basis for evaluation. Here's how your list might look:

Metric	Performance indicator
Happiness	Spend more time with family Work closely with new interesting people Be an active part of creating a needed solution
Status	Awards Recognition by colleagues Profile in my trade association
Innovation	Job flexibility, Use of creative energies Be part of a team
Get in on the ground floor	Age of the company Resources allocated to company's growth Company's plans, missions, and direction
Money	Remuneration, Benefits, Stock options Retirement package

Assign values
Once you have identified what you want (your metrics) and how you will evaluate its potential (your performance indicators), next you need to assign a value to each opportunity. You can then analyze its ability to help you support your performance indicators.

Look at each metric and ask yourself how well this opportunity allows you measurement. Rate this metric on a scale from one to ten. One represents a low probability of being able to meet your performance indicators and ten indicates a high probability.

Now you can put it all together. Your final chart will look like this:

Metric	Priority	Weight	Performance indicator	Value	Score
Happiness	Want to	2	Spend more time with family Work closely with new interesting people Be an active part of creating a needed solution	9	18
Status	Nice to	1	Awards Recognition by colleagues Profile in my association	10	10
Innovation	Nice to	1	Job flexibility Use of creative energies Be part of a team	8	8
Ground floor opportunity	Want to	2	Age of the company Resources allocated to the company's growth Company's plans, missions and direction	7	14
Money	Have to	3	Remuneration Benefits Stock options Retirement package	9	27
Opportunity score					77

Step 3: Understand your action framework:

When opportunities come your way, you need to blend what you have learned about how you handle risk with the evaluation of the opportunities in order to develop specific strategies.

The following grid will help you rationally decide which opportunities fit best with your career decisions.

a. You now have a score that tells you your propensity for risk. You have also created a rating system for each opportunity. It is now time to marry the two numbers into a meaningful form. Plot the information you have learned on the grid below.

Based on the example above, the grid would look like this:

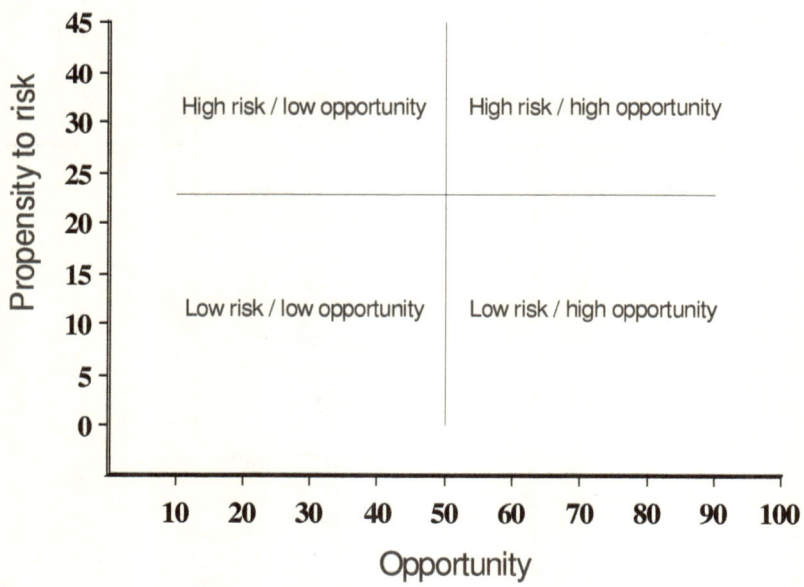

Interpret your strategies for change:

1. High risk/ low opportunity: Opportunities that fall into this category are best ignored as they will bring you a minimum amount of growth potential.

2. High risk/high opportunity:

If an opportunity falls into this category, then you should be asking yourself: How comfortable are you assuming this risk? Having a great sales career and dying young as a result of stress, fatigue, and excess worry doesn't make a lot of sense. That's why knowing your propensity for risk is so important.

By completing step one; you have calculated your propensity for risk. If you are conservative or moderately conservative in your risk tolerance, you may be missing some opportunities because of your discomfort with taking risks. If you are on the aggressive or very aggressive end of the scale, then you need to be careful that you are not jumping at opportunities just because it is in your nature to do so.

What actions can you take to mitigate the risk while taking advantage of the opportunity? If taking an opportunity puts you outside your comfort zone, you have two choices: 1. Ignore the opportunity, or, 2. Explore methods of mitigating the risk.

The best method of accomplishing this is to get feedback. Talk to your employer, colleagues, mentors, role models, and customers. Be open and frank about your concerns and talk about what you can do to lessen the risk. These may include working on a project jointly with other colleagues, putting off the decision until you have received further education or exploring methods of dividing the opportunity into smaller chunks so you can accomplish smaller goals — one at a time.

3. Low risk/ low opportunity:

If opportunities fall here, there's a small upside and a small risk. These might be things that are simply fun to do such as trying out for your company's sporting team or volunteering to be on a committee. As long as they don't distract you from your main path — go for it.

4. Low risk/high opportunity:

These opportunities are those that give you the best chance for growth. With a manageable level of personal risk and a huge up side, opportunities that fall into this quadrant are those worth exploring.

You have now learned the steps that will help you overcome your sense of helplessness, examined your propensity to risk, found the courage to act, and developed your persistence. In the next chapter, we will explore the pursuit of happiness.

Grab Success by the Horns

5
Pursue Happiness with Gusto

"The three grand essentials of happiness are: Something to do, someone to love, and something to hope for."
Alexander Chalmers [120]

You spend approximately 30 percent of your life selling. That's a lot of time and a big investment. Why are you doing it? Perhaps you work to make enough money to support a lifestyle, to make a difference in your community, or simply because you believe that working is what you are supposed to do. Regardless of your reasons for working, one thing is common to us all: We want to be happy. James M. Barrie, author of Peter Pan, wrote, "It is not doing what you like but liking what you do that is the secret of happiness." [121]

There is more to happiness than an occasional smile and a good belly laugh. We live in a culture that continually bombards us with the promise of instant happiness. If we drink the right beer, take the right pill, drive the right car, or land a new account, happiness can be ours.

Yet, how many of us are truly happy? Many people have grown cynical and see no reason to be happy. They may be in a bad relationship, disappointed with the cards that life has dealt them, concerned about the environment , or unhappy with their political leaders... the list is endless. Then there are those who grumble that they feel stuck in a daily routine that has grown as predictable as the punch line to a bad joke. Happiness is not universal. You can be happy at work and yet remain an unhappy person. We don't have to look far to see examples of this; it's everywhere.

---

[120] Alexander Chalmers, (1759 – 1834). Among his accomplishments was the creation of a 32 volume A General Biographical Dictionary. No, I didn't read the whole thing (in case you were wondering).

[121] James M. Barrie, *Peter Pan*, (Henry Holt and Co (BYR)); 100 Anniversary edition, 2003.

Finding happiness does not mean you have to quit your job or abandon your daily routine. On the contrary, it often doesn't require such drastic action. Often, you can find happiness by simply taking small steps. This chapter looks at POAs who took action to bring happiness into their lives. In some cases, the pursuit became their primary focus; for others, it involved small daily steps towards their goal. All of the POAs in this chapter share a willingness to go out and seek happiness. Here are two great examples.

Laura Robinson's Story

Laura was born in Kingston, Ontario and moved to London, Ontario, where she attended public high school. Her high school years were typical of a self-professed overachiever; she was president of her sorority, active in gymnastics, and a cheerleader. She also had a knack for languages and was active in theatre productions. Mostly, she loved the dynamics of being part of a group. Laura's early style became a thread throughout her life as she worked with colleagues and partners.

Laura came from a musical family. Her father played saxophone professionally as did her brother. Her mother was a writer and actor. Her family taught her to dream and perform. At every event, they always sat in the front row cheering her on. "They gave me the guts to do what I did," Laura said.

In high school, Laura was fortunate to have writer, teacher, and Jungian Analyst, Marion Woodsman as her mentor. When Laura had to make her career choice between acting and studying languages to become an interpreter, it was Marion Woodsman who steered her towards acting.

Laura obtained her Bachelor of Fine Arts Audition in Dramatic Arts, (BFA) at the University of Windsor, Ontario, Canada. "I did a lot of full-scale productions."

After university, Laura went to Toronto and quickly landed an agent, who found her work at Canadian Broadcasting Corporation (CBC). During that time, Laura learned about the American Broadcasting Corporation's Development Program. This program accepted young actors with potential, put them under contract, and groomed them for a career in show business. Laura went to New York City to audition. Out of 1,000 candidates she was chosen, so off to Los Angeles she went. She spent one year with the program and landed a role in a television pilot.

She assumed the pilot would ultimately turn into a series. She would be a big star, fame and fortune would be hers. Laura freely admits that she simply didn't know "how tough things are." When the pilot, like so many others, was not picked up, Laura came back to Canada. Her dad was sick and she wanted to be closer to home. There, she landed a role in CBC's popular television series Night Heat. She spent three years with that series.

Then, in 1985, she met Paul Toyne. Laura and Paul became a couple. In addition to a romantic life, they were also interested in other endeavors. Paul had a friend who was one of the original investors in the board game, Trivial Pursuit. When this newly minted millionaire revealed that he was looking for investments, Laura and Paul jumped on the opportunity.

Laura's mother loved board games. As a triplet, she had played games all of her life. When Laura was growing up, board games were part of her family culture. Based on a dictionary game she played in her youth, Laura and Paul developed Balderdash. "We worked non-stop; we were obsessed," Laura said. To support this venture, Laura worked doing television commercials. "In 1985, we showed Balderdash to a distributor. He offered to launch for Christmas 1986. We didn't understand how long it took to launch a game. We couldn't wait, so we walked out. The distributor chased us and agreed to do a test in 1985. I was cocky."

Since 1986, when the game was first launched, it has sold over 10 million copies in 17 countries. Balderdash put Laura in the board game stratosphere along with Trivial Pursuit developers, Chris Haney and Scott Abbott, and Monopoly developer, Charles Darrow.

Eighteen years later, Laura launched a new game called Identity Crisis. In the interim, she has did simply sit idly by, cashing her royalty checks. Laura invented a game under the Pictionary label called Pictionary Mania, developed a television game show (NBC), and produced games for board game wannabes, all the while raising two children.

So, with all this success, Laura still pursues her happiness in acting because, as she says, "Acting is who I am." She also writes, and in the next few months, she plans to get into a studio to record her music.

Laura's philosophy is, "If you expect it: it will come. I get into a mental place and create the life I want. I caution people from spending time in their head trying to figure out what they want."

Laura continues, "I focus on the weird things like the color of the box." At public school, Laura always saw the title page of her projects long before the project was finished.

Laura is actively promoting Identity Crisis, has another board game in development, is shooting a pilot for a game show, and still finds time to tend to her music. She says, "My music is a gift and deserves the time I give it." As lunch concluded, I was obviously impressed by Laura's accomplishments, but what stayed with me was that she was able to balance her career and personal life so well. She seems truly happy finding new challenges and at the same time being there for her husband and two boys. She is a go-getter who got it all through learning, trying, and persistence.

"A friend once said that instead of the old adage Ready, aim, fire," Laura said, "I'm the opposite. 'Fire, aim, ready.'.."

Mike Schultz's Story

Mike was the third of four boys. His father was an investment dealer and his Mom stayed at home to care for her family. "Ours was a nuclear family with traditional values," Mike says. Mike attributes his tenaciousness to being the third born. He had to try harder to prove himself.

As a child, Mike was active in sports and average in school. He worked as a camp counselor, and much like our previous POA, had a knack for being in the right place at the right time. For example, at eight years old, Mike remembers being chosen to be the model for a brother – sister team for a specialty book called We Live in Greenwood Village.

Mike and a young girl were taken to various spots and photographed for the book; they posed as brother and sister. Little did Mike realize that this would not be his singular journey into the field of publishing.

Mike's family was close, and yet, each one was very different. Mike's brothers followed in their father's footsteps; one became a CFO for a large corporation, another became an investment banker, and the third a computer specialist.

Mike's brothers all went to their hometown university. Mike chose to leave the fold. He spent his first year studying geography. He was a C+ student with good social skills, but geography wasn't his passion.

He loved working in the outdoors during his summers at a vacation resort. By the time he had finished his second year, at another university, Mike had still not found his niche. The third year of university changed all that. Mike discovered history. "I became a voracious reader," Mike recalls. "I read everything, and for the first time in my life, things began to click for me."

His affinity for history sparked a lifelong passion for his country, but he still lacked direction. So, he took his time. While all his brothers focused on financial careers, Mike worked at a number of jobs. He married and eventually enrolled in teachers college. Once again, Mike's sense of timing was working. He learned that teaching gave him the same satisfaction and joy he received as a camp counselor. "Counseling is the same model," Mike explains. "You have a number of kids in your cabin, you take them on trips, teach them crafts, help them experience nature, and then report back to their parents."

What he liked about being a counselor was the sense of camaraderie and the chance to give to the kids under his care. There was a continuous learning curve and he enjoyed the competition and the quest for exploration. "It was a Ulysses thing," Mike explains. His personal odyssey unfolded before his eyes and he was able to see the connections between his counseling skills and what he needed to be a teacher. For the first time, Mike found a direction he felt he could enjoy for the next 25 to 30 years.

He approached teaching as a chance to continue his quest to do novel things. This euphoria was what Mike describes as the "kick" in life. "It's like a drug. The first time you get goose bumps. Then you ask, what's next?" Mike goes on to say, "My dad died at 59. What he gave me was his "do or die" mentality. You don't wait around for things to happen. If you wanted something important, then you had to go out and get it." It was 1977, and teaching jobs were hard to get. Mike responded to a newspaper advertisement for a one-year contract teaching history. Mike was married and expecting the birth of his first son. He had a family to feed and he wanted to try teaching.

Mike thought he would like the classroom setting where he could apply what he had learned as a camp counselor. "With my teaching job,

I got involved on committees that were looking into curriculum changes. We were helping them revamp." After the year was over and his contract was not renewed (the person he was replacing was on a one-year sabbatical), Mike was once again left to float alone. He toyed with broadcasting, but with a family on the way, he needed a steady source of income. Once again, luck interceded and Mike landed a sales job with a book publisher, John Wiley and Sons, in their school division.

With a background in history and one year of teaching, he was a good candidate to handle this new challenge. At that time, Wiley was a fast-growing company and Mike saw an opportunity to grow. "I like to start things, initiate them, incubate them, nurture them, and then bow out," Mike said. He loved the corporate life and travel, developing suitable lists and working with authors. At Wiley, he learned how business is conducted and how ideas are initiated and what skills are necessary for success.

Mike was with Wiley from 1978 to 1984. He was constantly challenged to develop new lists of books, while continually focusing on where his department was going. The lesson that was frequently reinforced was: "You have to be proactive in business." Then Mike had another realization: "I thought I would become a VP of Publishing someday, mainly because it mirrored my dad and brother's careers, but what I realized was that maybe that's not for me. I functioned best in sales where I had some independence."

During this era, the publishing world was in upheaval. "Men like Rupert Murdoch were building massive international communications empires," which meant buy-outs, re-organizations, turmoil. Mike saw the writing on the wall, but hadn't made a move. [122]

Luck entered again, but this time it held a pink slip in its hand. Mike took his severance package, walked out the front door, and went to pick up the new suit he had, bought a newspaper, and drove home.

In the 1990s, one of the curriculum changes in schools was an emphasis on entrepreneurialism. "At that time teachers were generally anti-business," Mike explained. "But, here was a chance for me to ride a new wave of thinking." Mike returned to teaching. Since that move,

---

[122] Rupert Murdoch, born in 1931 in Australia. The communication company Mike referred to is of course News Corp.

Mike has become active in Junior Achievement and their "Dream Big" program. He has taken kids to such exotic locations as Fiji, Korea, and Japan to share work experiences. In the summers of 1997 and 1998, he taught an entrepreneurial program at Cambridge University in England. He has developed many web-based teaching programs, written a series of articles for a national newspaper, and was instrumental in the development of the co-op high school program where students were credited with time spent in industry as part of their studies. Mike helped develop courses in entrepreneurialism, and co-wrote a textbook called *The Entrepreneurial Spirit.*

"What I've learned is that I can use all the skills I have honed. As a co-op teacher, I am active in business as well as with my students. Sometimes I feel like I'm piloting a 747 to get my programs and my students in the air and then they are ready to complete the flight on their own. At other times, I feel like a juggler who spins a dozen plates in the air at one time. Each plate is one of my students, and I need to be constantly running from one pole to another to make sure none of them fall." Mike went on to say, "There are lots of things that can derail kids today. What I try to instill in them is that to get what you want you have to park your frustrations and focus on what you can do. Then I help them do it."

"My best moments are when a student comes back for a visit and takes the time to tell me how my work affected their life. I have a collection of notes and projects from students that I cherish. That's my payoff."

In Laura and Mike we have two entrepreneurs, one who collects royalty checks and the other notes from grateful students. Both have an impressive C.V. and both are happy. Laura and Mike each wanted a life filled with accomplishment. They were not able to stand for second best, and therefore, were proactive in making career decisions by using their skills in a manner that brought them happiness. If Laura and Mike can build a career measured in satisfaction and happiness, why can't you?

Happiness and your well-being

If you look at happiness as a "nice to have," and not a crucial element in your sales career criteria, perhaps you should rethink your rationale for not including it.

University of Illinois psychologist and expert in the area of subjective well being, Professor Ed Diener says that happy people tend to be more extraverted and agreeable than unhappy people. Happy people earn higher salaries and have stronger marriages. Happy people are physically stronger and may live longer. 123

David G. Myers, in his book, *The Pursuit of Happiness*, confirms Dieners' theory finding that happy people, as compared to unhappy people, are more trusting, loving and lenient, and are less frustrated and less likely to be abusive. 124

Dr. Sheldon Cohen, Professor and co-director of the Brain, Behavior and Immunity Centre at Carnegie Mellon University in Pittsburgh, Pennsylvania, conducted a study of 334 healthy volunteers over a period of two weeks. The volunteers were asked how they felt the day of the interview in three positive emotion areas: vigor, well being, and calmness. They were also questioned about three negative emotion areas: depression, anxiety, and hostility. After the assessment, each volunteer got a squirt in the nose of a rhinovirus, the germ that causes colds. The volunteers were then monitored during the next week to see how many of them manifested a cold. Cohen found that "study participants who had a more positive emotional outlook weren't infected as often, and experienced fewer symptoms, compared to people with a negative emotional outlook." 125

According to the Dahlai Lama: "The purpose of life is to be happy." Buddhism sees the pursuit of happiness as a life goal. The Dahlia Lama advocates "cleaning up our mental environment so that the real happiness can be both uncovered and sustained." Happiness, according to the Dahlia Lama, is an incredible gift we all can earn. 126

For many Western thinkers, happiness is held up as a right. It's embodied in The American Declaration of Independence, which states, "We hold these truths to be self-evident, that all men are created equal, that they are endowed by their Creator with certain unalienable rights, that among these are Life, Liberty and the pursuit of Happiness."

---

[123] Coles, Clifton, *Science Pursues Happiness*: Happiness Pays Off, Studies Show, *Futurist*, (July, 2002), Volume 36, Issue 4.
[124] David G Meyers, *The Pursuit of Happiness*, (Harper Paperback, 1993).
[125] Dr Sheldon Cohen, "Happy People May Have More Immunities to Common Cold", Center for the Advancement of Health, July 22, 2003.
[126] Who doesn't know the Dahlia Lama but in case you have been out of touch he is the spiritual and political leader of the Tibetan people and the current incarnation of a long line of Tulkus (Buddhist Monks).

What will make you happy? Is it money, fame, success, recognition, possessions, children, a trophy spouse, lots of amazing sex, good health?

Philosophers, for generations, have written about the basic need to move toward pleasure and away from pain. If something brings us pleasure, we do everything possible to possess it, particularly in material form. However, it can create a perceptual dilemma if we view the pursuit of happiness as shallow, superficial, and nothing more than the flavor of the month. According to the Dahlia Lama, "Happiness is a fundamental drive as basic as sex or companionship." When you feel stuck in a job and stifled by the demands of the material world, you may, as a result, change jobs, spouses and cars at an alarming rate. The average American changes jobs 10 times, moves six times, and is married more than once — all in the pursuit of happiness.

What is happiness?

Happiness comes when you pursue something that will both challenge you and bring satisfaction and reward through the doing of it, not just the end result. Happiness is about doing, not just possessing. Some people find that one special thing that will bring them happiness early in their lives, while others have to search through life's smorgasbord of possibilities until they finally hit on something. It's true for our POAs and it is true for most people. If you feel that life has treated you unkindly and not put happiness in your path, take heed. Here is a list of famous actors. Match the name with what you assume was their original career choice. The answers follow. [127]

1. Angelina Jolie	Veterinarian
2. George Clooney	Chef
3. Courtney Cox	Tennis professional
4. Toby Macquire	Architect
5. Julia Roberts	Funeral director
6. Matthew Perry	Professional baseball player
7. Hugh Grant	Priest
8. Tom Cruise	Advertising copy writer

The correct answers. 1 – Funeral Director, 2 – Professional baseball player, 3 – Architect, 4 – Chef, 5 – Veterinarian, 6 – Professional tennis player, 7 – Advertising copy writer, 8 – Priest.

---

[127] You can always find celebrity trivia is such magazines as: People, Star, Hello, Inside E and Life and Style.

Herein lays the dilemma. We look for happiness, particularly when we feel stuck in a corner, and yet can't see past the feeling of unhappiness. If we put our life on a scale, happiness on one side, unhappiness on the other, when the scale tips in the right direction, we accept what we have. Reaching for happiness is often mistakenly assumed to be our proactive act. However, Buddhists teach us that striving for happiness, in fact, blocks us from finding what we are searching for. Rather, we can find happiness by taking measurable steps to attain some material good, all the while acknowledging, not blocking out, the negative. Zen Buddhism teaches us 'attempts to downplay the negative by focusing only on the positive are faulty thinking'. Negative and positive experiences are simply two sides of the same coin. Each is necessary to balance your choices. [128]

The Microsoft Encarta Dictionary defines happiness as "feeling or showing pleasure, contentment or joy." [129]

This seems to suggest that there are two kinds of happiness: One is at an emotional level (feeling) and the other at a demonstrative level (showing). Let's consider both.

Robert Solomon, professor at the University of Texas at Austin, says, "We can deceive ourselves into thinking we're happy when we're not and we can be happy without realizing it." [130]

For example, it's easy to fall into a rut of everyday behaviors. Wake up, brush your teeth, eat breakfast, go to work, call customers, wait for a coffee break, complain about senior management, back to work, make more calls to customers, wait for lunch, etc. Every day is the same. I once heard a speaker refer to this as "hell with florescent lights." [131]

---

[128] The origins of Zen Buddhism are said to have a direct link to a speech given by the Gautama Buddha - The "Flower Sermon." The story is that when his followers gathered around to hear their Buddha speak he remained silent. Then after a protracted period of time, he held up a single flower. When his followers tried to make sense of the Buddha's action they were frustrated until one of them got it. He told the Buddha that he had gained special insight – beyond words. The Buddha apparently pleased by the response, smiled.
[129] Microsoft Encarta Dictionary, (St. Martin's press, 2001).
[130] Robert Solomon, University of Texas professor and author of 40 books including *On the Passionate Life*, 2003-2004. {Publisher, location of publisher and date published}
[131] That is a perfect description for what many people experience and I am sorry that I don't remember the source of the quote.

It is easy to fall into the numbed-out worker groove and think you are happy when, in fact, what you are really doing is accommodating yourself to the situation you are in leading a life of "quiet desperation." Yet, the risks of doing the same thing day in and out can also be detrimental to your physical and mental health. Performing the same movements over and over again can cause ailments as carpal tunnel syndrome. Performing the same task repetitively can also add to discontentment, unhappiness, and depression. [132]

Work stress, both mental and physical, is derived from a fast-paced, role-ambiguous, excessively worrisome environment, and monotonous tasks. As our economy focuses more on career specialization rather than being the generalists of the past there is danger. This discussion goes beyond the repetitive work on an assembly line, call centre, or data entry jobs. Recently, I had a total knee replacement. My orthopedic surgeon specializes in knees. If I want to talk to him about my back he has to refer me to someone else. Yet, I am grateful I chose to have my procedure by the best knee doctor around. From his point of view, how will he feel after doing knee replacements for thirty or forty years? Will it become repetitive? Will one knee look like the next?

Passion: one road to happiness

Here's a question. Have you ever felt so strongly about accomplishing something that sitting back and doing nothing was not an option? Most of us have issues or situations that spark something deep inside that demands to be listened to. It might be the kind of work you've chosen or the company you work for, concern for equality and social justice, the environment, day care, employee benefits, or general working conditions. There are times when one of these passions will guide your actions. The problem is that many of us don't follow our passions. We often miss the opportunity to act and later slap ourselves on the forehead asking ourselves, "Why didn't I do something?"

When I think of people who are passionate, I conjure images of the caring eyes of Mother Theresa or the commanding voice of Martin Luther King Jr. or even chest-thumping Tony Robbins. To me, these people draw upon a deep sense of commitment to find the motivation to take action. Where does this commitment come from? What is the fuel that creates their spark? How does it drive their productivity?

---

[132] Virginia Galt wrote "3 A.M.: Where are the happy workers?" For the *Toronto Star,* (October 20, 2006). She also reported higher than average rates of dissatisfaction among sales reps, and service employees.

The Microsoft Encarta dictionary's definition of passion is "A keen interest in a particular subject or activity." [133]

If passion leads to persistence, then you might assume that you would stick to any subject or activity you felt strongly about. Passion may be the spark that ignites a long journey. In fact, it may even be the fuel that maintains the fire, but passion alone is not enough. Passion needs the bellows of persistence to keep the roar of the fire going. So, to invoke the lessons in persistence that we learned in chapter three, we need to understand the role of happiness and passion.

While there may be some connection between passion and persistence, they differ in that persistence is a skill that we can all learn. The same cannot be said of passion. I cannot teach you to be passionate nor can you convince yourself that you are passionate about something. You either are passionate about something or you are not.

What is passion?

Most of us have had moments when we have felt strongly about something. It might be an injustice we have noticed such as employment inequity, corporate greed, or poor stewardship. The assumption that feeling strongly will motivate you to action is part of a philosophical discussion that has endured millennia. Plato simply stated that if you judge one course of action as the best, then why would you do anything else? If you were strongly passionate about something at work, for example, you would follow this passion as long as you thought this was the best course of action for you.

According to Plato, people will always move in a direction that's right for them. If so, why do people sometimes act wrongly? Surely every rational being would only choose what's best for them. [134]

This is where Aristotle joined the debate. In the Nicomachean Ethics, Aristotle wrote about something called "akrasia." Akrasia addressed this inconsistency acknowledging that sometimes people know what they should do, but do not follow their own reason. [135]

---

[133] Microsoft Encarta Dictionary, (St. Martin's Press, 2001).
[134] Sheldon Wein, *Plato's Moral Psychology* (Saint Mary's University), www.bu.edu.htm.
[135] Richard Kraut, "Alternate Readings of Aristotle on Akrasia", *Stanford Encyclopedia of Philosophy* (2005), http://en.wikipedia.org/wiki/Akrisia, Deborah Kerdeman, *Educating Ethical behavior*: Aristotle's Views on Akrasia, (University of Washington, 1992).

Feelings overpower reason and will act in ways that will not necessarily give the right result. For example, what stops the majority of workers who are aware of unethical or illegal activities within their organizations from blowing the whistle? Is it fear of reprisal, loss of income, or being ostracized by their peers? Surely, there has to be more than one person in an organization that knows when things are wrong.

Yet, it is often the sole courageous person who stands up and says enough is enough. Even if you feel passionate about something, but are not motivated to act, there is still the potential for change. Take, for example, an employer who recognizes leadership potential in one of his sales people. He supports and encourages this sales person by providing training and opportunities to lead teams and handle difficult presentations. There may be times when this sales person gets bored, overworked or simply wants to give up. Then, this same employer encourages and cajoles the employee either through threats ("If you give up, you will be throwing away any chance for advancement") or encouragement ("Just think about the satisfaction you will feel when you land the new account"). The question is whether this employee would have become a leader without the interference of his manager.

By contrast, actively passionate sales people will approach their boss and ask for training, or purchase books on sales techniques, and learn as much as possible on their own. They are motivated internally to pursue what they feel is important.

A great example of passion in North Americans is the automobile; they're highly symbolic of their owner's psyches – fears, hopes, and dreams. No one understands the love affair with the automobile better than Mike Yager.

Mike Yager's Story

Mike Yager parlayed a passion for cars into a $35,000,000-dollar-a-year business that employs over 170 people. "Most people *have* to go to work – I *get* to go to work," Mike laughs.

Mike was the youngest of nine children, growing up in Effingham, Illinois. In the '60s, getting your driver's license and having a car was a ticket to freedom, and Mike grew up in a household that was crazy about cars. With six older brothers, there were always cars around their house, everything from jalopies to hot rods. When one of his brothers purchased a 1960 Corvette, Mike fell in love. "I remember seeing my first Corvette," recalls Mike. "I just went bonkers over it, and I knew that someday I would own one."

Mike bought his first Corvette in 1970, when he was 20. His infatuation led him to start a Corvette Club in Effingham, which soon grew to almost 200 members. This led to his involvement with the 15,000-member National Council of Corvette Clubs, where he became a regional officer and then later served on the executive board.

Mike was a proud Corvette owner and talked to fellow enthusiasts at the automotive events they attended. He soon became aware of a need for Corvette-related paraphernalia like pins, hats, shirts, and more. And he learned, "There didn't seem to be anyone offering these products."

Mike decided to do something about it. He borrowed $500, and on February 23, 1974, started his own business, which he christened Mid America Enterprises. His idea was to make just enough money to cover his expenses while indulging his passion.

At first, Yager operated out of the trunk of his Corvette. In fact, the UPS van would make pickups and deliveries from the parking lot of the tool-and-die plant where Yager worked as an apprentice toolmaker. But the demand for his products increased and he soon moved his operations to his apartment. In a little less than a year and a half, Mike realized that his part-time hobby was growing into a full-time concern. "You know what?" the 24-year-old said to himself, "A person could make a living doing this."

Mike quit his tool-and-die job to devote himself, full time, to his passion for Corvettes. He renamed his company Mid America Designs and it quickly outgrew his apartment, then his home, and finally his rental building. In 1979, the company moved to its own permanent headquarters outside of Effingham.

Today, Mid America boasts a 36,000-square-foot automated distribution center, which includes the office and showroom complex, a manufacturing facility, and a Garage Museum. In the museum, you will find such cars as a 1997 Porsche Tweekster, a 1988 Callaway Turbo Corvette, and the original shaking "Herbie" car—the star of the popular movie of the same name. The company is the largest supplier of Corvette parts and accessories in the world. [136]

"I had no clue I would ever get to where I am today," says Mike." And now, 32 short years later, I am where I am!" Mike's philosophy is that success comes in filling a void in the marketplace and doing it with

---

[136] Mid America Motorworks. If you are a Corvette enthusiast, or just like cars in general then check out www.mamotors.com and enjoy the ride.

style. "If you believe in the product, if you meet your customer's expectations, and even exceed them, the marketplace will reward you."

Mike knows his passion for Corvettes has been the key to his success. "When you deal in a business that is passion-driven to begin with," Mike says, "you overcome a whole lot of obstacles. I have customers today that have been with me ever since I started the business. I'm very hands-on. I know an awful lot of our customers personally. I'm very involved within the hobby. I do what my customers do: I collect cars, I drive them, I race them, and I restore them."

"Passion can get you only so far," Mike says. "To be an entrepreneur, you also have to have a vision and steer towards that vision—and not be afraid." For Mike, the road from his initial business idea to his current success has not always been straight and it hasn't always been smooth. He has had his share of potholes along the way. "I can't imagine anybody being in business who doesn't find obstacles day in and day out," Mike reflects. "But it's from these challenges that you grow your strength and develop your ambition and philosophy.

"I think," continues Mike, "that a lot of entrepreneurial-driven people get scared at a certain point and give up just when, if they had pushed through a little bit harder, if they had persevered, they would have gotten results. Most of my life has been a two-person race and I've finished second more often than first. An awful lot of people give up if they don't finish first. But if you look at why you finished second, next time you'll prepare a little harder, be a little smarter and win the race."

Mike's advice to anyone starting a business is to channel their passion. "Get involved in your trade association. Be a visible person in your profession or hobby. Set the pace and be the leader. And then, be prepared to have people attack you, emulate, or copy you. If you're always innovative, then you'll always be a step ahead."

Mike's passion is not limited to four wheels. He describes himself as his company's "chief cheerleader." "I lead people," Mike declares. "I don't know what presidents do, but I know what leaders do. To be a leader, you have to be more concerned about helping and developing others than being self-centered." Mike's personal mission statement is to make sure he helps everyone he is associated with achieve his or her ultimate goals, dreams, and successes in life. "I'm not worried about myself," Mike maintains. "I'll get there. I have a goal, a vision that when I walk out of this building to retire someday, a bunch of millionaires will walk out with me. I want to retire when I'm 95 or 96, so I'm at the halfway point and planning my next career!" Whatever he decides to do, it's a safe bet that he'll be leading the pack for a long time to come.

Passion into action

Sometimes the link between intention and action is not a problem. It's as if a person's commitment is hardwired and passion is ingrained. Formed early in life, it hangs on to the human spirit like a well-tailored suit. Henri Dunant was a man who wore his passion on his sleeve. While his name may not ring an immediate bell of recognition, the results of his passion surely will.

Henri's Story

Henri Dunant was born in 1828 in Geneva, the son of a businessman and devoted Calvinist. His parents stressed the value of social work. His father, Jean-Jacques Dunant, was active in helping orphans and parolees. His mother, Antoinette Dunant-Colladon, worked with the sick and poor. An influential moment in his early life was a visit to Toulon where he witnessed the suffering of prison inmates. [137]

Henri grew up in the Réveil (The Awakening) period. This was a time of religious awakening, and at the age of eighteen, he joined the Geneva Society for Alms Giving. The following year he founded the "Thursday Association," a group of young men dedicated to Bible studies and helping the poor. In 1852, he joined the YMCA and was active three years later in founding its international organization.

Vocationally and financially, things were not as smooth for Henri. He failed out of College Calvin. He became a moneylender by profession and ultimately declared bankruptcy. Despite his many accomplishments, in his later years he was forced to live off the kindness of distant family members.

But in 1859, Henri's travels took him to Solferino where a battle had just occurred. There were 38,000 dead and injured soldiers on the battlefield. Outraged, Henri organized local citizens to erect makeshift hospitals, find supplies, and tend to the wounded, regardless of which

---

[137] Henri Dunant, (1828-1910). To learn more about this fascinating man check www.icrc.org, www.ourstory.info and www.britannica.com.

side of the battle they fought. The locals coined the term "Tutti Fratelli," (All are Brothers) as they began their relief mission. 138

Once he returned to Geneva, Henri wrote a book about his experience. "Un Souvenir de Solferine (A Memory of Solfernino). In the book, he described the need for a neutral organization that would care for soldiers. In 1862, he published 1,600 copies at his own expense. 139

Henri began traveling to promote his book and expound on his idea. Ultimately, the President of the Geneva Society for Public Welfare created a committee to explore Henri's idea. Their first meeting in 1863 is considered to be the founding date of the International Committee of the Red Cross. In 1901, Henri was awarded the Nobel Prize for his efforts and passion.

Passion and intention

The Dahlia Lama says that as long as we try to eliminate displeasure and preserve only pleasure, no lasting happiness is possible. The trick, according to Buddhism, is to understand how you fit into the big picture. I'm not suggesting that you need to give up everything for a career based on passion alone. Many of us are not prepared to do that.

If you can give your passion context and allocate a degree of commitment, but fail to act you are missing the third ingredient— intention. Without intention, your unfulfilled passion puts you in the league of the millions of Monday morning quarterbacks. You will have lots to say about how things should have gone, but very little involvement in the game. If this describes you, then you will need to act on your passion or look elsewhere for happiness.

Good news for the silent majority

If you have a passion for something, then acting on it will ultimately bring you satisfaction. This is opposed to the disheartening feeling in the pit of your stomach — knowing that you have left your passion simmering in a pot on the stove and it is now smoldering with neglect.

---

[138] The battle of Solferino was fought on June 24, 1859 which paired Napoleon 111's army against Victor Emmual 11 of Sardinia.
[139] Henry Dunant *A Memory of Solferino*, , (Published by the International Committee of the Red Cross, 1986).

While many of us feel passionate about something, the majority of us do not. We may be concerned citizens, but we go through life missing that one big issue to motivate us to action.

If you have no particular passions or are not prepared to act on your passions, then what will make you happy? According to psychologist Ed Diener, there is no one key to happiness, but there are several important elements: [140]

1. Family and Friends
The wider and deeper the relationships with those around you the better. Research suggests that friendship can ward off germs. Our brain controls many of the mechanisms in our body that are responsible for disease. Just as stress can trigger ill health, it is thought that friendship and happiness can have a protective effect.

2. Marriage
Marriage is also important. According to research, the positive effects of marriage add an average of seven years to the life of a man and four years to a woman.

3. A sense of meaning
A belief in something bigger than yourself from religion, spirituality, or a philosophy of life contributes to happiness.

4. Goals
Having goals that you are working toward and that you also find enjoyable embedded in your short - and long-term plans is an element of happiness.

5. Meaningful work
This means spending that third to half of your life doing something you feel good about. Knowing that you are making a difference and having an opportunity to display your competencies.

Our next POA found happiness by going back to his younger years and renewed a childhood activity to change his career direction.

Nathan Sawaya's Story

Ever since his boyhood in Veneta, Oregon, Nathan was hooked on playing with Lego. He started out copying little houses and boats from

---

[140] Coles and Clifton, *The Futurist, Science Pursues Happiness*, (July 2002), Volume 36, Issue 4.

Lego packages. Before long, his parent's living room held entire Lego villages. When he was nine, Nathan had a life-altering experience. On a family trip to the Alameda Square Shopping Centre in Denver, Nathan saw his first traveling Lego display. Here he saw the Washington Monument; the White House and the U.S. Capital buildings all built in Lego perfection. Nathan was dumbstruck. From that moment on, while other kids rode their bikes and played sports, Nathan was building Lego models on his parent's living room carpet.

Like many good little boys, when it was time for a career, Nathan looked for something solid and respectable. He became a lawyer specializing in mergers and acquisitions for a New York City law firm. But the love of Lego never left him. With 25 years of Lego parts that he had collected as presents or bought on e-bay, Nathan had enough Lego to build a giant self-portrait. "It was easy. I knew the subject and had access to him," Nathan jokes. He found building large-scale models brought balance to his life. "It was a left-brain, right-brain thing," Nathan said.

His left brain, the analytical side, helped him in his law practice. His right brain, the creative side, helped him in the evenings and weekends spent creating Lego models. For Nathan, building Lego models was therapy. "After a long day practicing law, this gave me a creative outlet."

Then came his big break. The Lego Company had a competition for the coveted title of Lego Master Model Builder. They held regional competitions around the United States and Nathan entered. Nathan was chosen along with 26 other finalists who went to Carlsbad, California for the national finals. Nathan won. He could boast that he was one of only 20 other individuals with the coveted title. The LEGO Group offered him a Job at LegoLand. [141]

He took it, and after seven months realized that he missed New York, so he went back home to his law practice.

Nathan continued to build models in the evenings and on weekends and posted them on his website. Before long, and much to his surprise, companies were asking Nathan to build models for them. He built a complete working air conditioner at a trade show in Las Vegas. At a

---

[141] Lego enthusiasts will enjoy a visit to www.legoland.com and learn about theme parks in Denmark, U.K, U.S.A. and Germany.

boat show, he built a 10-foot speedboat for the Chris Craft Corporation in 10 days and with 250,000 pieces of Lego Nathan assembled the boat as people stopped and watched. He has also built a six-foot tall scale model of the Iwo Jima Flag Raisers for the National Museum of the Marine Corps, a working personal computer which was photographed for the cover of PC magazine, and a grand scale city for F.O.A. Schwartz in New York City. [142]

Ask Nathan how big a project can be built out of Lego and he answers, "As big as your imagination and wallet."

You would think that building Lego for 18 hours a day would be tough work, but according to Nathan, it's not. "Who needs sleep?" he jests. He thought building models would have its limitations but it hasn't. "Who would have thought that a boy from Oregon would be building props for movies?" He just finished doing just that for a movie starring Natalie Portman and Dustin Hoffman. "It blows my mind," he comments. When I asked what about his favorite project, he answered "the next one." Building Lego started out as a child's hobby and Nathan (literally) built it into a career. He's having the time of his life.

We've seen that Mike Schultz returned to his first love — teaching, and Laura Robinson learned about board games early in her life. Mike Yager found his passion in cars and Henri Dunant found success in giving to others, while Nathan Sawaya discovered Lego was the key to his happiness. Going back to your early childhood interests to find something that makes you happy now, and will continue to do so in the future, often makes sense.

The other side of this coin is when we project our happiness into the future. You might say, "If I could work for a more understanding boss, I would be happier," or "If I had a million dollars life would be good."

There is no way of knowing how the future will work out. There are lots of examples of people who move from job to job looking for the right boss and are never happy. There are stories of people with wealth who are not happy.

According to Daniel Gilbert, author of Stumbling on Happiness, "We are lousy at predicting the future. Thinking something will bring us pleasure is a fantasy with no shred of evidence that it will." [143]

---

[142] Visit Nathan's site www.brickartist.com and see his amazing gallery.
[143] Daniel Gilbert, *Stumbling on Happiness*, Alfred A. Knopf, 2006.

Have you ever wanted something really badly, and then when you got it, wondered what all the fuss was about? If you answered yes, you are not alone.

Perhaps your daydreams once included thoughts of working for a fast-moving tech company, going to work in blue jeans, having a basketball hoop in your cubicle, meetings around a pool table, espresso bars, a hefty salary with stock options, and the chance to punctuate every new idea with, "cool."

You embellished your daydream with, "no boring jobs for me." Your dream job sounded idyllic, and yet, when the fiscal fantasies of the high-tech sector hit reality, they issued pink slips just like General Motors and workers and investors alike learned they weren't immune to bankruptcy and worthless stock options.

It's important to remember that any sector has its share of office politics, competitions for revered promotions, and overbearing, under-appreciating bosses to work for. After the crash in 2001, the fantasy job lost its sparkle. Boring, but stable jobs once again looked pretty good.

Which countries are happiest?

Adrian White, analytic social psychologist at the University of Leicester, attempted to answer that very question. White analyzed over 100 different studies with responses from over 80,000 people which were conducted by such organizations as UNESCOI, the CIA, the New Economics Foundation, WHO, the Veenhoven Database, the Latinbarometer, the Afrobarometer, and the UNHDR.

From this data, she created the first ever World Map of Happiness. This map includes 178 countries.   [144]

Adrian found that the three most prevalent indicators of happiness are health, wealth, and education. Those countries with high GDP, good health care, and access to education scored highest.

---

[144] World Map of Happiness, This is really interesting to look at. Visit www.physorg.com and see where your country is ranked.

Ten Happiest Countries

Denmark
Switzerland
Austria
Iceland
Bahamas
Finland
Sweden
Bhutan
Brunei Darussalam
Canada

Ten Least Happy Countries

Burundi
Zimbabwe
Congo Dem. Rep.
Moldova
Ukraine
Sudan
Armenia
Turkmenistan
Belarus
Georgia

Happiness Ranking for Other Notable Countries

23. The United States
41. The United Kingdom
90. Japan
82. China
125. India

Happiness and your brain

Happiness isn't part of our hardwiring and doesn't come naturally. According to an article in England's *Sunday Times*, homo sapiens evolved during the Pleistocene era (1.8 million to 10,000 years ago), a time of hardship and turmoil. During the Ice Age, our ancestors endured long freezes as glaciers formed, followed by ferocious floods as ice masses melted. We shared the planet with terrifying creatures such as mammoths, elephant-size ground sloths, and saber-tooth tigers. But, by the end of the Pleistocene era, all of these animals were extinct. Humans, on the other hand, had evolved large brains, and used their intellect to make fire and sophisticated tools, to develop speech, and social rituals. [145]

During our evolution, we developed a "catastrophic brain," which was always on the lookout for what was wrong. There is a good reason negative thinking is deeply ingrained in our psyche. The ability to feel negative emotions derives from an ancient danger-recognition system formed early in the brain's evolution and was important to our survival as a species. The pre-frontal cortex, which registers happiness, is the part of the brain used for higher thinking, and it was the area of the brain that developed later in human evolution. It's not surprising that the happiness area of the brain developed later.

If an ancient Homo Sapien were to stop and take a momentary leave of his defense mechanism to smell the flowers, he would very likely become lunch for a passing carnivore.

But how does this affect us today? Experiments show that we remember failures more vividly than successes.[146] We dwell on what went badly, not what went well. When life runs smoothly we are on autopilot; we're only in a state of true consciousness when we notice the stone in our shoe. Scholars call this a "Hedonistic Treadmill." [147]

Professional speakers talk about "being in the zone." It's a place where the audience and the speaker are one. At that moment, the speaker feels invincible. They can do no wrong. Often, they receive

---

[145] Dorothy Wade, "So What do you Have to do to Find Happiness?" *The Sunday Times Magazine*, (May 29, 2006). In this same article you will also find reference to the "Hedonistic Treadmill."

[146] William J Cromie, "Bad Times Make for More Accurate Memories", *Harvard University Gazette*, (May 11, 2006).

audience feedback from such a presentation showing that 99% of participants thought the speaker was the next Messiah. However, if one person's comments were lukewarm (perhaps they made a negative comment about the speaker's style or PowerPoint) what do you think the speaker ruminates over? I have read many biographies of writers, actors, and celebrities who claim not to read reviews because, when they do, they focus only on the negative comments.

Often, the more possessions or accomplishments we have, the more we need to boost our level of happiness. Once again, this goes back to the evolution of the brain. Daniel Nettle of the Royal Institute,[148] noted that the brain systems for wanting and liking are separate. Wanting involves two ancient regions of the brain, the amygdala and the nucleus accumbens, which communicate by using the chemical dopamine to form the brain's reward systems.

Liking involves different brain chemicals. Real pleasure is associated with opiods. Happiness is different again. It involves a third chemical pathway. Is happiness a matter of chemistry? In part, yes. Serotonin can reduce fear, panic, and sleeplessness and increase sociability, cooperation, and happy feelings.

Happiness may be a matter of selective memory. The challenge is to go backwards in our personal evolution to weed out all the messages about what went wrong and focus on what went right—and then savor them in your memory. In order to move forward, we need to open our happiness drawer for clues. Nathan Sawaya found happiness in a childhood fascination with LEGO, Laura Robinson's came from her family's love of board games, for Mike Schultz, it was camping, and Mike Yager found his happiness in cars. It's not always easy to find what you are looking for, but the search is worth the effort.

Professor Ed Diener says, "We need to train ourselves not to make a big deal of trivial little hassles, to learn to focus on the process of working toward our goals and not wait to be happy until we achieve them and to think about our blessings."

Sustaining happiness

Happiness comes from within. There is no external measurement for happiness. Only you can decide whether you are happy or not. Have you ever gone to a movie, listened to some music, or read a book and

---

[148] Daniel Nettle, *Happiness: The Science Behind Your Smile* (Oxford University press, 2006).

were filled with joy? What happens when you reread the same book? Does it give you the same emotional charge? Do you read the words and see new things that you missed the first time? What happens when you read it a third or fourth time? Does the feeling of joy remain the same? The answer for many of us is that it doesn't. The initial feeling of happiness dissipates the more we repeat the experience. Does it mean that we are destined to be on the constant lookout for new things to keep us happy? Are we emotionally fickle? Does our low attention span mean we require a constant barrage of new stimuli in order to feel alive and happy? The answer is, maybe. Irving Biederman and Edward Vessel wrote a paper for the periodical, *American Scientist*, where they presented this argument. [149]

Beiderman and Vessel conducted experiments using functional magnetic resonance imaging (fMRI), which allowed them to observe the subject's brain p atterns when exposed to various stimuli. One group of subjects was presented with a series of images, but not observed on fMRI, while the second group was connected to the fMRI scanner. The first group was asked their preference re various images presented. These images were presented a number of times and the subject's preference for each image declined the more times it was presented.

The second group, connected to the fMRI, was subjected to the same scenes. This group was asked not to voice their preference. As Beiderman and Vessel's hypothesis predicted, scenes rated high- elicited activity in the posterior portion of parahippocampal cortex region of the brain. The same decline in preference observed in the first group could now be seen in specific brain patterns.

We see similar patterns emerging from our personal everyday experiences. When we see the same thing over and over again, it loses its emotional punch. If variety were all there was to pleasure, then we would all be on the constant lookout for new and exciting things to amuse us. Marriage is a good example. Think back to your early courting days. Were they filled with excitement, charged with anticipation, so that being with that one person was the only thing that occupied your thoughts? Then, as time passed and your relationship matured, did you notice that those initial feelings were replaced with feelings of comfortable warmth? The initial urgency of being with this one person changed because he or she was now constantly available.

---

[149] Irving Beiderman and Edward A. Vessel, *Perceptual Pleasure and the Brain, American Scientist*, (May/June 2006).

Those who understand this natural change can adjust their lives (and expectations) to the reality of the experience. Those who don't, continually search for happiness in new experiences and conquests. However, as we've seen, POAs such as Nathan Sawaya were able to maturely integrate the source of their initial happiness (in his case, building Lego), into his adult life. By so doing, his love of Lego has remained strong throughout his lifetime. Active doers can prolong the pleasure of the experience by their ability to find the hidden challenges that are uncovered when they delve further into those things that bring them passion. Nathan is no longer building the same Lego he did as a child, but he's still doing what he loves.

Money and happiness

Steven Page, lead singer for the rock group The Barenaked Ladies, once quipped, "Money won't buy you happiness but it will let you park your yacht beside it." For most of us, lack of money is a convenient excuse for inaction. We say we don't have the money to start that new business, travel to India, go back to school – whatever our dream may be. So, we buy lottery tickets, or the very prudent will open a savings account and sock away bits of money with the hope that someday they will have enough to buy that illusive happiness. Then there are people like Robert McDuffie who wanted something badly enough that he found a way to raise the money to buy it.

Robert McDuffie's Story

Robert McDuffie is a world-famous violinist and distinguished professor of music at Mercer University in Atlanta Georgia. His talent landed him, like other prodigies of his time, at the Julliard School. There, he studied with classmates of the caliber of Nadja Salernao-Sonnenberg and Nigel Kennedy. [150]

His drive and talent grew over time, and now McDuffie plays concertos with some of the leading orchestras in the world. So, with talent, good looks, fame, and respect, what else could he possibly want to make him happy? For McDuffie it was a violin. Now, if you are

---

[150] Robert McDuffie, John Terauds, "The Price of Fame: $3.5 Million", *The Toronto Star*, (June 4, 2006). "College of Liberal Arts: McDuffie, Robert, Symphony", *The American Symphony Orchestra League's bi monthly magazine*, (May/June 2001). Melinda Whiting, "The Advocate, Symphony", *The American Symphony Orchestra League's bi monthly magazine*, (May/June 2001).

thinking of buying a world-class violin, the first name that might come to mind is Stradivarius. But, McDuffie's sights were on a violin made by Guarneri del Ges in the eighteenth century and was once owned by the classic composer Paganni. Violins of this caliber are actually preferred by soloists over the Stradivarius because of their depth of sound. The only drawback for McDuffie was the price tag of $3.5 million was way outside McDuffie's financial snack-bracket.

After trying unsuccessfully to raise the money to buy the violin, a friend suggested a limited partnership. It would be legally structured so that McDuffie would sell enough shares to raise the $3.5 million. Then, McDuffie would lease back the violin for 25 years. His payments would cover the $14,000 per year in insurance. After 25 years the violin would be sold and the moneys disbursed among the partners.

McDuffie has created such a partnership so he can achieve his musical dream. It is estimated, that at the end of the lease period, the violin will have appreciated in value to somewhere between $10 million and $25 million. But isn't McDuffie only buying temporary happiness? In an interview with Melinda Whiting, McDuffie said, "I believe that the next 20 years are going to be the best of my playing life." When the lease expires, he will be 65 years old, and with his share of the profits, there might be another violin that will suit his post-del Ges period. His partners not only get to share in the proceeds from the sale of the violin; in the meantime, they can also experience an intimate connection to the arts by knowing that they're actively involved in helping a talented musician achieve his artistic potential.

McDuffie did what entrepreneurs have always done – raised venture capital to create their dream. But this lesson applies to everyone. The investment you make can be on a smaller scale, and still add to your happiness. It can be as simple as investing in training, getting new posters for your walls, a good sound system, better lighting, ergonomic furniture, or new computer software. You can invest in your personal professional development; attend classes, travel, or go to events in your industry. For Robert, the violin brought happiness. How else might you bring happiness into your work? No person or material thing can guarantee your happiness. But, bringing as much happiness as possible into your career has its rewards. Benjamin Disraeli once said, "Action may not always bring happiness but there is no happiness without action." [151]

---

[151] Benjamin Disraeli, (1804 – 1881), British statesman and writer.

Lessons Learned

- Embrace happiness
- Identify your happiness triggers
- Rearrange your mental furniture

Happiness makes your work more satisfying; it is the underlying element to a healthy life. Sometimes early passions form the direction of your life and work from the get-go, while, in other c ases, you may need to go through a process of self-discovery to get in touch with your happiness. One common thread among all the POAs in this chapter is this: the seeds of happiness were planted in their youth.

Laura Robinson played board games with her family. Nathan Sawaya played Lego on his parent's living room rug. Mike Yager fell in love with a Corvette. Henri Dunant, Mike Schultz, and Laura Robinson found happiness in lessons learned from their families' interests and values.

Some find happiness by following their passions. Mike Yager built an empire on his passion for Corvettes and Henri Dunant's passion to help led to the creation of the Red Cross, which changed the world.

From Robert McDuffie we learned that money can lead to, if not actually buy, happiness. Sometimes we have to invest in our happiness.

However, in all of the POAs in this chapter, we see that the real currency of happiness is proactivity. Not one of them found what they were searching for through inactivity. They all went out and made it happen, and you can too.

Lessons into action: your career action plan

Step 1: Embrace happiness

Happiness is often an illusive goal. While it would seem absurd for someone to say, "I want to be miserable," I have heard people say, "I don't deserve to be happy," or "Happiness is not my primary goal in life." Embracing happiness is your inalienable right, but reaching out to get it is often difficult.

Read the following quotes. If you've ever said these words, or even thought of them, place an X in the box that precedes each statement.

- ❑ My approach to work is very serious and happiness isn't a consideration.
- ❑ I'm willing to put up with the negative aspect of my job because I have security.
- ❑ I'm too busy working to support my family to worry about personal happiness.
- ❑ Parts of my job are not great, but overall, it's not that bad.
- ❑ Self-employed people have a much easier time pursuing happiness than people who work for someone else.
- ❑ I'm reasonably happy in my career, so there is no point spending more time looking for ways to feel even better.
- ❑ My job is what it is; my real fun starts after 5:00 o'clock when work ends.
- ❑ The first thing I'd do if I won the lottery is quit my job.
- ❑ The old adage, "One step forward and two steps back" is a perfect description of my career path.
- ❑ I can spend as much time as I like doing the things that make me happy after I retire.
- ❑ I've tried to make my work more fun, but haven't had the right breaks.
- ❑ I like my work and I guess I'm pretty happy.
- ❑ Happiness hasn't played a role in my career.

If you read each quote and did not check any of the boxes, you can proceed to the next chapter. However, if you checked one or more of the 15 boxes, you have recognized that something is missing. If you choose to ignore the signs, it may result in detrimental consequences to your career. Take this as an early warning signal. Perhaps you are not quite as happy as you could be. With this understanding you are ready to proceed to step two.

Step 2: Identify your happiness triggers

We saw that each of our POAs discovered happiness in their youth. Some maintained their early passions and built a career around them. Others followed a different path, only to find a turn in the road that led them right back to the beginning.

Think back to your childhood. What did you do that was fun? What activities or hobbies brought you real happiness? As you recall, make a note of the activities and what you liked about them.

Step 3: Rearrange your mental furniture

Now it's time to rearrange the furniture in that private part of your mind that ruminates on everything but what will make you happy.

Rearranging your mental furniture helps you focus on new priorities. How do you do this? Start with a personal diary. Your first entries come from the following steps.

a. Imagine the possibilities

Imagining is all about seeing things that you cannot see with your eyes. It is about your potential, your dreams, and your possibilities. Without imagination, you will be stuck in the present and be focusing on one of the quotes in step one that you marked with an X. If you are having difficulty imagining, just ask yourself, "What would my life be like if the statement I highlighted in step one was not true?"

Sit in a quiet space and write an answer to this question. For example, if you related to the statement "I am too busy working to support my family to worry about personal happiness," think about how your life and work would be different if your family's priorities also allowed you an opportunity for happiness.

Perhaps you can imagine that selling would be more joyful and satisfying. Perhaps you see yourself going home without feeling burdened and resentful that you have sacrificed your happiness for your family's sake. Perhaps you can picture yourself being open to and enjoying them. Let your imagination run wild and record your thoughts in your diary.

Understand that you are unparalleled.

We on this planet are special – there are 6+billion people who are unique. No two of us are exactly the same. This step is your opportunity to explore your innermost self and ask yourself, "What guides my decisions?" Let's use the same example.

You might see that putting your family first is something you learned from one or both of your parents. It's pretty typical behavior of the baby-boom generation, whose parents went through the great depression in the 1930s and did everything they could just to make sure there was food on the table. If this was your reality as a child, then examine these actions in light of the 21st century.

Ask yourself, "Is this belief still valid in the life and work that I have undertaken? Are circumstances sufficiently different now that I can shed this belief and replace it with one that includes my personal pursuit of happiness?" Once again, write out your thoughts in your personal diary.

Activate your thoughts

In this step, you will list things you can do to help activate activities that you can do differently to bring happiness into your work. Perhaps you might allow yourself the luxury of getting involved with some of your organization's extracurricular activities, such as the bowling team, or a charity drive, or you might take work-related courses. Maybe there is a chance for you to bring your family to work and have your son or daughter shadow you for a day.

Write at least five things (more if you can) in your diary that you can do differently at work — immediately. If you're having difficulty with this step, return to the exercise you did in step two and consider hobbies and passions you enjoyed as a child for clues. What can you do that would bring some of that early happiness into your life now?

Be a conscious doer

When you implement your new action steps, you are bound to stumble occasionally. Not everything is going to work as you planned. It's like taking golf lessons. When I spend time with a golf pro and learn something new about my swing, the next time I am on the course my game is often worse than it was before the lesson.

That's because I'm focusing on the nuances of the swing rather than playing the game. In the game of golf, I have an expert who can guide me. In the game of life, we are all guiding ourselves. Sometimes we are completely on our own and at other times we have the benefit of a professional career coach, mentor, or role models. Don't be discouraged if some things don't instantly work out well.

Don't give up if you don't get the immediate response you imagined. Every day, try at least one of the things you listed and let happiness find you. Professor Biederman says that once we actively pursue happiness, the pursuit itself will become addictive and you will spend the rest of your life pursuing it. How bad can that be?

Let's review. You have learned how to overcome the helplessness that sometimes accompanies career advancement. You saw how you can develop your courage and persistence, and learned how to spot or create opportunities to bring more happiness into your work and life. In the next chapter, you will learn how to reframe adversity, transforming it from an enemy into a teacher.

6
Succeeding in an Imperfect World

"That which does not kill me, strengthens me."
—Friedrich Nietzsche [152]

Many of us look at the world as comprised of two groups of people: winners and losers. In the world of selling there are the winners who have carved out a successful and profitable career or achieved the status of sales leaders. The reward for their efforts is status, power, money, or recognition. The losers go quietly to work, don't complain, and wait until retirement. They never seem to be able to climb to the next rung of the corporate ladder. This faulty and unrealistic view of the world may be a result of expectations. Our society places accolades on the winners—the best in business, the best under 40, the employee of the month, sales person of the year, and so on.

Self help books, and the gurus who write them, tell you that by following simple steps you can pave your own road to fame and glory. Motivational speakers relate heart-wrenching stories about their turnaround from an impoverished past, an eating disorder, a life threatening illness, or an act of violence, and how they built a new life. They claim that if you are daring enough to take the same steps as they did, you too can change your life. Set your standards high, they tell you. Don't fall with the meek and fearful, take bold steps, and to paraphrase the Star Trek introduction, "Go where no man has gone before," and the career you want is yours for the taking. [153]

---

[152] Friedrich Nietzsche, (1844 – 1900) German Philosopher.
[153] Star Trek is the product of Gene Roddenberry and its reference here is a perfect addition to this chapter. While the original Star Trek television series became one of the biggest cult phenomena of the 20th century, it suffered its own setbacks. After being in development for six years it aired and lasted only three seasons when it was cancelled due to poor ratings. Yet this apparent failure led to four additional spin offs and eleven feature movies.

It sounds idyllic and yet millions of us start our careers with a plan in place and buy into the myth that as long as we stick to the plan, success will follow. The problem is that we live in an imperfect world. The workplace is continually changing. Businesses are constantly centralizing and then decentralizing. One day they divest and the next they merge. They downsize, upsize, and then capsize. Life continues to surprise us by throwing obstacles in our paths that can easily derail the best of plans through mishap, lapse in moral judgment, or a miscalculation of risk.

The road from here to where you want your sales career to head is long and precarious. It is filled with setbacks. We learn as we go that hopes, dreams, and ambitions end, that plans get changed and people disappoint us. Sister Joan Chittister[154] said, "We learn that life is a balancing act lived between the poles of unreasonable hope on one hand and disheartening despair on the other." The truth is, that without this range of possibilities, life would probably be a dull trip. A straight road poses the risk that the driver will soon become drowsy and swerve into a ditch. A more interesting life and career is like a winding road that's often filled with roadblocks and setbacks. Things are thrown in your path that offers you a choice that will either end your journey, or force you to detour, and perhaps, alter your destination.

It is important to distinguish between setbacks or challenges that are beyond our control such as illness, war, or being born into poverty, and setbacks or challenges that are a result of our own actions. These include things like lacking certain life skills, poor educational and career choices, and bad marriages or relationships. The first group we will refer to as circumstances beyond our control. The second group is self-created circumstances. In either case, when you are faced with a challenge, no matter what its cause, you always have a choice — sink or swim.

We all face both kinds of setbacks. We get sick or make bad decisions and yet society pressures us to be perfect. This expectation often results in us tiptoeing around customers operating on autopilot, feeling safe yet stagnate, or not quite alive. While corporate culture preaches innovation, pursuing the cutting edge, and expanding the envelope, many of these same managers hover over their over-worked

---

[154] Joan D. Chittister, *Scarred by Struggle, Transformed by Hope* (William B. Eerdmans Publishing Company, 2003).

sales people primed to pounce at the slightest "mistake." The sales person who is willing to try new things that don't work out is not rewarded for his or her imagination. So, if the culture you work in abhors taking risks and trying new ideas that may fail, it's no wonder you might avoid them too. But, there is a difference between failing and being a failure. Everything from vaccines to fighting deadly disease to the invention of Velcro was the result of an initial failure.

According to author Harold Kurshner, the key question you need to answer is not whether you can go through life without some failures and rejection, but how you will respond to those disappointments. [155]

Whether the circumstances are beyond your control or self-created, they are only setbacks. The key to your success is how you choose to handle them. Will you let them defeat your efforts or will you rise above the setbacks and move on? Here's a good case in point of someone who turned his failures into gold. His name is William Joseph Martin Joel, but the world knows him better as Billy Joel.

Billy Joel's Journey

Billy Joel[156] is a man who has released 15 albums and 40 singles, many of which reached number one. He has won numerous Grammy's and received the Living Legend award from the National Academy of Recording Arts and Sciences, along with such notables as Quincy Jones, Johnny Cash, and Aretha Franklin. He has earned hundreds of millions of dollars and has a career that has spanned over four decades. But Billy's rise to fame and fortune has seen many setbacks. It is well worth our time to take a closer look at his remarkable saga.

Billy was born in 1949, in Long Island, New York. His father, Howard, was a survivor of the concentration camp at Dachau. After the war, Howard and his wife Rosalind emigrated to the United States and settled in Levittown, New York. When Billy was four years old, he discovered the piano and his parents enrolled him in classes to study classical music.

---

[155] Harold Kushner, *Overcoming Life's Disappointments*. (Alfred A. Knopf, 2006).
[156] There is so much written about Billy Joel, two good sites to visit are: www.classocbands.com, and www.sing365.com.

During his youth, he was involved in gang crime with lots of general disruptive behaviors at home and school. At one point, Billy ran away from home and was arrested for suspicion of burglary (the charges were ultimately dropped). He even took up boxing as a teenager to release his anger. Billy had a total of 22 fights and had his nose broken once. Oddly, his younger years were an unlikely mixture of piano lessons and welterweight fights.

In 1964, Billy witnessed an event that would steer his career for the rest of his life. He, like millions of Americans, tuned in to the Ed Sullivan Show to watch the "British Invasion" with the first performance by the Beatles. Billy knew instantly that playing rock and roll/pop music was what he wanted to do. His classical piano lessons morphed into a love for rock and roll. [157]

Billy joined a band called The Echoes. Dressed like the Beatles, their heroes, Billy and his friends played at the Holy Family Church. They went through a number of name changes, but did not spark the interest of the teenage girls they were hoping to impress. About this time, his father died, leaving Rosalind with the responsibility of caring for her family. Billy took whatever jobs he could, at night, to help with the family's finances and attended school during the day. It was an impossible schedule, and ultimately, Billy didn't get his high school diploma because of absenteeism.

When he was sixteen, Billy joined a band called The Hassles. The group cut two albums. Both failed to launch his career. Then after a breakup with his girlfriend, he attempted suicide by drinking furniture polish. He must have sensed his impending doom, because Billy checked himself into the Meadowbrook Hospital for a psychiatric evaluation. During his three week stay, he reaffirmed his own sanity and resolved to make music his life's work.

Billy bounced back, but his success did not come quickly. He continued to record albums and married his first wife, Elizabeth Weber in 1972. Finally, in 1973, Billy had his first big break with an album called Piano Man, which included his first hit, New York State of Mind. His career continued to build slowly, and in 1977, he was catapulted into super stardom with his album The Stranger, which rose

---

[157] The Ed Sullivan Show was originally called "The Toast of the Town, and aired on CBS from 1948 to 1971.

to number two on the pop charts. It had been a struggle getting that far, but he was finally a success.

Was the rest of Billy Joel's career path paved with gold? Hardly. It was riddled with setbacks. During the next few years he sued his former manager (and ex-brother-in-law) for mismanaging his funds, divorced his first wife, suffered a broken wrist in a motorcycle accident, married and divorced his second wife (Christie Brinkley), and had to cancel numerous concerts because of throat ailments. Yet, despite all of his problems, Billy Joel has earned a place in the hearts and minds of millions of fans throughout the world.

Billy's story is remarkable. While many of us will never reach the career heights of Billy Joel, we can learn valuable lessons in how he managed to maneuver through the setbacks and continued to forge his place in history.

His circumstance beyond his control was being raised in an urban social housing environment. This would have left many people perplexed and possibly damaged and unable to find a way out. But Billy took this setback and channeled his anger from his fists to his fingertips. He was also fortunate to have parents who saw his talent and directed him to piano lessons despite their financial restraints. His self created circumstances were the decisions Billy made, his suicide attempt, his choice of manager, the groups he played in, and his choice of wives. Each of us can relate to this story at some level. No one has a perfect upbringing and we all make mistakes. It is what we do with these setbacks that differentiate those who create a career they want from the rest of the pack. That is what this chapter is all about. Helping you understand your setbacks and the steps required to move on. According to Harold Kurshner, the trick is to "concentrate on what you have left and not on what you have lost." Here is another example.

Sister Joan Chittister's Big Disappointment

We have all experienced unreasonable bosses. At some time you may have been given an order to do or not do something that seemed, at the time, completely arbitrary and unreasonable. You may have assumed that a grin-and-bear it attitude was your only option. Nobody knows this better than Joan Chittister.

Joan was born into a Catholic home in Upper New York State. Her father died when she was three and at his funeral her mother told her that the nuns were "special friends of God" and would stay with her father until the angels took him to heaven. Joan was hooked. From that moment her life's direction took hold. She wanted to be a nun. But, at the age of seven, her mother married a Presbyterian who never converted to Catholicism. A story about Joan that was reported by Mark Roth of the Pittsburgh Post-Gazette, described Joan as racing home from school concerned about her stepfather's fate. She needed to talk to her mother.   158

"The nuns told me," Joan said, "Only Catholics go to Heaven."

"What do you think of that?" her mother asked.

"I think it's wrong."

"Why?" her mother asked.

"Because the nuns don't know Daddy," Joan replied.

Joan brought a questioning, and personally focused approach, to her religious beliefs. Even at an early age she was fearless in her approach to her religious beliefs. She wasn't afraid to challenge the Catholic establishment; an attitude that continued for the next seven decades. But; I get ahead of myself. When Joan was 16, she joined the Benedictine Sisters of Erie, Pennsylvania. She arrived on September 8, 1952. On October 15, 1952 she was stricken with polio and spent the next four years in and out of hospitals. It was four years before she could walk unaided.

But Joan's time in the hospital was also time to let her imagination run wild. She kept a diary and wrote notes on everything. Her passion for writing was blooming. Joan felt her gift for storytelling needed to be nurtured. More than anything she wanted to be a serious writer.

"I lived to write," Joan wrote in her book, *Scarred by Struggle, Transformed by Hope*.   159

She wrote and read constantly. When she was released from the hospital, her monastery assigned her to teach in a rural grade school.

---

[158] Mark Roth, "A Life Dedicated to Faith and to Questioning its Policies," *The Pittsburg Post-Gazette*, (June 27, 2005).

[159] Joan D. Chittister, *Scarred by Struggle, Transformed by Hope* (William B. Eerdmans Publishing Company, 2003).

Afterwards, she applied and was accepted to complete her undergraduate degree, and then applied and was accepted at Iowa State University to study for her Master of Fine Arts Degree. Her dream was coming true. Her life of struggle, loss, sickness, and dreams was finally evolving towards that moment when she was to be a writer.

Many of us dream of something we would like to accomplish or where we would like our careers to go. We hope, pray, and learn. We read all the right books and attend all the right lectures and are caught up in the fantasy that we can have anything we want.

However, in Joan's case, and for many of us, dreams are not always meant to be. In her second year, Joan received a phone call from her superior telling her that she was assigned to work in a summer camp as a third cook and needed to leave school: one phone call and her dreams and hopes were smashed. Her superior did not explain the rationale behind her decision. It seemed arbitrary and unfair to Joan but like many of us when faced with a similar predicament she acquiesced and went to the summer camp and became a third cook.

Out of the ashes of disappointment, Joan built a life in her monastery that is remarkable. She has authored 32 best-selling books on spirituality and was Prioress from 1978 to 1990. She became an outspoken advocate of world peace, women's rights and change within the church, while never losing touch with her faith.

But her life was not without struggle. Her stepfather was killed in a car accident in 1971 and her mother died in 1995 after suffering with Alzheimer's disease for 28 years.

Joan writes, When something happens in your life, the question you often ask is 'Why me?' When the real questions are:
What am I supposed to learn from this setback?
How do I grow beyond this?
How do I find meaning in my life after an experience like this?

Joan asks, "Do we worry ourselves into failure?" There is a good argument for this last question. Often, we are so focused on doing the job right we make costly mistakes.

Dr. Debbie Crews, a psychologist from the University of Arizona was intrigued by this phenomenon. [160]

The story goes that she was watching the 1996 Masters Gold tournament and watched professional golfer Greg Norman blow a six-shot lead in the final round. What happened to Norman was simply that he "choked." Choking is a physical phenomenon where the muscles tighten, the breath becomes shallow and overall performance suffers. Choking happens under conditions of extreme stress.

Dr. Crews took this concept one step further and conducted an experiment with 10 amateur golfers. She subjected them to a pressure sensitive exercise. On a flat green each golfer was asked to complete 20, 2.5 meter putts. Then, these same golfers were asked to hit 20 more, only this time they were told that they would be filmed for a current affairs program and they would be on national television. They were also told that if they managed to beat their initial score, they would receive a prize of $300.00, but if they did worse than the first round they would owe Debbie $100. The pressure was on. They went to the green and putted. Five golfers did better in the second round. Tests showed that in these players the brain activity between the left and right sides of their brain was evenly distributed. The left side is referred to as the analytical and the right the creative. Those who did worse discovered that the left side was doing most of the work. When the left side of the brain is dominant, it causes you to ask questions like, "What am I doing? Am I going to look like a jerk when my friends see me on TV? Am I going to choke?"

You may be doing the same thing when the voice in your head says, "I could never do this," or "They are probably waiting for me to screw up," or "Who are they kidding? I can't do that." It's easy to talk yourself into what psychologists have called a "self-fulfilling prophesy," when you choke and limit your chances of success. [161]

A lot that happens to us is directly related to what we do when a setback occurs. Our reactions can work for or against us. Further, our response doesn't seem to have any relevance to the severity of the setback. You can lose your job, end your marriage, or experience the death of a loved one. But, what if you experienced all of them at once?

---

[160] Debbie Crews, "Golf Brain", www.abc.net.au/science/features/golg/. Also visit, archives.cbc.ca.

[161] The term Self Fulfilling Prophesy was coined by sociologist Robert K Merton in his book, *Social Theory and Social Change*, (Free Press, 1968).

We all agree that that kind of catastrophic event would have a major impact on our lives and our ability to go on. There are, of course, countless stories of acts of terrorism, wars, famine, and disease that affect people's lives. In recent times, one of the deadliest acts of nature was Hurricane Katrina. As a result of the hurricane, more than a half a million people were evacuated from the New Orleans area. There were 1836 confirmed deaths. It was the worst natural disaster in the United States in seven decades and the most costly in American history.

Ronald C. Kessler, a professor of health care at Harvard University Medical School and an expert in survey design and epidemiology, along with a group of colleagues, conducted a study of the Katrina survivors. [162]

Kessler and his colleagues studied 1,043 Katrina survivors to track the speed and effectiveness of hurricane recovery efforts. Kessler used the K6 scale, which is the most widely used screening scale in the United States. It looks specifically for mood disorders. Kessler compared the post-Katrina responses to another study of New Orleans residents' responses prior to Katrina. What Kessler found was a "significantly higher prevalence of serious mental illness than respondents to the earlier survey."

Among those in this higher level of mental illness, he found that 8.4 percent had a prevalence of "suicidal ideation," that is, they had serious thoughts about, or had attempted, to take their own life. With the added stress of Katrina, we might assume that this number would rise.

But, Kessler found that the statistics proved the opposite. The suicide ideation dropped to .7 percent. What caused this remarkable change in thoughts were two factors: "Faith in one's ability to rebuild their lives and realization of one's inner strength." What motivated these post-Katrina survivors and formed the backbone of their resilience can be quantified as follows:
   81.6 percent became closer to their loved ones
   95.6 percent developed faith in their ability to rebuild their lives
   66.8 percent became more spiritual
   75.2 percent found a deeper meaning to their lives
   69.5 percent discovered their inner strength

---

[162] Ronald C. Kessler, *Mental Illness and Suicidality after Hurricane Katrina* in the *Journal of the World Health Organization*, (2006).

Why some people bounce back after they experience one of life's setbacks and others fold under the pressure of change seems to be directly related to how well they have developed their beliefs. This, in turn, leads to the conclusion held by experts that resilience is a learned trait. The question that needs to be addressed is whether you have to wait until disaster strikes before you can find resilience or can you start to develop those characteristics now?

When Barry graduated from university he found himself working in the residential construction business. One person in the company who made a lasting impression was Arthur Zimet, the vice president of construction. Here was a man who was responsible for overseeing the construction of 1,000 homes per year. He didn't fit into the mold of other vice presidents I met. He drove a Checker automobile, which you see all though North America as the taxi of choice. He cut a dashing figure, well dressed but not stuffy, and wore his Stetson hat with panache. He never stood in one place for long. His office was covered in boards reclaimed from old farm barns. When you entered his "den" you felt the power that this man exuded.

Barry got to know him through my work, and while his praises were rare, the recipients revered them. Barry recalled a small hand-written note complimenting him on a report that he had completed. The note was three words in length, "Nice job, Barry," but to Barry it was the equivalent to winning an Academy Award. He pinned it to his bulletin board, and while he was working on new reports, he often glanced up and was motivated by that note.

In 1971, he set out to build his own construction empire. He recruited Barry, who joined his firm as office manager. Within three years Barry was vice president of administration and finance, and they were building high- and low-rise condominiums across the country.

Things were good. The market was strong and we felt invincible. Arthur had a personal net worth in the millions (when millions really meant something). But the market turned. Interest rates were climbing and sales of new homes plummeted. Barry watched his boss grow weary under the constant strain and worry of losing all that he had built. The bank eventually closed his business. Barry knew that no matter what life threw in the man's path he would survive.

The next time we heard from him, he had become a partner in a development project in Arizona. A few years later, with a new fortune intact, he was back in the saddle of wealth, power, and comfort. His survivor quality is, in my opinion, what helped him stand out in the crowd. Survivors are resilient. It was his resilience that brought him from the brink, not once, but many times throughout his career. Our best guess is that the one overwhelming characteristic he possessed was his faith in his ability to rebuild his life — one of the five resilience characteristics identified by professor Kessler.

Resilience is so important that we do it an injustice when we describe it in clichés such as "keep a stiff upper lip," "pull yourself up by your bootstraps," "tough it out" or "grin and bear it." Some writers have said that resilience is what differentiates those who lead successful careers from those who don't. That's hardly a cliché. [163]

Three characteristics of resilience

Diane Coutu, a senior editor at *Harvard Business Review*, in her article, *How Resilience Works,* identifies three traits of resilience: See the world as it really is; find meaning; and, be ingenious. [164]

Let's look at all three and how they relate to your career decisions.

1. See the world as it really is

A Japanese fairytale, "The House of a Thousand Mirrors,"[165] says it all. The story goes like this. A long time ago in a small village there was a place known as the House of a Thousand Mirrors. In this village lived a puppy. He was frisky, adventuresome, and secure in a loving home. Overall, he was pretty happy. The puppy heard of the House of a Thousand Mirrors and decided it was a place he wanted to explore.

He rushed quickly to the front door of this house, bounded in, and to his surprise, found that the house was filled with a thousand happy puppies just like him. When the puppy smiled, the thousand puppies smiled back. When the puppy wagged his tail, the thousand responded by wagging their tails. "What a great house this is!" the puppy thought. When he left, he promised himself he'd return to this house soon.

In the same village there was another puppy. Only this puppy wasn't quite as happy as the first. He had a tough life. Abandoned at an early age, he had been forced to survive by begging food from strangers. He slept in an alleyway and at night he shivered in the cold. This second

---

[163] David Jenson, Developing Resilience, Science Careers.org, Nov, 2005.
[164] Diane Coutu, *How Resilience Works, Harvard Business Review,* (May 2002), Volume 80, Issue 5.
[165] "House of a Thousand Mirrors," http://forum.erraticwisdom.com.

puppy also heard of the House of a Thousand Mirrors and decided it was a place he should explore. When he entered he was faced with a thousand puppies that were sad and lonely. He left quickly saying, "This is a terrible place! I'll never go there again."

We are often like one of these two puppies. We see our world through distorted eyes. The world becomes a reflection of our circumstances. Yet reality is in a constant state of fuzziness. It's becomes difficult to tell what is real and what is not. Reality television is an example. We watch programs like Survivor, The Apprentice, and The Great Race. We see people faced with difficult situations, who attempt to overcome them and we think it's real. It is not.

All the situations are staged to minimize any harm coming to the contestants, thereby avoiding a flock of civil law suits. Reality television creates the illusion that perhaps you can eat a jar of bugs or jump off a cliff and be all right. After all, if seemingly ordinary people can become the new American Idol, it's easy to believe that maybe you can too since you think you sound pretty good singing in the shower.

We also misinterpret reality every time we see an advertisement for a product, watch a movie, read the newspaper, or watch a political debate. Someone is touting an agenda. Most North Americans get their daily dose of news from television. We watch CNN to see earth-shattering events that are happening, in real time. Is this reality?

It gets blurred so easily because we tend to mix up all the perceptions that stimulate us. What is the real difference between watching a bomb go off in Baghdad and watching a bomb ignite in a Bruce Willis film? It's hard to tell. Millions of people think reality is what American Idol's Simon Cowell dishes out when he tells hopefuls they either have or don't have what it takes to follow their dream.

Ever since we first contemplated if a tree falling in a forest when nobody is there to hear it makes a sound, the issue of reality has been discussed ad nauseam from philosophers to scientists. And yet, no one has been able to nail reality on the head and say, unequivocally what reality is. Albert Einstein said, "Reality is an illusion, albeit a very persistent one." [166]

Dead pan comic Steven Wright's quip on this age-old question is, "If you tell a joke in a forest and nobody laughs, was it a joke?"

---

[166] Einstein, "See The Nature of Reality: Three Positions," www.chemistrycoach.com.

If the definition of reality is difficult to grasp, then acknowledging the reality of a complex situation is often impossible. We often lull ourselves into a false sense of security because of a tendency to focus on good experiences rather than bad. It is a human tendency to want to move ourselves towards pleasure and away from pain. A study conducted by Daniel Schacter, professor of Psychology at Harvard University, may answer the question; Is our natural tendency leading us in the wrong direction? [167]

Schacter recruited 76 men and women ranging in age from 18 to 35 to compare the phenomena of emotions and memory. They were sports fans with no history of psychiatric or nervous disorders. Some had strong feelings about the New York Yankees and some had similar feelings about the Boston Red Socks. The 76 fans filled out a questionnaire within six days of the last game in the American League Playoff series in October of 2004 (the Boston Red Socks beat the New York Yankees) and then again 23 and 27 weeks later. Emotions and vividness of memory were rated on a scale from one to seven. Lower numbers indicated negative feelings and higher numbers positive. The survey showed that the Red Socks fans gave their memory ratings of 5.5 or higher while the Yankees fans memory ratings were 2.5 or lower.

Schacter went one step further and checked if recall had to do with personal or event details. Personal details would include such things as what the person was wearing or how many beers he or she consumed. Event details related to specific players and their performance on the field. Studying both the happy and unhappy fans revealed they remembered an equal number of personal details; however, the Yankee fans recalled more event-related details than did the Red Sox fans. So, it seems that if you want more accurate details on what is real and what is not, you will have to rid your memory of negative things. That's often impossible to achieve. We are, in fact, a combination of both positive and negative experiences. That's what makes us human. One good case in case in point is Kimiko Soldati.

Kimiko Hirai Soldati's Story

The Aquatic Times[168] magazine described Kimiko as "... one of the most elegant and electrifying platform and springboard divers in the world." She is a United States national champion on the 3-meter

---

[167] Daniel Schacter, "Bad Times Make for More Accurate Memories," *Harvard University Gazette*, (May 11, 2006).
[168] "Aquatic Times, 2004". http://www.aquatictimes.com/atfeature.html.

springboard, the 10-meter platform, and in synchronized diving. She has been honored with both "Female Athlete of the Year" and the United States "Diver of the Year" award. She was also Valedictorian for her graduating class at Indiana University. But this over-achiever's story wasn't always filled with fame, glory, and accomplishment. Her story is filled with failure and disappointment, and yet she was able to deal with life and face reality in her own unique way.

Her story really started in 1941 after the bombing of Pearl Harbor. Kimiko's grandmother, Mae, and her husband were born in the United States. Like many other Japanese-Americans after the bombing, they were unceremoniously uprooted, told to sell all their possessions and sent to an internment camp for no other reason than their Japanese heritage. Mae was quoted in an article published on MSNBC by the Associated Press as saying, "They were allowed to take the clothes they could carry and nothing else." Mae's husband was allowed to work at a local sawmill earning $16 per month, but the rest of the family lived behind a fence. During this time, their son Gary was born.

Gary grew up in Idaho and described his life as "typical American." But there were obviously some scars from the family experience. In college, he wrote a paper about America's policy towards Japanese-American citizens. He was clearly disturbed by what had happened to his family and this was a way to share his story.

After college, Gary married Judy and had two children: a son named Chris and a daughter, Kimberley Mae. Kimberley (Kimiko) was a natural athlete and her first love was gymnastics. She came to athletics honestly. Gary played college football and her grandfather played semi-pro football. She loved gymnastics, but a series of knee surgeries short-circuited her plans to continue with the sport. Gary encouraged her to try diving. He recognized her strong physical attributes and encouraged her towards a sport that she could do.

At first Kimiko was lukewarm to the idea, but as time went on, diving became a passion. Kimiko's "just make do" attitude towards life helped her make the transition from gymnastics. Kimiko remembered her grandparents' stories about leaving everything behind and being forced into an internment camp during World War Two.

They sold the family car for $200 and they had to leave in such a hurry that her grandmother remembers leaving the doilies under cups on her dining room table. And yet this uprooted family, with no physical assets, had each other. Had they been unforgiving and bitter about their experience, they might have left a scar deep in their family's collective hearts. But, they never felt victimized. Instead, they developed a community in the camp and made do. Kimiko attributes her strong heart and willingness to accept reality and continue trying, to her upbringing.

Diving became a passion, but not without a price. Shoulder injuries requiring four surgeries and two knee operations plagued this aspiring Olympic hopeful. During her teenage years, her mother died of breast cancer at the age of 43. To this day, when Kimiko competes she wears her mother's wedding ring as a reminder of her mom's strength.

Kimiko's shoulder and knee problems persisted, and in 1994, what started as an eating problem became bulimia. "I felt that I went from the penthouse to the doghouse," Kimiko recalls facing one obstacle after another. But she faces each new obstacle as fuel that will propel her towards her goals. The average person suffering from bulimia takes four-and-a-half years to seek help. "After two years, I knew I had a problem and sought help," Kimiko said.

"But," I asked her, "How did you know your dream was real and achievable?" "It was a deep down burning desire that was never going to go away," she said. Many people counseled her to quit because of the struggle — both physically and emotionally—but her desire to reach her maximum potential prevailed. She always knew that she "wasn't going down without a fight." She readily admits that she didn't know if she could achieve her dream, but she had to give it her "best shot."

Then, she discovered her spirituality and once embraced, Kimiko saw the connection between spirituality and diving. Both were interwoven, and because of her faith, she realized that diving wasn't just about her anymore. She was gifted, but there was more to diving. She learned to trust in an ultimate plan. "If it doesn't happen, it doesn't happen and that's okay," she said.

Now, Komiko is retired from the world of competitive diving and has channeled her talents into the Purdue University diving team where she and her husband are coaches. She has a son and her days are filled. "I used to think God made me to be a diver," Kimiko said. "Now I know he made me to be a mom."

Like Kimiko, facing the truth means understanding who you are and what each situation means in your life. How does it affect what you stand for? How will it affect your family? How do you think it will affect your career? At the end of the day, that's probably the only truth that matters. But Kimiko's story teaches us something else. Not only did she have the ability to face up to her truths along the way, she discovered the second ingredient to resilience — meaning.

2. Find meaning

Viktor Frankl identified three sources for meaning in one's life: work, love, and courage. [169]

Frankl went on to write that even when forces beyond your control take away everything, there is always one thing left — your freedom to choose how you will respond to the situation.

Viktor Frankl's Story

Viktor was born in 1905 in Vienna. At the age of three he declared that he would become a physician. As a teenager, Viktor's thoughts turned to philosophy and psychology. At age 16, under the tutelage of Sigmund Freud, he published his first professional manuscript in the prestigious International Journal of Psychoanalysis.

That same year, while attending adult education classes, he was invited to give a lecture on the meaning of life. His belief that humans must assume responsibility for their existence became the cornerstone of his life's work. It was no wonder that as a teenager he decided to focus his vocational aspirations on psychiatry. He had a gift and was encouraged by friends and teachers to use it to help others.

Viktor founded Vienna's first private youth counseling program where he had secured his first counseling job. From 1930 to 1937 he worked as a psychiatrist for the University Clinic in Vienna caring for suicidal patients. By 1939 he was head of the department of neurology at the Rothschild Hospital—the only Jewish hospital in Vienna.

When the National Socialist government closed the hospital in 1940, Viktor knew he was at risk of being arrested and deported to a NAZI concentration camp. In 1942, Viktor applied for, and received, a U.S. immigration visa which would allow him to escape from Austria to the United States. Emigration meant that he could build a new life in a new country. Professionally, it would give him the freedom to finish the book he was writing on "Logotherapy." [170]

---

[169] Viktor E. Frankl, *Man's Search for Meaning* (Beacon Press, 2006).
[170] Logo is from the Greek word for "meaning." Logotherapy was Victor's thesis, which focused on the curing of patients by leading them back to the meaning of their lives.

Yet, Viktor chose to let his visa lapse and remained in Austria to care for his aging parents.

Victor was born with a positive environment (circumstances beyond his control). It was his self-created circumstances that led to his arrest and incarceration in the next three years at four concentration camps — Theresienstadt, Auschwitz-Birkenau, Kaufering, and Türkheim.

He was starved, beaten, forced to witness countless atrocities, and was under the threat of death. He lived day to day in conditions reminiscent of the horror felt by millions in Germany and by many others who have experienced atrocities in such countries as the former Yugoslavia, Cambodia, Chile, Argentina, Uruguay, Rwanda, and Sierra Leone.

Miraculously, Victor survived his ordeal. The guards confiscated a manuscript he was working on so, he found scraps of paper and scribbled bits and pieces of information so that someday he could rewrite his book. He helped fellow prisoners and was able to see his logotherapy in action. He noted that the prisoners, who were able to reframe their suffering and find personal meaning in their predicament, had a greater change of survival. Once a prisoner lost meaning, he or she was dead within a couple of days.

After the war, Victor wrote *Man's Search for Meaning*, which recounted his time in the concentration camps. His moving and honest account transformed this small book into a non-fiction classic that has passed the 12 million mark in international sales.

In his book, Frankl quotes from a two-year survey of nearly 8,000 students from 48 colleges conducted by scientists at John's Hopkins University and sponsored by the National Institute of National Health. The report stated that when these students were asked what was "very important" to them in their careers, 16 percent said it was the amount of money they made while 78 percent said it was "finding purpose and meaning in life."

While most of us will never know the horrors of such an extreme situation as a concentration camp, many of us feel trapped in our self-imposed employment prisons. Getting through the experience, as Frankl discovered, in even the most extreme situations and finding meaning in a difficult experience is the crucial common denominator to survival and moving on.

3. Be ingenious

Being ingenious, for most of us, means looking at things with clear eyes to see what is often lying right before us. Nineteenth century philosopher Bernard Baruch wrote, "Millions saw the apple fall but Newton asked why." [171]

We have heard over and over again from our POAs that their choice was based on knowing that what they were doing was right. A feeling in their gut drove their decisions. This feeling that we have all experienced at one time or another is also called intuition.

Our next POA is a good example of someone who followed the three steps we've discussed to find her resilience. She faced her reality, found meaning, and used her ingenuity to take her career in a new direction.

Remember your mother telling you to eat all your vegetables because there were children starving somewhere in the world? Many of us have heard that message. Messages from parents have three effects.

They are quickly forgotten.

They remain in our consciousness and haunt us throughout our lives.

We recall these messages at a moment of personal epiphany and realize there was real truth to the message.

Peggi Pelosi-Gardiner's experience falls under the third effect of parental messages, and her epiphany changed her career in a direction she never thought possible.

Peggi Pelosi-Gardiner's Story

Peggi was the only girl among five siblings. Her parents led a typical "Christian lifestyle." They worked hard, went to church on Sunday, and took care of their family. She attended the University of Guelph in Canada and studied genetics. Peggi married young, and by

---

[171] Bernard Baruch, (1870 – 1965), US financier, statesman and advisor to Presidents Wilson and Roosevelt.

the time she was 28, she was a stay-at-home mom to five boys, all born within six years. She became interested in a company called Discovery Toys which produced high quality toys that Peggi bought for her children. She was intrigued with their business model.

Discovery Toys sold their products through direct sales networks. Because she lived in Canada, Peggi did not have ready access to Discovery Toys for her boys, so she approached the company and asked to be their representative in Toronto. She was turned down because doing business in Canada was not yet on Discovery Toy's radar. Frustrated by their decision, Peggi decided to create her own company manufacturing high quality toys. Her plan was to model the sales techniques used by Discovery Toys.

With a partner, she began like most entrepreneurs, working out of the basement, then the garage, and finally moving into rented warehouses and so on. Within three years the company was selling $3 million dollars of toys per year. Peggi had a natural knack for sales and business was good. Her husband, seeing her success, suggested they switch roles. He became the stay-at-home dad while she became the breadwinner. Peggi and her five sons were a great media story and the constant attention helped stimulate her company's growth.

The toy business is exceptionally seasonal. Eighty percent of sales are made during the last 10 weeks of the year. In 1998, Peggi had over a million dollars worth of inventory in her warehouse when the world discovered Nintendo. Nintendo became the toy of choice among Christmas shoppers, which left many companies like Peggi's with huge amounts of unsold inventory. Out of sheer desperation, Peggi ended up selling her inventory and company for 10 cents on the dollar. She was 37 years old and had gone from full-time mom to a small business to a big business to no business within a decade.

Peggi didn't let this setback stop her. She went into what she calls her "survival mode." She took jobs doing contract sales with large companies looking to supplement their sales force. "I became a student of people," Peggi said. She loved the interaction she had with customers and sought out places to learn more. She took courses from Dale Carnegie, Tony Robbins, and anyone else she thought had something to help her develop her skills. Her life changed again as her marriage ended, and she was now a single mom with five sons. In 2004, Usana Health Services, a manufacturer of high-end nutritional products, approached her to sell their products in Canada.

Within one year, she was invited to join their management committee as the general manager of sales, which meant moving her family to Salt Lake City, Utah. When she joined the company, Usana had plateaued. The company, with annual sales of $120 million per year, had stalled.

Now Peggi was sitting on a management committee, which reported to a board of directors. For the first time in her life she was outside her comfort zone. But, she stuck with it. While the committee looked at new products, new processes, and new markets to grow their company, Peggi was struck by the vision of 400 people who came to work everyday and were not happy. It seemed to her that they were just coming to work for the paycheck. So Peggi did what she always did — she trusted her instincts. Rather than simply focusing on the top and bottom financial line she looked elsewhere. The company had quietly been involved in some corporate giving programs, but it had nothing to do with the employees.

Peggi's company was in the nutritional business so she asked her committee if there wasn't something they could do to get involved with bringing nutrition to people in need who couldn't afford Usana Health Services' products. When she was a child her mother said, "Eat all your peas; children are starving in Africa." It made no sense. Where was Africa? Who were these starving children? The concept of starvation is unimaginable to a child in a society where fresh milk is as close as the corner store. Peggi believes that most people want to help, but often fall into the "Someday I'll" syndrome. Someday I'll help. Someday I'll give my time. Someday I'll volunteer. Many people, according to Peggi, want to help and yet, most don't.

Her act of ingenuity was to create an environment at Usana Health Services where people could work for more than a paycheck. She gave them a way to get off the "Someday I'll" treadmill and do something. She developed an inspirational workplace where everyone wins: the employees feel good about how they are spending their working lives; the company is growing; the customers take pride in purchasing the product; and the world is a better place.

How did she do it? Peggi wanted to partner with an organization that could help her accomplish her altruistic goals. She found such a partner in the Children's Hunger Fund in Los Angeles. [172]

---

[172] To learn more about the Children's Hunger Fund visit www.childrenshungerfund.org.

The Children's Hunger Fund provides "solutions and sustainability for people in the developing world." She took on the world and offered to the company, the employees, customers, and shareholders an opportunity to get involved. They could provide cash and/or products to help people who desperately needed it.

Each year Peggi and her CEO would travel to one orphanage that was receiving help from The Children's Hunger Fund. They would videotape the experience and share it with their stakeholders. Whenever they have any sort of corporate event, the CEO of the Children's Hunger Fund attends and makes a presentation. The stakeholders shifted their focus from improving their bottom line to helping rid the world of pain and suffering. How did it affect their bottom line? During the next two years the company's sales doubled, while share prices rose from $1 to $70.

"It just made sense," Peggi admits, as she looks back with the advantage of hindsight. Did she think that by becoming a sharing company her sales would double? Not at all. She had simply thought it was a chance to change focus and to give people a reason to help grow the company in a new direction.

In 2006, she was organizing a trip to Uganda to visit an orphanage when she had an inspiration. She called each of her sons and offered to bring them along. They jumped at the opportunity. While in Uganda, Peggi had an epiphany. Her mother's words finally struck home: "Children are starving in Africa." Peggi said to herself, "This is what I want to do with my life. This is what I am here to accomplish." I want to help companies feed children as Usana has done.

At the time of our meeting Peggi was about to release her new book, *Corporate Karma*. [173]

She was busy planning speaking engagements and had hired an assistant. Her career went from full-time mother of five to mother to thousands of undernourished orphans. Peggi faced reality, found meaning, and used her ingenuity to do her job at Usana and ultimately take her in a new career direction.

Peggi relied on her instincts to develop a solution for Usana Health Services. Intuition is something familiar to all of us. The problem is

---

[173] Peggi Pelosi-Gardiner, *Corporate Karma*, (Orenda Publishing, 2007).

that some of us listen to intuition's voice and some don't. I remember heated discussions with medical professionals about the presence of a higher source influencing their actions. Some would admit to listening to this higher source while others said, "We are scientists and need proof. No proof, no action."

But recent studies and much discussion have seen a sharp change in attitude. These professionals now readily admit to using their instincts to assess and treat a problem. Common sense might dictate that this intuition is really the result of years of experience in all sorts of situations, which gives the professional a warehouse filled with examples from which to draw. We have heard that some of our POAs knew an answer or felt that they had found their direction. But where does this insight come from and can we quantify and describe it so all of us can better tap into our intuitive abilities?

In 2007, Professors Lisa Ruth-Sahd and Elizabeth Tisdell published a study in the *Adult Educators Quarterly*, *"The Meaning and Use of Intuition in Novice Nurses: A Phenomenological Study."* [174]

Here, they studied 16 novice nurses who claimed a predilection to intuition that they used in their everyday work with patients in addition to skills they had learned, observed, and experienced. Using novice nurses for the study added credibility since they lacked a depth of experience from which to make decisions. The authors postulated that it's easier to isolate "pure" intuition without the layers of experience that might appear to be intuitive action.

While the study concluded that the nurses all showed intuition when dealing with patients, the truly interesting question is, "Where did their intuition come from?" As a result of extensive interviews, the researchers concluded that intuition was influenced by prior life or work experience, a result of greater meaning in their lives, and directly lived experience. Let's look at each.

Prior experience refers to experience that went beyond the nurses' traditional medical work in which they deal with life-and-death situations on a daily basis. The participants also spoke about life

---

[174] Lisa A. Ruth-Sahd and Elizabeth J. Tisdell, *The Meaning and Use of Intuition in Novice Nurses:* A Phenomenological Study, *Adult Education Quarterly*, (Feb. 2007), Volume 57, Number 2.

experiences, work experiences, and the presence of mentors. Often there is a mental disconnect between work and play. We tend to compartmentalize these experiences, but this is a fallacy. All of our experiences make us who we are. We cannot say to ourselves, "That happened to me on a personal level; therefore, it has nothing to do with my work."

Barry recalls: My relationship with my maternal grandmother is a good example. In her mid-70s she suffered a massive stroke. I was in my early 20s at the time. She lost control of the right side of her body and her speech. All she could mutter were a few seemingly unrelated words. I'd visit her often, hold her hand and look into her eyes. A doctor told me, "Don't pay much attention to her reactions; her mind is gone." I was told that no matter what I said, she couldn't understand me. But I looked into her eyes and knew the doctor was wrong.

On the day I was married I went to her bedside, dressed in my rented tuxedo. I walked into her room and her face lit up. She held my hand, and at that time, I knew that she knew. No doctor, no matter how authoritative, could convince me otherwise. This story seems so strange now because the attitude of the medical community has changed so drastically. They encourage the families of victims of stroke, coma, or other debilitating brain diseases, to talk to patients, tell them stories, even sing to them and hold their hands. While medical science cannot say for certain whether the patient is aware of these attentions, they intuitively believe that they are cognizant. Nine of the 16 novice nurses reported that previous experiences added to their awareness of their own intuitiveness.

The second aspect in looking at intuition in this study was the role of meaning in the nurses' lives. Seven of the 16 subjects reported using visual metaphors when connecting their intuitiveness to an "inner wisdom or spirituality." Several others used songs, poems, or scenes to make the connection. Many of us do this unconsciously. We hear a song and play it over and over again, perhaps because it has a catchy tune, or the words resonate deep within us, or rekindle a moment in time. Each time we hear the song it reminds us of who we really are. Couples do this all the time. They often have what they call "our song," which can bring back the memories of their courting days when their love was young and fresh. Often, the lyrics and melody can trigger feelings they may have thought they had forgotten.

We all have ways of connecting to meaning. Just as Victor Frankl did in a concentration camp, we can use these connections to help us build the life and career we want. These connections are always there.

It is up to each one of us to find what works for us. For me it is music. When I am feeling overwhelmed or anxious about a project, I sit back and listen to Neil Diamond. His voice and words center me and somehow remind me that there is meaning in what I am trying to do. That's what we all need to be reminded of.

I needed to remind myself of this connection when I first began this book. I assumed that getting people to share their personal stories would be easy. After all, I was offering them their 15 minutes of fame. But when I began, three out of four people I approached turned me down. The harder I pushed for new profiles, the tougher it got. So, rather than spending a lot of time searching, I closed the door and listened to music. I reminded myself that the best things in my life found me, not the other way around.

With that reminder I relaxed and let my POAs discover me. And they did. Each time I come in contact with some new interesting person with a strong story to tell, I know that it is a result of the synchronicity in the planet. You can do this in your job too. Use your newfound proactivity to bring the world to your doorstep. This may sound like your proactivity is passive when you let things find you. What I have found is that sometimes that's just what's needed. Deciding when and when not to act are all part of the same process. Both are deeply rooted in proactivity.

The third area identified in this study focused on the dimensions of time, space, and touch. For instance, sometimes your interaction through real-life experiences is through your senses as opposed to an academic, intellectual approach. The nurses did not do their work by reading files and medical histories alone. They stood at the end of the patient's bed. They combed the patient's hair, or held their hand, or just sat for a moment, in the presence of their sleeping patient, and watched.

These three areas—prior experience, meaning, and directly lived experience—lead to an intuitive understanding of reality. Think how different your decision making would be if you tuned into your intuition and ingenuity. Peggi Pelosi-Gardiner did it when she went into the field and actually experienced the children she was helping. She couldn't bring her Usana's employees to Africa, so she did the next best thing—she brought Africa to them. Peggi is a good example of a POA who used her intuition to fuel her ingenuity. Are you looking for your own ingenuity? Perhaps it's fast asleep within your intuition. If you have been ignoring your intuition too long, give it a shake and wake it up.

Lessons Learned

- Face reality
- Find Meaning
- Be ingenious

There are two types of setbacks: Circumstances Beyond our Control and Self-Created Circumstances. POAs possess a learned skill that keeps them coming back; it's called resistance.

We saw how Billy Joel and Joan Chittister were able to overcome their setbacks and carve out careers in their respective fields.

We met Kimiko Soldati who taught us the importance of facing reality, which often roots itself deep within the gut.

Viktor Frankl took a lifetime of work and gave it the ultimate "field test" as he learned, firsthand, that even in the most horrific circumstances, people with meaning in their lives have a greater ability to survive than those who don't.

And we met Peggi Pelosi-Gardiner who used her ingenuity to develop a win-win solution that benefited her company, its stakeholders, and thousands of orphans whom she will probably never meet in person.

These are powerful lessons and the sum total of all these experiences leads us to the one skill that we can all learn — resilience.

Harold Kushner writes that there are five elements to a complete life: families, friends, faith, work, and the satisfaction of knowing you are making a difference. Perhaps through resilience you can have everything. [175]

Lessons into Action: Your Career Action Plan

Step 1: Face reality

a. On a piece of paper, or in your personal journal, describe a sales setback you are now facing in as much detail as possible. Describe all the incidents that led up to the setback. Ensure that your description answers the following questions:

---

[175] Harold Kushner, *Overcoming Life's Disappointments* (Alfred A. Knopf, 2006).

What are the salient facts? (Pretend you are an investigator looking for evidence. List only those things that are facts—no guessing. If your description is filled with blame and recrimination you are on the wrong track. At this point just take a cold, impartial look at the evidence that you know for sure.)

How do you feel about the setback? (Are you disappointed, angry, upset, sad, frustrated, etc.?) What do you want to happen? (Here's where some soul-searching is necessary. By stating an outcome, you are on the road to resilience. Be careful of wanting to throw in the towel and quit too soon. If anything were possible, what would you like to see happen?

b. In Part A of this exercise you dealt with evidence, but there is a difference between truth and reality. Truth emerges when two detectives are searching a crime scene, each with the responsibility of unearthing clues. Reality goes to the heart of these truths and takes us one step closer to meaning. Take some time with this and answer the question, "What possibilities do these clues hold for me?" It's what psychologist Rollo May calls a "pattern of potentiality." [176]

We saw how Soldati found her reality buried deep in her gut. The evidence said one thing and her gut another. What does your gut say?

c. Now state your intention. You know the truth and you have learned the possibilities. Now it's time to become a POA and finish this statement, "I will make the following changes..." There is strength in stating your intention. Once you verbalize what you are prepared to change, your whole being is reprogrammed in a new direction. This may not happen quickly, but you have taken the first step and there is no turning back.

d. Look again at your possibilities and ask yourself, "Does my intention validate what I believe about myself?" You are the sum of all your experiences. If you were valuable before you encountered the setback, you are still valuable no matter what anyone says. Everyone suffers setbacks and what you will come to realize is that it's how you handle them that defines who you are. The way to a truly happy career is to love what you are doing and not how well other people say you are doing it. Your sales career is your reality.

---

[176] Tracey Marks, *The Meaning of Life*, Tufts University, (spring, 1972), www.geocities.com. Rollo May, *The Discovery of Being*, (W.W.Norton, 1983).

Step 2: Find meaning

a. Each of us has something that makes our journey worthwhile and important. It can be a sense of worth, a need for mastery, a belief in a higher power, or a commitment to family. Meaning is individual to each of us.

A close examination of your life will point you in the direction of what's most important to you. Take some time with this and articulate why you do what you do. Go beyond simply saying, "I have to earn money to eat." There's more to life than that.

Now develop a conscious relationship with your meaning and complete the following sentence. "I do what I do because..."

For instance, you could complete the sentence by writing, "I want to be a role model for my kids" or, "it's what I believe."

Now it's time to commit to your meaning. Answer the following as either yes or no:

I am willing to go through certain things that are not consistent with my meaning.   Yes ☐   No ☐

I'm willing to accept who I am as I've defined myself. Yes ☐   No ☐

I am willing to accept this is who I am and it's what I am all about.
     Yes ☐   No ☐

If you said "yes" to these statements, you have taken a huge step towards building your resilience. If you said "no" to any of these statements, it may be an indication that you have not accepted the reality you stated in step one. Go back and ask yourself "Why?" See if you can find what is in your way. Not being able to commit is, in itself, a setback. You need to work through it or resilience is nothing more than an illusion.

Step 3: Be ingenious

When you face your reality and know it's meaning, you will feel safe and comfortable with yourself. It is like the feeling you get when you are home after a long day of struggle. It's your home. You know who you are and what you can do. You know what you can change and what you can't.

Ingenuity is all about making changes that will move you closer to home. Ingenuity does not require the IQ of Einstein, but rather the good sense to undertake change that adds meaning to your life and career.

Look back at the situation you outlined at the beginning of this exercise and make a list of those things you have some control over that you would like to change. Next to each item, list the possible actions you can take. On a scale from one to five with five being the highest probability of success and one being the least, state the solution's ability to move you closer to home which is a place where you feel comfortable. Often resilience, when pointed in the right direction, will reveal truths in time that you are not able to see immediately.

Things you have control over and want to change	Possible action you can take.	Probability of Success (1-5)

Now make a commitment to yourself to do what you have said you will do. Complete the following chart.

Change	Priority	Implementation Date

Congratulations, you are now on the road to resilience. By repeating these steps each time you face a setback, you will find, that eventually, they become automatic and that's when you can say, "I am a Person of Action."

One last review before we look at a final step. You have learned how to overcome the helplessness. You saw how you can develop your courage and persistence, and learned how to spot or create opportunities to bring more happiness into your sales career.

You have also learned the importance of developing resilience to overcome the setbacks you are sure to encounter. In the next and last chapter we will take one final step which is finding a way to activate all that you have learned to make sure it fits with your values and sales career plans. We will take this final stage by looking at all you have learned from the inside out.

7
Turn Your Proactivity Inside Out

"Think not of yourself as the architect of your career but as a sculptor. Expect to have to do a lot of hard hammering and chiseling and scraping and polishing."
B.C. Forbes [177]

Sometimes we find ourselves in work situations that are, in part, unpalatable. Consider the surgeon who wants to do everything possible to help his patients, but must grapples with inefficiencies in the health care system. Think about the accountant who witnesses evidence of corporate greed or the pilot who is focused on safety, but realizes the inefficiencies in the air traffic control network or the soldier defending his country, while politicians debate the morality of his actions.

Think about the customers and clients you have to smile at while not really liking these people. The problem is that no matter how much we may object to the difficulties within our chosen field, few of us are willing to topple the status quo to take action.

There are always the whistle blowers and vocal career mavericks, but they're often viewed as nothing more than troublemakers. speaking out or taking action can be career suicide. So what do we do? Most of us either resign ourselves to the reality of our situation or we leave.

There is a third option that we have already explored in depth: being proactive. So far, we have learned about 35 persons of action (POAs) who took an intelligent approach and made a difference. In this chapter you will meet a few more who overcame a sense of helplessness, found courage, developed persistence, balanced risk and opportunity, pursued happiness, and became strong and resilient. Now it's time for you to take the lessons you have learned and put them to work.

I believe in that old adage, "If you work hard and focus on your strengths, you can have the career you want." I'm living proof. Years ago I acquired the "teaching bug" while I was at university. I taught

---

[177] B.C. Forbes, (1880 – 1954), Scottish financial journalist and founder of *Forbes Magazine*.

English at night school to new immigrants. The instant satisfaction I felt after giving a good class was unbeatable. After I graduated, I put my teaching on the back shelf and went in a different direction. Years later the desire to teach was still there. Occasionally, I would be reminded of it, like an itch that needs scratching, but I pushed it back into the recesses of my brain believing it was nothing more than a pipe dream. I believed that teaching would not provide me with the rewards and freedom I sought. I was wrong.

Twenty-two years ago, while experiencing a career crisis, I took another look at teaching. During the next few years I honed my speaking, presentation, and sales skills and now deliver 150 to 200 keynotes and workshops each year. The adage that hard work and focus can lead to the career you want was true for me and can be true for you as well. But, it takes commitment and self-awareness.

I learned from my own crisis that we have two choices. You can develop your career from the outside in, allowing external forces such as peer pressure, parental expectations, status, or perception to guide you. Or you can develop it from the inside out, basing your decisions on who you are by understanding your strengths and weaknesses and knowing what gives you the most satisfaction. Working from the inside out gives you control over the elements that govern your career in sales.

From a corporate perspective, people who work from the inside out have an understanding of the corporation's values, goals, and methods and find ways to work within the existing structure, while slowly guiding it to change. Those working from the outside in, buck the corporate culture and try to change it all at once. This is a faulty approach because it makes your success contingent on things that are often beyond your control. The alternative is to place the control where it belongs — inside yourself. It takes time and patience to be an insider. Insiders build a successful career in sales one step at a time. A good example is the story of a 12-year-old girl from Japan.

Sadako Sasaki's Story [178]

It was 1943 and the world was engaged in its Second World War. A barber living in Kusunoki-cho, Japan gave birth to his first daughter,

---

[178] Sadako Sasaki, I first learned about Sadako from my granddaughter who did a paper on this remarkable young woman for school. If you want to learn more, here are a few sites for you: http://homepages.which.net, and www.sadako,org, and www.pcf.city.hiroshima.jp

Sadako. Soon after her birth, he was drafted into the army and his wife took over the running of the barbershop. Three months later, the atomic bomb was dropped on Hiroshima. The blast was felt 1.7 kilometres away and destroyed their home. Miraculously the family escaped harm as they fled to the home of a relative living in Miyoshi. However, on their way, while crossing the Misasa Bridge, they were caught in the fallout's "black rain."

During the next decade the family rebuilt their lives. Sadako was a vigorous girl who took part in school activities and was an excellent athlete. She could run a 50-meter race in 7.5 seconds. Her dream was to teach physical education in junior high school. Suddenly, in November 1954, her parents noticed lumps on Sadako's neck and ears and spots on her legs. The diagnosis was leukaemia.

In Japan, paper cranes were sent to hospitals by the citizens of Nagoya to cheer up the patients. Inspired by these bright and cheerful cranes, many patients began folding their own. In the beginning, Sadako folded her wish "I want to live," into each crane that she made. But surrounded by death and suffering, she changed and wished for a world blessed with peace. She wanted to end the nightmares she knew from Hiroshima and Nagasaki. She wanted a world where there were no wars. By the end of August, less than a month after she began making cranes, Sadako had folded over 1,000 cranes that hung from the ceiling of her room and around the hospital. Her disease progressed quickly and by October 1955, she was dead.

After her death, Sadako's friends and family continued the tradition of folding paper cranes in Sadako's honour. Sadako's story spread quickly and every year, on November 17, World Peace Day, people around the world send thousands of cranes to be placed on her statue in Hiroshima Peace Park. Sadako did not achieve her lofty goal of world peace, but she managed to bring the issue to the consciousness of children around the world as they retell her story.

---

[180] B.C. Forbes, (1880 – 1954), Scottish financial journalist and founder of *Forbes Magazine*.
[181] Sadako Sasaki, I first learned about Sadako from my granddaughter who did a paper on this remarkable young woman for school. If you want to learn more, here are a few sites for you: http://homepages.which.net, and www.sadako,org, and www.pcf.city.hiroshima.jp

The change from inactive victim to a person of action is gradual. As we saw with Sadako, she changed her perspective and made an impact on the world—one crane at a time. In your sales career, you can sit back and wait until you lose your job, miss the promotion, or lose a client. You can wait until you face an earth shattering experience like Sadako did, or you can learn your lesson and begin the process of folding your pieces now.

Change can be a scary proposition, as it often means losing something and replacing it with something completely unknown. This can lead to the trap we often fall into called complacency. We get comfortable with the way things are and venturing beyond our personal comfort zone can create uncertainty. There are no guarantees and that's what really scares us about change. The good news is that by exercising our proactive mental muscles, we strengthen our resolve to find a better way to manage our sales careers. That's the payoff. Our next two POAs changed their respective worlds just as Sadako — one step at a time.

Frederick Smith's Story [182]

In 1971, Frederick Smith came up with a revolutionary idea. He wanted to start a company that would deliver packages from sender to receiver within 24 hours. By 2004 his company, FedEx, was delivering packages to 210 countries, owned over 600 airplanes, 46,000 vehicles, and boasted 170,000 employees. Today, FedEx handles over 3 million packages each day. But the 30-year road from idea to mega success that has earned Smith a place on Forbes' list of the 400 richest people in the world was not without its glitches.

Frederick was born one of four children in Marks, Mississippi. His father, Fredrick Smith Senior, was a successful entrepreneur who established the Dixie Greyhound Bus Lines and later the national Toddle House Restaurant Chain. But when the young Frederick was four, Fred Sr. died. Before his death, Fred Sr., concerned that his children would not have the maturity to handle a large amount of money, stipulated that they were not to receive their inheritance until they reached 21 years of age.

---

[182] Charles Fishman, "Face Time with Fred Smith", *Fast Company*, (May 2001), issue 47. "Interview: Fredrick W. Smith", *Academy of Achievement*, (May 1998), www.achievement.org. Meg Green, "Fred Smith 1944 – Early Life", www.referenceforbusiness.com, (2007).

Frederick Jr., born with Calve Perthes disease, a form of arthritis of the hips, spent his youth walking with the aid of crutches. Fortunately, by the age of 10, he had outgrown the disease. At school, he was interested in athletics and academics, particularly history. He developed an early interest in flying and at the age of 15, became a skilled amateur pilot. In addition, while at high school, Frederick and a group of friends formed the Ardent Record Company. In 1962, Frederick left Memphis to attend Yale University. An economics class term paper changed Frederick's life forever. His thesis was to develop a company that would guarantee delivery of time-sensitive goods within 24 hours to major cities in the United States. An unimpressed professor gave him a "C" for his effort. In 1966, Frederick entered the Marine Corps and fought in Vietnam. In 1969, after two tours of duty and decorated with several metals, he was honorably discharged.

In 1970, Frederick took another look at his university term paper. Originally, his idea was to offer the Federal Reserve System a method of transporting, sorting, and rerouting checks. With a solid business plan in place, he presented a case that would have saved the Federal Reserve an estimated $3 million per day. While the institution thought it was an interesting idea, they were not convinced that it could work.

On paper, the proposal was simple. On a practical level, it was fraught with challenges. First, it required an incredible amount of up-front money to cover the cost of airplanes, trucks, and personnel. It needed a system designed to ensure that packages got to the right destination. Frederick took the plunge with his inheritance and with an additional $90 million raised from venture capitalists, Federal Express was born. Within the first three months of operation, the company had lost nearly one third of its investment.

There was skepticism from the public that Federal Express could do what it promised. There were many challenges such as the high cost of advertising, the Arab oil embargo of 1973, trade unions, and aviation regulations. Federal Express posted an operating loss of $29 million during its first two years of operations. Frederick was steadfast. Rather than trying to change the system all at once, he approached it from the inside out, tackling one challenge after another. It took five years before FedEx turned a profit. Six years later, its annual profit exceeded $1 billion.

While Frederick had a revolutionary idea, he knew the importance of moving his dream ahead one step at a time. The most important lesson he learned was that FedEx's real strength was its people.

While Frederick was born into privilege and received an Ivy League education, his time in the Marines taught him how to lead blue-collar people, a skill that he was able to transfer to his civilian life. He developed a philosophy called P-S-P (People, Service, and Profit), which every day, each one of his 170,000 employees live by. He could be seen walking around a FedEx facility at night shaking hands with employees. Frederick initiated a "breakfast with the boss" program, where any employee with over 10 years of service can request and have breakfast with him.

Unlike Frederick Smith, who was born of privilege, our next POA wasn't, but he is also a master of working from the inside out.

Jack Welch's Story

Jack was an only child born in 1935 to parents of Irish ancestry in Peabody, Massachusetts. It wasn't until Jack was nine that his parents bought their first house across the road from a factory in Salem, Massachusetts. From these humble beginnings, Jack built a life and career that reached the pinnacle of success as the CEO of General Electric.

His mom was strong, loving, and principled. She taught her son early lessons that carried over for the rest of his life. She wanted Jack to grow up strong, tough, and independent. His dad was a railroad conductor on the Boston and Maine commuter line. He would bring home newspapers left by passengers on the train and Jack soon became a self-professed "news Junkie." His father also introduced him to a lifelong love of the game of golf. They were a close knit family.

His younger years were filled with reading and sports, including hockey, basketball, and football. While he didn't excel athletically, his competitiveness kept him playing. Jack's true game was golf. His dad got him started and he honed his skill by caddying for players at the local golf course.

As his dad worked long hours, most of Jack's parental influence came from his mother. Her parenting went from being a "real sweetie" to very strict. She instilled in Jack a set of values that became the hallmark of his business career.

Missing out on a Reserve Officers' Training Corps (ROTC) scholarship and the opportunity to go to Dartmouth or Columbia, Jack settled for an undergraduate education at the University of

Massachusetts. His sophomore years and beyond saw him in a fraternity that majored in "beer consumption and late night poker games." Yet he managed to maintain a 3.7 GPA and a place on the Dean's List. With an undergraduate degree in hand, Jack went to the University of Illinois for his Masters in Chemical Engineering, and ultimately, a Ph.D. In 1961, and fresh out of school, he found his place working for GE at an annual salary of $10,000. From those early beginnings Jack moved quickly up the ranks. At the age of 45 he became the CEO of General Electric.

Jack's time as CEO of GE is well documented in his book, *Jack, Straight from the Gut*. [183]

The first step as CEO, according to Jack, was to define his direction, which started with the overall feel of the company. What he found was a heavily bureaucratised culture with too many levels between the CEO and the workers. Introducing changes was, in Jack's words, "like trying to change a super tanker into a speedboat."

Change took time. An early initiative saw Jack take 14 senior executives on a two-day golf/business retreat where they could talk and get to know each other. This would become the beginning of GE's Corporate Executive Counsel, which, during Jack's tenure as CEO, would guide GE's growth and change.

Jack took on a massive bureaucracy that was deeply entrenched in its slow-moving pace. He had to fight people, products, companies, and public perception, in some cases for years, before he realized the changes he wanted. In his words, he threw "hand grenades" at the system rather than igniting an atomic bomb. During his tenure, he took a big company with earnings of $2 billion to an international conglomerate with earnings in excess of $10 billion. Throughout his book he talks about the struggle to break through and change the bureaucracy, change people's thinking, and refocus the company on being a world leader. And he did it one step at a time.

Influential Women

It's not just a man's world. Proactive women, as well as men, have found bountiful opportunities to carve out careers in spite of prejudice, culture, timing, industry standards, and cultural norms that one

---

[183] Jack Welsh, *Jack Straight From the Gut*, Warner Business Books, 2002.

generation ago were merely pipe dreams. What these women have in common is that they all worked their way up in the system.

No one was handed her career on a silver platter. They took a serious look at their respective worlds, understood the system, and slowly, methodically worked toward change.

Here are 14 examples of women who have overcome personal hurdles, sold their beliefs to their corporations and its customers, excelled as leaders, and along the way, smashed every myth in the book about women in high places.

- Sharon Allen is the chairman of Deloitte and Touche USA
- Colleen Barett is the President of Southwest Airlines
- Cathleen Black is President of Hearst Magazines
- Theresa Gutting is CEO of Telecom, New Zealand Group
- Ruth Bader Ginsburg sits on the Supreme Court
- Dawn Hudson is President/CEO of Pepsi Cola North America
- Neelie Kroes is the European Commissioner for Competition
- Rochelle Lazarus, Chairman of Ogilvy & Mather Worldwide
- Amy Pascal is Chairman of the Sony Entertainment Group
- Christine Poon is Vice Chairman of Johnson and Johnson
- Condoleeza Rice, former U.S. Secretary of State
- Auug San Suu Kyi is a Nobel Peace laureate
- Wu Xiaoling is Deputy Governor of the Peoples Bank of China
- Margaret Whitman is the Chief Executive of E-Bay

Working from the inside out came naturally to some and required learning by others.

It can also be argued that many POA's were not following a set plan. However, at one time or another, all these POA's experienced difficulties, yet they were able to overcome their helplessness, develop their courage and persistence, find opportunities, and overcome setbacks.

You can do this too. Your change begins today with your understanding of your Personal Sales Action Cycle.

The Sales Action Cycle

Taking action from the inside out is a cyclical process. There are natural places to get on board and there are checks and balances along the way to keep you focused in the right direction. Taking charge of your sales career doesn't happen in isolation. It is part of a continuous cycle of events that you tap into along the way. The Sales Action Cycle will help you understand where you are now and what you can do to improve.

The Sales Career Action Cycle

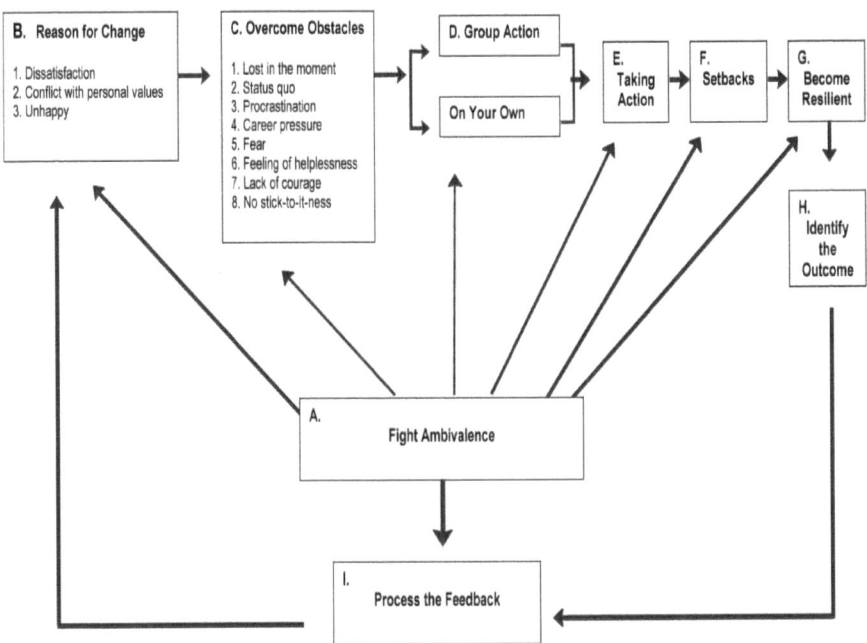

Understanding how the cycle works is the key to putting all you have learned into action. But, behind every stage of this cycle lies an enemy: ambivalence.

Fight ambivalence

If your sales career is moving along nicely, don't assume that you have nothing left to do. It's so easy to let ambivalence victimise you. Ambivalence is what sets in when the fires of passion burn out.

We see it happen in relationships, commitment to causes, and in our sales performance. Here is an example. A few years ago the serenity of my community was threatened with the plans for the development of a nearby gravel pit. The neighbours were outraged. "How dare they!" they cried. The gravel pit meant a huge increase in truck traffic, increased dust and pollutants, a potential of harm to underground water tables, and a loss of the peace and quiet that our community had always enjoyed. So, we enraged and conscious citizens did what anyone would do. We formed an association, hired a lawyer, and mounted our fight.

At the first meeting we had over 400 angry ratepayers in attendance. But the developer was confident and he quietly said to our newly elected president, "You have 400 people now; give this a year or two and you will be sitting in a meeting by yourself." The developer, well experienced with ratepayer groups, knew that the initial surge of interest soon dissipates, and in time, ambivalence sets in. The battle continues to this day because some individuals have kept the flame burning and helped the ratepayers fight their own ambivalence. It's a common ailment, which is why we need relentless leaders who continuously beat the drums that keep important issues at the top of our mind and in our hearts.

If you find that you lack the energy or enthusiasm to tackle the challenges you thought were important in the past, you are probably suffering from ambivalence. When ambivalence sets in, it becomes an enormous obstacle to change.

Ambivalence is a silent intruder that appears when you start to take things for granted. It can appear at any point in the Sales Action Cycle. Imagine you are driving your car and notice a small noise coming from under the hood. You know you should have it looked after, but you don't have the time to get to a mechanic. So you grow familiar with the sound. Eventually, you hardly notice it at all. If a friend joins you for a ride he might say, "What's that sound I hear?"

You might respond, "Huh, what sound?" In your sales career these "noises" are often minimized and relegated to "the cost of doing business." Fighting ambivalence requires regular tune-ups to make sure you haven't lost sight of why you chose the direction you're following. Make sure that little noise isn't symptomatic of some bigger problem.

We all sometimes see and hear things that are offensive or conflict with our values. These can be comments about sexual orientation, race, colour, and ethnicity, work habits, and so on. What should you do? You have choices. You can either speak out or remain silent.

Working from the inside out means you choose issues that are non-negotiable and demand your immediate attention, rather than others that are better dealt with in a different manner. One tried and true strategy is to pick your fights. When you confront everything, you risk losing credibility. For example, how would you handle hearing a derogatory remark from your customer about one of their co-worker's sexual orientation? You could choose to ignore the remark or you could say something and confront the issue head on or even choose to drop the customer from your sales route.

Trying to change from the inside out doesn't happen in a day. In this example, you could confront the issue head-on or take smaller steps such as participating in gay activities or lead by example and show tolerance for other people's sexual choices, whether gay or straight. If you're offended by religious intolerance, you can honour co-workers' and customer's religious holidays or reach out to other religions and celebrate their customs within your customer's organization.

The trick is to start small and change the things that you can. This helps to create a sense of hope and a confidence level that you are making a difference. Twentieth century philosopher and theologian Reinhold Niebuhr aptly wrote, "Grant me the serenity to accept the things I cannot change, the courage to change the things I can and the wisdom to know the difference." [184]

A departmental waste recycling program will not solve the problem of global warming, but it will begin a very important process of identifying the problem and finding solutions that are manageable. Changing your language may look like a small step, and while there have been many jokes about politically correct language, the

---

[184] Carl Paul Reinhold Neibuhr, (1892 – 1971). US Theologian.

underlying principle is sound. When you change Workman to Workers you are taking one step towards the recognition of an inequity.

Assess reasons for change

The next step in the cycle is to recognise the signs that indicate you need a change in your career.

1. Job Dissatisfaction

Why did you choose a sales career? According to an article on the Mayo Clinic website *"Job Satisfaction: Strategies to Make Work More Gratifying,"* you likely chose your career for one of three reasons: [185]

- It was a job, and at the time your focus was probably on the job's financial rewards, location, or the benefits awarded by your employer.
- If the career itself was your motivation, then the prestige, status, power, and challenge that came with the job probably motivated you. You chose a direction for your working life that gave you an opportunity for continuous growth and achievement.
- If you felt that selling was a calling, then your focus was on work that fulfilled a personal need.

Regardless of the reason, circumstances tend to change. What was compelling to you in the beginning of your career may have lost its importance. In the same Mayo Clinic bulletin, nine reasons are listed as to why dissatisfaction sets in. They are:
- Increase in conflicts with colleagues
- Conflicts with supervisors and managers
- An inequity between reward and effort
- Working conditions falling behind those of rival companies
- Shrinking promotional opportunities
- Lack of power
- Fear of losing your job
- Boring work
- Work that is no longer suited to your personality.

If these sound familiar, it may be a signal that you are ready for change. But be careful. We all have a feeling of dissatisfaction from time to time, so don't jump at the first sign. It's when the signs become persistent that action is warranted.

---

[185] Mayo Clinic Staff, "Job Satisfaction: Strategies to make work more gratifying", Mayoclinic.com, (2007).

2. Conflict with personal values

A value is a belief or philosophy that is meaningful to you. You learn your values from family, religion, schools, and friends. While values may change over time, they guide your everyday actions.

Corporations and institutions also have values. These are often found in published mission statements which, if enacted properly, become the corporate soul and underlie all decision making.

Prior to joining your workplace, presumably you did some research and satisfied yourself that your own values and those of the company were compatible. But, what happens when values change? And they do. There are countless examples of ethical corporations under the leadership of people who bend and ultimately break away from core values. We've seen executives commit fraud and lie to employees and shareholders. We've witnessed countless corporations who have moved away from their focus and become burdened with unmanageable debt. We have seen religious leaders act in ways that conflict with the values of their institutions. We've seen politicians who lie or cheat, while using shallow words that attempt to justify their actions.

Our values change—as our lives change—and not always for the worse, as in the examples above. What happens when your values change as a result of your life journey? One day you are focused on your career and willing to make sacrifices to move ahead, and the next day the most important thing in your world is your child. Do you make excuses for missing a sales call to attend your child's baseball game?

Or do you discuss more flexible work hours with your boss who says he supports work-life balance? Some people begin their career filled with idealism and hope. But these same people often get caught up in the daily struggle to meet mortgage payments and maintain their life style. Do they now accept conditions that would have been unacceptable to them in the beginning? Have they lowered their bar of tolerance as to what's acceptable and what's not?

A conflict in values can result in lost motivation, lack of self-respect and lack of focus. When values are in crisis, trouble lies ahead. If values butt heads, like two goats trying to prove their superiority, no one wins. The trick is to know your values, be aware of how they change, and make sure you are in a healthy and nurturing environment. If not, perhaps it's time to move on.

3. Unhappiness

We learned in Chapter 5 the difference between pursuing happiness and being happy. Pursuing happiness, at some point in the future, is faulty because we cannot predict what will make us happy. We can set goals and strive for them, but once we reach them, we may still be unhappy. Surely, if you won a large lottery you would be happy. But for how long? Let's suppose you win a lottery with a staggering seven or eight-digit payoff. You might pay off your mortgage, quit your job, take a trip around the world or buy an expensive sports car.

But when the initial euphoria dies down, you are like any other rich person straddled with the decisions rich people make. Some rich people are happy and some are not. Your happiness is no longer directly linked to the winning. You've already won. Now you have to look elsewhere.

So, where will you find happiness? The answer is in the journey. You can (and you will have to take my word on this) experience happiness when you buy a lottery ticket and dream about how you are going to spend the money. It is all tied up in what you do in the moment. This can be a two-edged sword, but the edge to focus on is the one that makes you happy. What can you do today that will make you happy? Of course, that all depends on whether you are convinced that you deserve to be happy.

I am not saying this flippantly. Some of us are hardwired to look at the gloomy side of things. We never see the sunlight because our heads are buried in the shadow of others who seem to have given themselves permission to be happy. The two universal truths are: 11. Nobody is happy all the time; and 2. You, too, deserve to be happy sometimes.

Try this. Think about what you really like doing. Is it taking a walk, playing a board game, going to a movie, or talking to customers? Find some simple thing that you like to do and do it now. But before you leave, put a bookmark on this page so you can continue reading when you feel happier.

In 1955, in the *Economist,* University of Singapore Professor of History Northcote Parkinson expounded his now famous Parkinson's Law, which says, "Work expands to fill the time available." [186]

---

[186] Cyril Northcote Parkinson, (1909-1993) British historian and author of sixty books. His famous Parkinson's Law first appeared as a tongue-in-cheek beginning of an article for *The Economist* in 1955. Realizing he was on to something important he expanded the line into *Parkinson's Law: and Other Studies in Administration* (Ballantine Books, 1987).

What Parkinson was referring to was his observations of the British Civil Service. He observed that while the span of the British Empire was shrinking, the number of employees in the Colony Office in Singapore was growing. It's an interesting principle that we see in many aspects of our lives. The most common is when we move to a new home or office and wonder how we will fill all that new space. Before we know it, every cupboard and closet is filled to the brim.

We can take this same principle when talking about happiness. When you are happy, you can fill your world with happiness. When you are sad and miserable, your world quickly fills with misery. To tell happy people to make room for happiness is redundant. Their cupboards are already overflowing. But, for others this is a powerful lesson. When you dedicate some room in your mental cupboard, you squeeze out a bit of unhappiness. When you realize how much more satisfying your selling career becomes, finding more room is the logical next step.

POA's like Laura Robinson, Mike Schultz, Mike Yager, and Nathan Sawaya have all found careers while never abandoning their desire for happiness. Henri Dunant's happiness was born out of the need to do something great. He overcame career and financial failure and focused on the source of his passion and his feelings for the suffering troops left behind and formed the Red Cross.

An anonymous author once said "One man's wilderness is another man's theme park." We have to watch carefully how much power we give to our unhappiness and take a firm stand when declaring, "I deserve to be happy."

Overcome obstacles
There are eight basic obstacles that each of us face at one time or another. Four of these obstacles have been dealt with in previous chapters and five are new. Let's look at each:

1. Lost in the Moment
Much has been written about "being in the moment," or "in the zone." Actors, athletes, sales people, and negotiators all find that place where they are completely focused on the task at hand.

Think about your typical workday. Review in your mind, hour by hour, how your day progresses. Are there times when you lose awareness of time, space and environment, and ignore or don't even hear outside distractions? Perhaps it was during a client presentation.

When you are in this zone, you are creative, focused, and uncannily able to produce great results. It sounds idyllic, but there is a dark side to being in the moment.

First, you can't be there all the time. Being in the moment is an energy drain. Actors and entertainers are often in the moment when they are on stage performing, but once the curtain goes down, they are exhausted.

Second, when you strive for these "moments," you lose sight of the rest of the world. Your focus is usually so narrow that things you value such as family, community, and environment are often relegated to second place. The mad scientist who is focused on a problem of higher mathematics and forgets to shave, brush his teeth, or eat is the stereotype of this state. We call this behaviour absent mindlessness. But, in fact, the scientist's mind, while absent from the trials and tribulations of every day existence, is hard at work in another world.

Being in the moment, therefore, can be a masquerade of focus, which cloaks your neglect of other aspects of your life.

The trick is to focus on what I call "the moment before." It starts with a clear understanding of who you are, what you want, and which values you hold. Your values are often clear the moment before and lose focus when you are in the moment. Then they become clear once again "in the moment" after.

To help you keep your perspective during the whole process (before, during, and after), you need to seed the situation with reminders. These reminders don't have to be earth shattering; small things will suffice. It's through small acts that big results occur.

It's like having a pebble in your shoe. When your mind wanders, the pebble brings you back to reality and ensures that your in-the-zone time is for pursuits that further your goals rather than intense, but escapist moments such as hobbies that you are passionate about.

2. Status Quo

We can blame our remarkable ability to become comfortable with the status quo on evolution. During the evolution of Homo Sapiens, certain characteristics were passed along from one generation to the next, which were based on their way of reacting to the world. For example, if our ancestors became oblivious to strange noises, clouds in the sky, or setting up camp in plain view on the open Savannah, they were doomed to a quick extinction. Those who developed the ability to sense change, survived. That's evolution.

In today's terms these changes in the environment to which our Neanderthal ancestors reacted have, over time, become part of our everyday experience. The problem is that we don't hear strange noises or notice changes as acutely anymore. We accept the subtle changes in our employer's practices with very little thought. Because these employment noises are slow and gradual, we hardly hear them at all. What was a significant signal to our ancestors is the norm to us now.

It's the same principle as white noise. Let's say that you are sitting quietly in your office and someone in the next office starts talking loudly on his or her telephone. You would obviously be distracted. If the noise persisted, you might turn on your radio to compensate for the noise from the other room. Now, let's say your office is in the middle of a hundred cubicles where there are a hundred different voices talking on the phone all the time. You will not be able to listen to individual voices, but the total becomes an audible hum, just like your radio that drowns out individual noises. This is white noise. Someone joining your beehive of activity will become accustomed to the white noise very quickly. This principle of white noise is what defines the status quo. In many ways we are hardwired to protect ourselves. For many of us, it is far safer living within the status quo than venturing out into strange territory where the risk of losing our job, reputation, credibility, and status is great.

The issue of global warming is a perfect example. We don't need thousands of scientists telling us that the weather is changing. All we need to do is look outside and see longer, hotter summers, shorter, wetter winters, and an increased number of tornadoes, hurricanes, and monsoons. Every day we hear about another global catastrophe from tsunamis to large chunks of Antarctica breaking away. We intuitively know that something is wrong, but short-sighted politicians and businesses have been slow to upset the status quo. Solving a problem that is 30 or 40 years away doesn't get votes in congress or the boardroom. Creating immediate jobs and profits does. The trick that many POAs have learned is the power of challenging the status quo little by little. Small steps often have large consequences. Rather than letting the status quo paralyse them, they move slowly and methodically. It makes sense to do this. After all, the status quo was established for protection. Stripping off those protective layers too quickly may expose you to unforeseen dangers.

3. Procrastination

What kind of procrastinator are you? If I created a test that would reveal what kind of procrastinator you are, one of two things would happen: 1. You might find excuses for not completing it, or, 2. You might complete it in order to avoid doing something else.

Instead of creating a test, why don't we just go directly to the bottom line and let me tell you the results? There are three types of procrastinators. [187]

The first group of procrastinators is very busy folks. They are industrious little beavers building dams everywhere. However, when these same people are faced with a problem, they rarely have time to address it because they are too busy. This group looks for the instant reward in doing little things that is lacking when they take on the bigger issues. With a career span of 30, 40 or maybe 50 years, many people don't see the real rewards until the later years.

Instant gratification junkies simply don't want to live in the future. They want to know that those things they are doing today have a result now. Imagine our industrious beaver building mini-dams out of twigs and branches. The job is done in a week or two. But, what if I said to that beaver, "How about building a dam that would make a real difference? It would be the pinnacle of your dam-building career. How about something the size of Hoover Dam?" He might shake his head at the magnitude of the project and realize that it would take years to complete. "No way man," the beaver would cry and waddle off with a twig in his mouth to stop another creek from emptying into a lake.

The next group of procrastinators do not work on the big issues in their life—their career, relationships, or family — because there is no guarantee that they will be successful. These failure-shy people would

---

[187] Paul graham, "Good and Bad Procrastinators." www.paulgraham.com, 2007, John Perry, *Structured Procrastination* (Sussex Publishers, 2006).

rather take a back seat to life than risk being proactive because they might not get what they want. For these people, there is a fear of wasting time. What if they invest a lifetime chasing a dream that doesn't pan out? So, they fill their time with other things to compensate. They stay busy doing things that are marginally useful.

They join a committee and attend meetings and volunteer for projects. They become the go-to guy who is always available to help. They will apply for positions for which they are not necessarily suited and join a throng of job hunters who do the same. They spend lots of time organizing their office so that every file is in its place. These procrastinators create a list of tasks, placing the hardest on the top and the easiest on the bottom. Rather than starting at the top of the list, they start at the bottom. Starting at the bottom is a way of avoiding the tough things on the top.

The third group of procrastinators does nothing at all. These couch potatoes would rather sit and watch the world go by than join in the parade. They have a list of important tasks, but unlike the second group who will list all tasks from hardest to easiest, the third group will only list the difficult and real important tasks. These tasks are simply overwhelming to them. They are too big and risky, so rather than tackling them, they ignore them.

Do any of these sound familiar? If not, maybe you are not a procrastinator. After all, chronic procrastination only affects about 20 percent of us, although periodic procrastination affects all of us. Regardless of the group you fall into, the critical thing is to ask yourself the question, "Is what I am doing important? Really important?" If it isn't, what's stopping me from making the change? Identifying the obstacle is the first step in overcoming procrastination

4. Career Pressure
Making decisions on your own is hard enough, but when other people try to pressure you one way or another, it can be even harder. Career pressure becomes an obstacle when your choices are a result of suggestions by others that lead you in the wrong direction.

Peer pressure is when people your own age try to influence how you act. Career pressure is something else. It goes to the core of why you have chosen a particular path to follow. Career pressure comes from one of two places—you or others. It's either internal or external.

Career pressure is different than peer pressure because there are no age or gender barriers. It can come from members of your family, mentors, role models, or colleagues. As much as you would like to think that the distinction between decisions you make on your own and those that emanate from others is clear, it is not. People influence all parts of your life, even if you don't realize it. They can affect your decisions in positive ways such as helping you find a career path that is ideally suited to your values, talents, and personality, or they can affect what you do in negative ways such as suggesting things that might conflict with your values, aspirations, and talents.

Why do we often give in to the suggestions of others? The simple answer is because one of our basic needs is to fit in. Affiliation is the third rung on Maslow's Hierarchy of Needs. [188]

Some worry that if they don't do what someone else suggests, they will disappoint that person. This is common when people turn to professions or jobs because their parents or a well-intentioned close relative was either in that field or believed strongly that it would serve them well. Then there is the curiosity factor. When you see the career paths of others you admire, it's normal to wonder what your life would be like if you modeled yourself after that person.

Career pressure can be positive when people in your network provide you with the confidence and courage to move forward. To assess your career choices, you need to answer these questions:

- Why did I choose this particular career direction?
- Was it consistent with my beliefs, aspirations, and talents at the time I chose it, or did others pressure me into it?
- Is my career still consistent with my current beliefs, aspirations, and talents?
- Is it a career that satisfies me or does it simply provide status and/or money while at the same time making me unhappy?

These are the kinds of questions that let you know if the pressure to maintain your career is coming from outside or within yourself. Internal pressure is generally a positive thing. Just be careful when it comes from others. Career pressure is an obstacle when you are drawn into a

---

[188] Abraham Maslow, (1908 – 1970). US Psychologist. His hierarchy of needs first appeared in an article published in 1943 called, "A Theory of Human Motivation".

career that really doesn't fit. The trick is to make sure you balance your decision between well meaning advice from others and your own needs. You are the one who has to live with your decision—no one else. It takes courage, conviction, and a strong sense of self to minimize the effects that others have on you and continuously make career decisions that are right for you, even though they conflict with a relative or friend's values.

5. Fear

Having a career in sales is analogous to raising a child. You conceive it, you nurture it, you advise and guide and eventually you have to let it go. That's what parenting is all about—knowing when not to parent, back away and let your children (and in this case a prospective customer) discover for themselves what they need to know. The fear of backing away sometimes grows like a seed and weakens your resolve to let go.

You can find all the tools and tricks for handling fearful situations, but at some point you will have to actually face the fear of letting go and see what happens. It can be terrifying. Will my child run out into traffic? Will she take on a challenge and fail? Shouldn't I be there to protect her? If you have taken on a new selling challenge, getting into it and giving it your best, means letting go of your fear. This is probably the toughest job a parent or career-minded individual will face. If all your preparations have lessened the fear, then all is well and it is no longer an obstacle. If you find that your fear is debilitating, then it is a warning that you have more work to do.

6. Feelings of Helplessness

Imagine you are a monkey living in the jungle, swinging happily day after day looking for coconuts and bananas. One day your daily swing gets interrupted and you find yourself in a small box with holes in the top to let air in. Day after day you are trapped in the box until one day someone opens the door and lets you climb into a larger box, decorated to look like the jungle you came from. Welcome to the zoo.

Regardless of how well constructed and designed, you are still living in a cage. Your daily life has changed. Rather than searching for food, it's brought to you once a day. If someone wants you to mate, then he or she chooses a suitable mate for you and watches as you do the act. At the end of the cage are windows or bars and on the other side are people standing, staring, and making stupid faces at you. There is no escape — no way out. This is helplessness.

What's really interesting about monkeys in the zoo is that no matter how helpless they feel, when an opportunity to get out presents itself, they will jump at it. If someone leaves the cage door open; the monkeys will escape.

We sometimes feel caged by rules, policies, miserable bosses, restrictive laws, responsibilities, choices, technology, and colleagues. These feelings of helplessness can be overwhelming and often cause us to close our eyes and give up. But it's when our eyes are shut that we miss opportunities. The trick is to take that leap of faith that tells you that no matter how hopeless things are, there is always an answer. Without that leap, helplessness becomes an obstacle. When you accept that there are answers, even if you don't see them now, you have reframed helplessness into hope. Hope is the backbone of a successful career in sales.

There is a behavior pattern common to all animals, which is known to psychologists as "critical reaction." [189]

It describes how all living things, when they are backed into a corner, fight for survival. Psychologists define critical reaction as "an acute emotional reaction to a powerful stimulus or demand."

Think about a situation you might find yourself in where the future of your career lies in the outcome. It could be a response to being asked to sell a product that is not right for a particular client. What would you do? When you are fighting for your career, it is realistic to imagine yourself shedding the chains of inhibition and timidity and come out fighting. Even if you are outnumbered and the situation seems hopeless, you will swing your arms and fists wildly hoping against hope that one of your blows will connect.

Your critical reaction says, "I am not going down without a fight." It's that attitude that helps you cope with helplessness. It's the rage or the burning need to complete something that fuels your critical reaction. We saw this behavior in Hannah Taylor, and Samantha Smith. While their situation wasn't life or death, the feeling of helplessness was clearly present. Our Toronto cop, Paul Gillespie saw death and overbearing odds every day at work and when sitting beside his son. When all else failed, our POA's needed one last try.

---

[189] Sora Song, "Are We Happier Facing Death?" *Time*, (October 30, 2007).

Our POA's were not fighting for their lives; they fought for what they believed in. When their back was against the wall they lashed out in one final attempt to defeat their enemy.

7. Lack of Courage

I recently saw a story in my local newspaper about a man who was attacked by a bear. He overcame his fear and successfully fought the animal off. In the same paper, there was a story about a woman bus driver who lost both her legs in an automobile accident. As part of her recovery process she went to night school to learn new skills to become an administrative assistant. She now has a satisfying full-time job. What do these two stories have in common? Both people found the courage to survive. Both were faced with overwhelming odds and both came away from the situation as winners. It's easy to imagine both these people wallowing in defeat and self-doubt. Had that happened, neither would be where they are today.

I remember a guidance counsellor in high school talking about the sacrifice needed to find a worthwhile career. He told us that it would take years of education and training to master any profession. He told us that once we left high school it would probably be 10 years before we felt truly comfortable and competent in our chosen career.

"Ten years!" one of my classmates said in dismay, "Who wants to spend that much time when there are no guarantees that we will get what we want?"

"Good point," answered my teacher, "But if you don't try, where will you be in 10 years?"

His words resonate with me to this day. It takes courage to commit to a career in sales that may take a decade to master. Our investment is in time which, once over, we can never have back again. One way or another, that magical 10-year mark will happen to all of us. The question is where do you want to be?

We have such a short time on this planet. And yet, in that cosmic millisecond, we have to make a gazillion decisions, everything from what toothpaste to use to how we want to spend our time. The little decisions are taken care of. It's the big decisions in life that need our attention. We can choose the kind of life we want to live, the kind of people we want to become, and the careers we should follow. We all have the power of choice. It's what makes us different than all the other living creatures on the planet.

Let's suppose that you were able to read the future. You could gaze on a candle or an Ouiji Board and somehow all the mysteries of the future would be revealed in your mind. What if you saw how you were going to die? Let's say you know that in your 78th year while crossing the street a car hit you. What would you do with that information? My guess is, that if you were like me, in my 78th year I would be very careful crossing the street. See, we have choices.

What if you could see that at the end of your career you would be in a senior management position with a comfortable retirement package and a happy family? How would that affect you now? Would you let go and be complacent saying that everything is going to turn out okay so why worry? Or, would you fret with each decision you make thinking that you may be doing something that messes up your ultimate plan. Or, would you simply do nothing. Making choices is difficult and requires a lot of courage.

Here is a bit of folklore to help make the point:
The young prince had never seen a dragon, but had heard of the dragon's great strength and the fire it breathed from their nostrils.

One day, when the prince was on his regular early morning ride on his favorite horse, he galloped down the path and into the woods. As he turned a corner, he found himself face-to-face with the dragon. He could have turned his horse and run, and maybe he would have escaped, but the dragon was heading for the town. The prince knew that his inaction would result in the townspeople being hurt or killed.

The young prince, his heart beating fast, charged straight at the dragon and drove his sword deep into its neck. The dragon was killed and the kingdom saved.

This familiar bit of folklore has been repeated often as cultures around the world have created their own version of dragons and courage. Dragons are something that we all face at one time or another. In today's terms, your selling dragons can take on many forms. They can include such things as:

- Saying no to an unethical practice
- Standing up for a colleague
- Speaking out in a sales meeting
- Changing employers or careers
- Sticking by your personal priorities

Letting go of a belief, a career direction, or an attitude that is not helpful is taking a step forward. But, it's the process of letting go, which requires real courage. We saw it in Fatos Lubonja, Rudolf Vrba, Paul Rusesbagina, Evelyn Personeus, Wayne Yetman, Penny Gonzalez-Green, Cathy Charaba, and Rosa Parks, who were all ordinary folks who found the courage to let go of their dragons and move forward.

8. No stick-to-it-ness

A recent article in Forbes magazine listed the 10 things that will change our life in the future. There are things on this list that I don't really understand yet, but I know they are coming: [190]

- Fuel cells
- Gene therapy
- Haptics
- Internet2
- Life straws
- Magnetoresistive Random Access Memory
- The $100 laptop computer
- The $200 barrel of oil
- VoIP
- WiMax

It seems that every day there's another reason to change. But that's not what stick-to-it-ness is all about. It entails an entirely different set of thoughts and actions whose sole purpose is to make you a better person, better at what you do. Stick-to-it-ness is not a reward system, where if you do everything right and stick to it you will ultimately be rewarded. Stick-to-it-ness is a constant vigilance for finding things that you can do to improve, regardless of changes around you.

Simply put, your sales career plan is not based on a point system; rather it is your personal system with a point. It goes back to a basic need to get the job done regardless of the changes around you. It's so easy to be overwhelmed by change. Managing a career is, after all, one of the greatest challenges most of us will face. But when we let everyday events get us off track, stick-to-it-ness becomes an obstacle. Simply not having the ability to stay in the game can be disastrous.

---

[190] "Ely Breckinridge", *Forbes.com*, (February 17, 2006). {Ely Breckinridge Story or author?}

I saw a recent documentary about a tribe of people somewhere in Australia with an interesting language pattern. For example they do not have words for tomorrow, when, or I'll get back to you. They live squarely in the present. If they are hungry they go fishing and catch breakfast while not giving a second thought to lunch. The past and the future hold no place in their language.

Children are like that. Give a typical two-year-old a box of cookies and he will stuff as many into his mouth as his little mouth will hold. Telling him to save some for later is not in his consciousness. Tell the same two-year-old that you will take him somewhere special next week and his response is "I want it now."

This tendency seems to be a remnant of our distant past. Food and water and impulses all had a short shelf life. So, saving money for a rainy day, or sticking to something for the long run, is contradictory to the very grain of being human. To be successful in sales means going against your primordial impulses. You need to be constantly vigilant in the face of the panicking crowds who jump to what turns out to be single occurrences and by those who blindly follow the crowd who dictates trends and values. Albert White, Wolfgang Amadeus Mozart, Mike Ackerman, and Dorothy and Jack Babcock were all in it for the long run. They moved beyond the need for instant gratification. They personified what it takes to be persistent and it paid off. Persistence can work for you too.

Group action or on your own?
POAs are not necessarily "lone wolves" who tackle the world and their careers on their own. There may be instances where it is advisable to develop a group to support your action. Think of such issues as gay rights or health and safety in the workplace. If you see a problem with these issues, chances are that others do as well. There is safety and strength in numbers. By mobilising others to work with you, you have a better chance of effecting overall change.

Let us suppose that you are given the responsibility of increasing the overall sales efficiency in your organization. The scope of the task involves many people and will require the expenditure of resources and time. You now have a choice. The first is to take on the task alone, where you develop the overall strategy, create a working model, secure the necessary resources, and implement the strategy by telling each person what is expected.

The second choice is to form a team that represents the various areas that will be involved and facilitate the process whereby everyone adds their input into the strategy. Which approach is better?

They can both work. The trick is to keep your options open. Clearly, there will be times when you need to make decisions on your own and there will be a time when building a group consensus is desirable. Unfortunately, there are no hard rules that dictate when one strategy will produce better results. Your experience is the best judge.

One of Jack Welsh's first changes at General Electric was to form the GE Corporate Executive Counsel. It started with 14 people and grew to over 200. Rather than working individually, these people shared their talents and experience with each other to create a more powerful whole. Nearly all great leaders need to work with groups at times. It is a sign of strength and commitment. So, if there is a mechanism in place to form or be part of a group to tackle a common issue, go for it.

Take action
Human beings are decision-making machines. They decide which partner to team up with, what travel destination to go to, which customers to pursue, which present to buy, which car to drive, which politician to elect, which education to pursue, —even which coffee and breakfast cereal to buy. Every 24 hours we make hundreds, perhaps thousands, of decisions.

If we spend our conscious life deciding, why are some decisions easier than others? One of the things we need to decide is whether the issue is "pressing" or "significant." [191]

Pressing decisions have immediate consequences. They demand your attention now. Pressing decisions may include what you will order for lunch, should you fill your car with gas or wait to see if you can make it to the next station or when should you pay the telephone bill so your service won't be interrupted. The consequences of going hungry, running out of gas, or having your telephone service disconnected are real and imminent.

Significant decisions are those that make a greater impact on your life, but often lack a short-term payoff such as what job to pursue, what

---

[191] Sri Ramh, How we do what we do", www.koaching.com, (2004).

exercise program to begin, or what further education you should follow. Often our attention goes to the small, but pressing issues first, leaving the significant ones on the coals smouldering with neglect. Sometimes significant decisions are ignited by outside forces such as pending company layoffs or a recent posting for a coveted job. Suddenly, there are deadlines and those decisions become more pressing.

The solution, with regard to your sales career path, is to bring significant decisions into the realm of immediate concern. You can do this by taking some time to create your long term sales goals. Ask yourself where you want to be in five or ten years and what smaller, immediate, measurable steps you can begin taking now that will help you achieve your long-term goals.

It's these smaller steps that have the immediate payoff. Establishing these steps in sequence helps move you in the direction you want to go. It also makes the process of deciding easier, because if you miss the next deadline, you will be responsible to yourself for the consequences. This kind of self-policing can be a tremendously useful tool.

Deal with setbacks
Gandhi once wrote, "Freedom is not worth having if it does not include the freedom to make mistakes." [192]

A mistake which can morph into a setback is just part of the great plan that has been laid out for your working life. Walking through your career path is like stepping on stones as you cross a stream. Sometimes you slip, and you just pick yourself up and learn something about walking on wet stones and continue on. If you don't, you will never reach the other side of the stream. For the rest of your life you will sit on the bank and look forlornly at the other side wishing you were there. Well, you can be. You need to get back on your metaphorical stepping stones and keep on walking.

All of the People of Action you have read about started out as you and I. They grew, found a sense of purpose for themselves and changed their world by taking action. I believe that through hard work and continuous self-improvement we can have the career of our dreams. None of our POA's got to where they were going by wishing. They

---

[192] Mohandas Karamchand Gandhi, (1869 – 1948) Indian non-violent political and spiritual leader.

approached their careers with passion and commitment and were prepared to do the hard work necessary to achieve their goals. They didn't fall victim to their own helplessness, they found the courage to act; they were resilient and persistent. They found opportunity, they pursued careers that brought them happiness, and they were willing to work from the inside out – they changed themselves and then changed the world one step at a time.

Become resilient

You learned in Chapter 6 that resilience is not an inborn trait; rather it is a set of skills and attitudes that you can learn. I know, because I've done it myself. In my career as a writer and speaker, rejection is a big part of the business. When I look back at the number of rejection letters I have received over my career, I shudder. For contrast, after each presentation I meticulously read through the participant feedback sheets looking for the constructive criticism passed along by a few. Focusing on the positive feedback puts the rejections in perspective and builds resilience. Early in my career, more than once, I found myself ready to pack it in and look for some other way to earn a living. But I didn't. Instead, I developed resilience.

What I did was remarkably close to what Dr.'s Maddi and Khoshaba wrote in 2005 in their book called **Resilience at Work**. [193].

The authors conclude that the three factors that lead to resilience are commitment, control, and challenge.

1. **Commitment.** Think back to the 10-year commitment we discussed earlier. In order to master a skill or a job you will need to invest 10 years of your life. That's a massive commitment, which can't be taken lightly. But, if you approach your sales career seriously, with your eyes wide open, then the setbacks along the way become expected and therefore bearable.

2. **Control.** The truth is, that whether you work for yourself or someone else, there are lots of things beyond your control: laws, the market, customers' attitudes, production methods, and banking regulations. There is no use beating yourself up when you are faced with an obstacle that is beyond your control.

---

[193] Salvatore R. Maddi and Deborah M. Khoshaba, , *Resilience at Work*, (Amaco, 2005).

The good news is that there is much that you can control such as how you spend your time, the job you choose to tackle, the colleagues you nurture and the organisations you join.

Try this helpful exercise. Draw up a list of all the problems and challenges you face and put them into one of two columns. One column includes those things that you can control, and the other includes those things you can't. Now, in order to make your life easier, take the items in the "no control" list and forget about them. You don't need to spend one more second worrying about them because there is nothing you can do about them.

3. Challenge. When things go badly you can let it overwhelm you or learn from the experience. When an editor says, "no," I try to make contact with him or her and ask "why?" Sometimes they give me a stock answer like, "It doesn't fit our editorial requirements." Other times their feedback tells me more about the market, the readers, publishers, and timing. With each rejection I learn something that makes my next pitch stronger. This trick works for me, and if you accept that you are on a constant learning curve, it will work for you.

In science there is an effect called albedo [194]

It is one of those things that have increased in our awareness because of global warming. Albedo is a measurement of the amount of sunlight that is reflected away when it hits an object. In global warming terms, when the sun hits the ice and snow at the poles it is reflected away helping to keep the planet's weather relatively stable.

However, we get warmer because the sun's rays get trapped in the environment and have nowhere to go. Eventually, the theory goes, as we warm, the ice and snow at the poles melt and are replaced with water which is dark and will absorb light with the results of further warming.

Albedo can be used metaphorically to describe your career in sales. A certain amount of external influences are important to maintain a healthy career. But sometimes things go wrong. In global terms, some times the poles are very cold and other times they are very wet. Your sales career will mirror this. Sometimes things will go along swimmingly and other times you will feel left out in the cold.

---

[194] "Albedo", www.arcticice.org/albedo.htm, www.Wikipedia.com

The trick we have learned is to harness the power of resilience. Planet earth is resilient. Throughout its history it has survived being plummeted with giant boulders from space, volcanoes, earthquakes, fires, and it will survive humans. All these apparent obstacles are merely temporary setbacks. Planet earth just keeps chugging along. The secret according to Mahatma Ghandi is to "Live as if you were to die tomorrow. Learn as if you were to live forever." [195]

Herein lies the secret of your resilience that our POA's, Billy Joel, Joan Chittister, Kimiko Hirarai Sodati, Viktor Frankl, and Peggi Pelosi-Gardiner all managed to harness.

Identify the outcome

In American folklore there is the story of a slave, born in 1840, who was freed after the Civil War. His name was John Henry.[196] The story reveals that John Henry was a physically powerful man and so, with his best assets to offer, he went to work for the Chesapeake and Ohio Railroad Company. He spent his days drilling holes by hitting a steel spike into rocks. He would crouch on all fours with his hand-drill penetrated in solid rock. Day after day John Henry built his reputation as the strongest man working on the rails.

The story unfolds that as the railroad was progressing Big Ben Mountain halted its path. It was decided, that rather than building the railroad around the mountain, they would drill straight through. It was a distance of one and a quarter miles. It was a ferocious task that took three years to complete. Before the tunnel would see the light of day on the other side, over a thousand men would lose their lives.

John Henry was relentless. Each day he swung his 14-pound hammer and helped advance the tunnel 10 to 12 feet. One day a salesman selling a steam-powered drill approached the boss. His claim was that the machine was more productive than the railroad's best man. The challenge was set. John Henry versus the machine. With one 20-pound hammer in each hand the contest began. For the next 35 minutes the contest between man and machine gathered momentum. At the end of the contest, John Henry had drilled two seven-foot holes, a total of 14 feet. The machine drilled a total of nine feet.

---

[196] "John Henry", retold by S.E. Schlosser, www.americanfolklore.net.

John Henry was victorious. John Henry's goals were such, that at the end of each day, they could be measured. One can only presume that his daily outcome was based on a realistic expectation for a man of his strength and experience. Rather than focus on the completed tunnel, he focused on his ten to twelve feet of progress.

A career in sales is like that. We try, but it's often difficult to focus on the end result. Often the changes are too subtle to notice, but when you can set realistic, short-term goals, measurement is often achievable. But don't mistake the process as being long, laborious, and monotonous. Careers in sales often throw surprises in your path that challenge you further—like John Henry and the steam powered drill.

Often these challenges are unexpected, so you need to be constantly vigilant for the break in your daily routine. Just as John Henry's challenge was met, your challenge, if handled with all your might, can propel your career a few notches further along. The trick is to take the time each day to ascertain whether you put your best effort into the task at hand to meet your goals.

Process the feedback

As a POA, you're constantly looking at the outcome of your actions as feedback for improving your future performance. Ask yourself, "Am I now content with the career direction I have chosen, or does the feedback fuel an additional search for action?" How do you want your sales career game to unfold? With intelligently proactive thinking, you have three choices: You can be a player, a wannabe, or a spectator.

Players are those who look at their sales career and pledge to themselves that they will take control and mold it into something that works for them. No, they all won't be Jack Welsh or Fred Smith. They will be tool and die makers, machinists, accountants, doctors and sales people who live a good life and have a career that is satisfying. Some play the game by rote — numbly walking through the moves because they have done them a thousand times before.

Others approach each new opportunity with total concentration and focus. It's like watching Tiger Woods line up a tough putt. You know he is there 100 percent of the time. Tiger Woods is a player, and so are Jack Welsh and Fred Smith, not because they became superstars in their respective businesses, but because they were able to focus on the job at hand and were not prepared to settle for anything less than perfection. Second best wasn't an option.

The wannabes sit on the sidelines. Their dialogue is filled with "If I only..." They sit warming the bench waiting for one of the players to fail and hoping to be invited to take their place in the game.

Wannabes really want to be in the game, but they hesitate. Perhaps it is because of one of the many reasons we have already discussed in this book; perhaps it's something else. What the wannabes need are the tools to help them reach out for the brass ring.

Then we have the spectators. These are the people who watch others play, but never want to get in the game. They find comfort in their timidity. They are perfectly happy to let life take them by the arm and lead them along until they retire.

It's all well and good to be a spectator, but there is a danger. Spectators assume that they live in a fair world. They assume that all employers are going to offer them a lifetime of employment.

Takeovers, mergers, and bankruptcies, that are a part of everyday life, can blindside them. It's the spectators who suffer the most through adversity; they are simply unprepared to deal with uncertainty and upheaval when it happens.

So, who are you? Are you a player, a wannabe, or a spectator?

What keeps POA's going?

Think of yourself as the CEO of a corporation—your corporation. You are now running Bob Inc. or Betty Inc. Every decision you make has to satisfy your Board of Directors and allow your shareholders to see a continuous improvement on their investment.

Most of all, your stakeholders have committed to a set of guiding principles and values so that no action passes without ensuring it is compatible with your corporation's direction.

Every decision, and therefore every action, must in some way improve your corporation's bottom line.

Intelligently proactive behaviour is not chasing a "flavour of the month." Choose things that are important to you. If opportunities don't pass your litmus test, then they are not worth the time you give them.

Ideas and initiatives can come from anywhere. They can come innocently as a result of a conversation with a colleague or intently as a result of a serious search for a workable solution. If an idea makes sense, then as CEO, you have to take on the role of the initiative's champion. Being a timid leader simply doesn't cut it.

Take a serious look at your stakeholders—your strengths and weaknesses. Your strengths are your best employees, but what about your weak employees; your weaknesses? Do what any CEO would do. Fire or replace them, but don't let them drag down your corporation's overall performance. Being successful is all about focus, passion, and the relentless pursuit of what is right for you and your career.

The impact of these initiatives will show up in your operating results. Your career will be on the right track and will perform as you expected it to. But, if you fail to meet your goals, do as a CEO would and go back to your Sales Action Cycle. Identify the problem, develop appropriate actions, and send in the army to fight the battle. Go about your new ideas with a vengeance. Tackle them as if your very survival depended on it.

Jack Welsh says that every corporation ought to fire the bottom 10 percent of its employees. You can do that too. Look at all your strengths and weaknesses and every year make it your goal to lose 10 percent of those characteristics that are a drag on your career.

It's tough making those calls, but that's a crucial part of a CEO's job. Being a POA is not an easy road. You can be a doer, wannabe, or spectator; it's up to you. But if you want real change you are going to have to go out there and get it. And whatever you do, don't tell me it's impossible.

About the Authors:

Barbara Siskind, celebrated author and consultant, has joined forces with husband **Barry Siskind**, an internationally recognized speaker and writer and president of International Training and Management Company, a firm that helps corporations achieve better results from events and trade shows. He's also the bestselling author of ***Bumblebees Can't Fly; Powerful Exhibit Marketing;*** and ***Eagles Must Soar***.

In ***Grab Success by the Horns***, the Siskinds note most careers are shaped by various external forces such as peer pressure and parental expectations. Their breakthrough book teaches you how to put the control where it belongs – inside yourself – one step at a time, utilizing inspiring advice of those who took a proactive approach to earn success.

Manor House
905-648-2193
www.manor-house.biz

Grab Success by the Horns